The New Indoor Plant Book

the NEW INDOOR PLANT book

JOHN EVANS

Photographs by Jacqui Hurst

Illustrations by Sally Maltby

KYLE CATHIE LIMITED

First published in Great Britain in 1993 by
Kyle Cathie Limited
7/8 Hatherley Street, London SW1P 2QT

Paperback edition published 1994

ISBN 1 85626 152 2

A Cataloguing in Publication record for this title is
available from the British Library.

Designed by Geoff Hayes

Printed and bound in Hong Kong
Produced by Mandarin Offset

Contents

Introduction   **6**

Indoor plants in the home   **10**
The kitchen   12
The bathroom   14
Dark hallways and corridors   16
Conservatories and garden rooms   18
Windowsills   20
Dry atmosphere plants   22
Trailing and climbing plants   24
Winter colour   26
Fun plants for children   28

Foliage Plants   **31**

Flowering Plants   **141**

How to care for your plants
Glossary   224
Light   228
Temperature   230
Watering and humidity   232
Feeding   236
Grooming   237
Propagation   238
Pruning   240
Training   241
Repotting and potting on   242
Compost and potting mix   243
Pests and diseases   244

Useful addresses   246
Index   250
Acknowledgements   254

Introduction

I have been involved with the growing and selling of pot plants all my life. The family business started back in 1876 in south London, moving to Sidcup in the early 1900s and to Ruxley in 1960. We had stands in Covent Garden Market for more than one hundred years, where our plants were sold to the London florists.

In the old days, before my time, the pot plants, loose on shelves, were loaded on to covered carts. Then in the evening driver, horse and cart would slowly wend their way to market. There the plants would be unloaded with the help of porters and set up individually on our stands, ready for my grandfather and his brother to sell them the next morning. I understand there was many a time when the horse found his own way back to the nursery with the driver snoring heavily as a result of a few too many at one of the multitude of ale houses which abounded in the Covent Garden area.

Now we have insulated temperature-controlled vehicles with air suspension. The plants are boxed, care carded, pre-priced, barcoded, sleeved, in fact given state of the art treatment to ensure that they are in peak condition when they reach the retailers' shelves.

Over the last twenty-five years a complete metamorphosis has taken place throughout the indoor plant industry due to a more affluent society, a change in retailing patterns and greatly improved distribution methods. Many books have been written on houseplants, and women's magazines, newspapers and periodicals all have articles on the multitude of species and varieties, which has helped both to popularize plants enormously and to dispel the mystique surrounding the care of plants.

Once upon a time, plants could be bought only at a florist's or at your local nursery. From America in the 1960s came the concept of garden centres. These sprang up in every part of the country and our own at Ruxley Manor was one of the first. Among the many items for sale were houseplants, standing on benches in glasshouse conditions. Never before had plants been sold from conditions similar to those in which they had grown.

Pot plant sales literally took off. From a once fairly limited range available, growers began to seek new plants from Europe and further afield to provide more choice for the customer in the home. The multiples saw their opportunity and Marks and Spencer were the first to sell pot plants in volume in the United Kingdom. But additional demands were then made upon the growers.

RIGHT: *Hedera helix* (ivy) in its variegated form and *Ficus benjamina* (Weeping fig) are two of the most common and versatile indoor plants, easy to grow and long-lasting. Here they are combined with a *begonia rex* and a cyclamen.

Gone were the days of a plant is a plant is a plant. Rigid specifications were placed on every pot: the height, the width, the degree of openness of the flowers, the colour range, the variety to be grown, the hardening off period – all so that the customer would get the best out of the plant once purchased.

This really set the trend for the future of the industry. Allied to the breeding of new varieties, the specialist growers, seed houses and research stations both here and abroad are placing more emphasis on providing plants that will keep better and be more able to cope with the change in conditions from the glasshouse to the home.

Today the glasshouse that produces houseplants is a highly sophisticated place, with computers controlling the heating, watering, lighting and ventilation to very fine limits, so that the plants are able to enjoy near natural conditions. Once in the home, conditions can be very different, but this the grower knows and so makes every effort to acclimatize the plants before they leave the nursery. The industry and the public alike have much to thank Marks and Spencer for.

Today, along with the garden centres, flower shops and market stalls, most multiples the world over sell indoor plants and more people than ever are enjoying the beauty, both in colour and foliage, that plants can bring to the home.

At home, experimentation is vital. How much time are you prepared to devote to caring for your plants? Are you prepared to learn from mistakes? And try again? I was asked to write this book because my editor had failed three times with the same plant, an extremely beautiful new indoor plant adapted from a cut flower. Acknowledging your contribution will direct you into either choosing plants labelled as easy in this book or into tackling the more challenging ones.

The range of pot plants I have chosen should be widely available, as all are grown commercially, though some may only be stocked by the larger garden centres.

Also, I have tried to provide a wide range of foliage plants in varying hues and leaf types, and flowering ones that will follow the seasons covering a wide colour band. After all, plants are like people – different shapes, sizes and colours. And, like people, they all have their aches and pains. Yet they are very adaptable and resilient, though, of course, some are more so than others. There are detailed care instructions about every plant in this book, but basically all that is needed is common sense and consideration for the plant's natural preferences.

Large plants, small plants, hanging plants, and specimen plants – they all have their place, providing the warmth, colour and sheer magic that only they can give.

Easy Care

A long term houseplant which in good conditions will last many years. **Light** — Bright natural light is best, direct sunlight may scorch leaves, in shade the plant will become spindly. The plant will grow towards the light, turn it occasionally to maintain its shape. Keep away from cold winter draughts. **Water** — Water only when the compost is almost dry. Overwatering or standing the pot in water will suffocate the roots and cause the plant to die. **Feed** — Weekly April - September with a houseplant fertiliser. **Other Information** — Keep leaves dust free, by wiping with a damp cloth. Leafshine can be used on this plant. **Do not place this container on a polished surface as scratching or staining may occur.**

MARKS & SPENCER PLC
BAKER STREET
LONDON
© 1992

G200

Most plants sold today have care cards giving instructions on how to look after the plant. These instructions range from being thoroughly vague to pertinently precise. Overall the standard has improved greatly and the major multiples and garden centres have gone to great lengths to provide concise information. I have chose the Marks and Spencer 'Easy Care' range as a benchmark.

The care card is split into seven sections, designed to suit all the plants the store sells, and the instructions are really as good as one will ever get on such a small piece of plastic!

An expression such as 'bright natural light, but keep out of direct sun' advises you to keep the plant in a bright area but away from the direct rays of the sun that may come through a window. 'Water only when the compost is almost dry' means water when the compost on the top has dried out.

A specimen plant can be used to great effect in this striking black Victorian fireplace. The blue *Hydrangea* will do fine away from the light it would get near the window for 2 or 3 weeks but should then be moved to a lighter position for the balance of its flowering period

Indoor plants in the home

Plants bring a home to life!

They have the most amazing range of colours – *natural* colours that can add a great deal even to the most beautifully decorated room. The indoor plant can be used as the focal point in an otherwise functional room or it can provide interest in a dull corner. It can bring colour to the view from a window or be used against a busy wallpaper to produce a sense of calm. And many together can create a dramatic effect, such as foliage plants conjuring up a jungle look. In fact there are so many opportunities for plants indoors – provided, of course, you can offer the conditions in which the plant will thrive.

Large plants will almost always have more dramatic effect if on their own and can even take the place of a piece of furniture. Some of the smaller plants make a better impression when grouped together within the room, the combination of colours adding to their 'noticeability'. In either case there should be sufficient space for the plants to grow and develop.

Natural clay and terracotta pots show off indoor plants particularly well, as do white china ones. There are many patterned china pots to choose from, too, and it is simply a matter of matching the colours of leaf or flower to those of the pot. Wicker or bamboo baskets make attractive alternatives but ensure they are lined to prevent water from seeping through on to the floor or furniture. Ethnic shops often sell beautiful pots which, though perhaps not originally intended for plants, can be adapted to effective use.

And don't forget that you can create interesting designs by displaying plants on glass shelves and against mirrors. The reflection also provides increased light, which is beneficial if light levels are low.

The following pages contain design ideas for plants in some of the less ideal spots in a flat or house. Obviously these are only suggestions and there are many other possibilities – but remember, it is important to match the conditions in which you expect a plant to grow with those the plant requires in order to stay at its best.

The kitchen

Good, no-nonsense plants, both foliage and flowering, are the order of the day here rather than the more temperamental ones. Temperatures near doors, around stoves or electrical appliances often fluctuate quite dramatically and sudden draughts can do their best to upset all but the most robust plants. Leaves can become coated in grease, blocking the pores, and plants by the sink often suffer tidal waves of washing-up water. The kitchen is normally a very busy place so do not place plants on the floor unless there really is enough room to walk around them easily.

That said, there are many plus-points for plants in the kitchen. As it is probably the most regularly used room in the house, the plants will not be neglected. The windowsill normally takes pride of place, often being used as a casualty clearing station for those plants that have had problems elsewhere in the house.

The herb family – basil, thyme, chives and parsley – do well here and miniature tomatoes grown in a hanging basket can also be very successful. A windowsill by the sink is ideal for *Saintpaulia* (African violets) and those plants that enjoy humidity. *Hypoestes*, *Tradescantia* and *Epipremnum* will do well. Throw in the odd cactus and wait for it to flower, and remember the magnificent scent of spring bulbs is accentuated by the warmth of the kitchen.

Philodendron scandens (the sweetheart plant) and the variegated *Hedera canariensis* (Canary Island ivy), together with others from the wide-ranging ivy family, can trail themselves through darkish spots and awkward places, breaking up the harsh edges of surfaces such as cupboards, kitchen counters or appliances.

Always make sure there are some flowering plants to add colour, highlight the changing seasons and bring vitality to that most important of rooms.

Here trailing greenery acts as a screen to divide living area from kitchen. Though little direct light will reach these pellaeas here, they will do well and look extremely effective for a few months.

RIGHT: Often the hard surfaces and paraphernalia of a kitchen can be cheered enormously by the use of foliage plants. This one is cheered by a clivia and an azalea. Kitchen plants need to be tough to withstand the changes in atmosphere and the fumes from gas and other cooking appliances.

The bathroom

Some bathrooms are heated throughout the winter, while others have no source of heat at all – both types of room have a range of plants that will thrive in them. Indeed, the bathroom is one of the best rooms for an indoor plant (provided there is sufficient light and heat) because there are few plants that don't welcome the humidity generated by the warm bath water.

If the window is small and the glass opaque there may be a problem with light. Choose plants that don't mind minimal light, such as *Philodendron scandens* (the sweetheart plant), *Davallia* (the rabbit's foot fern), or *Epipremnum*. *Philodendron scandens* and *Epipremnum* will grow easily as climbers or trailing plants, quickly transforming the starkness of bathroom surfaces. *Adiantum* and *Begonia* are more delicate but like moist air, warmth and shade. They should be removed from the bathroom in winter.

Bathrooms with large windowsills are a joy and many of the ferns and palms will welcome these conditions. I particularly recommend *Syngonium* 'White Butterfly', *Chrysalidocarpus lutescens*, asparagus, *Pellionia*, *Peperomia* and both *Maranta leuconeura* and *Maranta tricolor*. It is often possible to fit an indoor plant into the corner of a bath surround, and all too frequently this is a fairly dark spot where *Aglaonema* (Chinese evergreen) or *Chlorophytum* (spider plant) would do well. *Tolmiea menziesii* (piggyback plant), with its pretty speckled leaves, is compact and well suited to an unheated bathroom though more demanding of light. It can also be grown in a hanging basket above the bath, as can the members of the *Nephrolepsis* fern family, the most popular varieties being 'Boston' and 'Teddy Junior', though 'Linda' which has a more delicate feathery appearance is worth looking out for.

Again introduce flowering plants to provide a kaleidoscope of colour throughout the year. *Saintpaulia* (the African violet) and *Streptocarpus* (the Cape primrose) will flower right through the summer. The humidity and warmth of the bathroom heightens the perfume of fragrant flowers. The first plant to kick off the New Year with would be the winter-flowering jasmine followed by the gardenia, then *Stephanotis* (the Madagascar jasmine) or *Exacum* (the Arabian violet) or *Hoya bella* with its beautiful porcelain-like flowers.

Once flowering is over, remove the plants from the bathroom and allow them to grow under better light conditions elsewhere in the house, or better still in the conservatory or greenhouse.

Here *Adiantum* (the maidenhair fern) thrives on the moisture from the bathroom, not minding the lack of light. The delicate *Streptocarpus* complements the shape of the fern fronds.

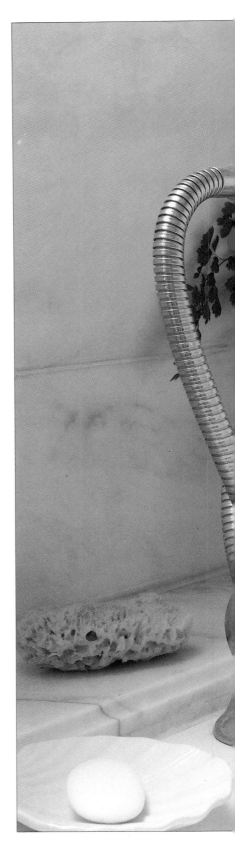

Dark hallways and corridors

Entrance halls often lack light and can be very draughty, with doors opening off in various directions. Temperatures at night may be cold, if there is any heating at all. So tough, shade-loving plants are required long term, with flowering plants used as short-term disposable items to provide dramatic focal points of colour among the more sombre green foliage. Together these plants will bring life and vibrancy to what could otherwise be a fairly soulless area of the home.

In looking for a long-term resident for dark corridors, choose a Swiss cheese plant (*Monsteria deliciosa*) or the smaller leaved *Philodendron pertusum.* You could also try, from the same family, the *Philodendron scandens* and *Philodendron selloum* or the *Fatshedera lizei* (tree ivy) with its rich glossy leaves. These can all be table plants, but are also ideal as feature plants, growing up moss poles to heights of around 2m/4–5ft – real sentries in the corridor.

The aspidistra, or cast-iron plant, is practically indestructible and is presently enjoying a new wave of popularity. Then there is *Aglaonema* (the Chinese evergreen), *Rhoicissus rhomboidea* (the grape ivy), and not forgetting the *Platycerium* (staghorn fern). You will find you have a plethora of plants to choose from.

Now for some flowering plants to add that spot of dash and brilliance – how about a basket of cyclamen or azaleas, a large azalea on its own, a container of chrysanthemums, a single hydrangea or the beautiful slipper orchid (*Paphiopedilum*) or moth orchid (*Phalaenopsis*). Again, choose the plant to fit the season, displayed either on its own or massed together with others according to the size of the hall or space.

For a plant that enjoys longevity as a foliage plant yet also produces a flower, you cannot beat the *Spathiphyllum* (white sails).

Use simple single foliage plants to maximize drama in a bland dark passageway. These will give more pleasure than a collection of straggly plants growing desperately towards whatever small light source there may be.

Always rotate the plants to which you give difficult conditions. A spell of two to three months in a more sympathetic situation will do much to restore their vigour.

ABOVE: A single plant – in this case a delicate pink *Primula malacoides* (fairy primrose) – can bring life to a dark corner.

RIGHT: *Nephrolepsis* (sword fern) does sterling work, here combined with *Spathiphyllum* (white sails) to provide interest in a dark hallway. On the shelf to the right is the indispensable *Scindapsus* (devil's ivy) and on the stairs the aspidistra complements two yuccas.

Conservatories and garden rooms

Many of us dream of having a room we can devote to a collection of rich, green, sweet-scented plants, and since the 1970s there has been a vast increase in the number of conservatories built. There are certain advantages in having a conservatory – chiefly that the light reaches the plants from all sides, similar both to the environment of their native habitat and to that in which they are raised in the commercial greenhouse. Also, today's conservatories often have proper ventilation systems to keep the air fresh and blinds to shade delicate plants from the midday sun, preventing scorched leaves.

Decide on the purpose of your conservatory – is it a formal dining room or a casual extension to the sitting room, a plant room where a jungle fantasy can be indulged or simply a hideaway? – and choose plants that complement that purpose. Having a conservatory is a luxury, but at the same time it requires a commitment of time and energy.

When choosing the plants, look for some of the exotic species that can't commonly be grown around the house. This will, of course, depend to some extent on the amount of heat you can provide in the cooler months of the year, but there is a very wide range of plants that can be grown in a room with a winter temperature of only 10–13°C/50–55°F. Also make sure that you have a supply of water within easy access of the conservatory as there will be a great deal of watering to be done.

A comfortable garden room making good use of sweet-scented *Citris mitis* and *Mimosa*

Some of the more exotic species that can be tried include *Agapanthus* (try *A. campanulatus*, a vigorous, blue variety which happily adapts to sun-room conditions); *Citrus*, with its beautifully scented white flowers and pretty small orange fruits; or some of the rarer orchids: try the vibrant pink *Cattleya bowringiana*. *Laelia purpurata* is the national flower of Brazil and can be brought into flower in late winter or early spring; it is not difficult for the beginner. The *Abutilon, Bougainvillea, Columnea, Gloriosa* and *Oleander* are other exotics well worth trying.

The jungle aspect of a conservatory is created by the foliage plants. Look to the palm family, and here I recommend *Howea* (the kentia palm) and *Chrysalidocarpus lutescens* (the areca palm). *Rhapis excelsa* (the lady palm), a relatively new addition to the commercial range, is worth looking out for. All the *Ficus* varieties do well, and of course I recommend *Ficus benjamina*, either variegated or plain green. *Ficus lyrata*, with its rich big leaves, can also create a strong impact. *Philodendron* is tailer-made for the conservatory, whether trailing or growing up a moss pole. Another good architectural plant is *Dracaena marginata*, which will provide stark contrasts with its whitish stem and spiky foliage.

Remember that the conditions in a conservatory will suit plants with variegated or coloured leaves, the light bringing up the intensity of their leaf patterns; so try to include *Codiaeum, Cordyline terminalis, Caladium, Dieffenbachia exotica, Hibiscus, Maranta* and some of the *Begonia rex* cultivars.

Terracotta pots are particularly effective in conservatories and garden rooms. Here, sweet scented geraniums are used to good effect; also the bold leaves of avocado are complimented by the purple flowers of *Bougainvillea*, which is happy only with plenty of light

Windowsills

At first sight the windowsill seems the ideal place for plants, but there can still be problems.

Sunny windowsills

Here there is a danger of the leaves being burned by the sun and of the plants drying out very quickly, particulary in summer. Where the windowsill takes the full face of the midday sun, a protective screen such as very light curtaining is well worth considering. There are few plants able to withstand such hot situations, the exceptions being *Coleus*, *Bougainvillea*, *Sansevieria*, *Beaucarnea* and *Yucca*, but these all need to be kept well watered. The *Echeveria*, coming from the dry Mexican plateau, can also hold its own in the midday sun.

Consider the conditions of a sunny windowsill in winter. In the evening the curtains are drawn, the radiators go off during the night and the plant is subjected to dramatically changing temperatures, so it is always best to bring the plant into the body of the room before closing the curtains.

However, as the sun is weak during winter a much larger range of plants can be displayed.

Windowsills with little or no sun

This location opens the doors for a wide range of plants.

Many of the foliage plants such as *Chlorophytum* (spider plant), the aspidistra, the *Dracaena* family, the *Schefflera*, *Aglaonema* and the *Philodendron* family will grow quite healthily in indirect light conditions.

Again flowering plants should be used to provide colour and then removed after flowering.

Where curtains and radiators are involved during the winter, move the plants into the room at night.

On this windowsill display a *Yucca*, *Sansevieria* and *Beaucarnea* are combined with two examples of *Soleirolia soleirolii*. During winter nights, when the curtains are closed and the radiators turned off, these plants should ideally be removed from the sill

Dry atmosphere plants

Plants need humidity, but there are a few plants that will do well in centrally heated rooms with little ventilation. The most obvious group of these plants is the cacti family as they are long-living and can put up with neglect. They are also plants which people seem to either love or loathe.

There are two groups in this family – the desert cacti and the forest cacti. Both originate from Central America, the former, and by far the larger group, growing in semi-desert regions; the latter growing on trees as epiphytes in the woodlands and jungles.

Of the foliage plants, *Phoenix canariensis*, *Yucca* and *Beaucarnea* will thrive in a dry atmosphere as will *Aloe* and *Brachychiton*. The *Eustoma* will bloom happily, as will *Bougainvillea*, *Hibiscus* and *Kalanchoe*, and the regal and zonal pelargoniums.

Plants will almost always be improved if placed on pebble trays, particularly those situated near a radiator. Look, too, at species which can tolerate room temperatures throughout the year and do not require cool winter conditions for the dormant season.

Consider what function you want your plants to fulfil. Dramatic branch shapes such as those of the *Dracaena marginata* can make a sparsely furnished room – either a living room or dining room – more 'furnished'. A group of palms can act as a divider between living and eating areas (but remember there must be enough room so that you don't constantly knock the plants). Alternatively, small plants could be used as centrepieces on dining-room tables, on side boards or on shelving. A simple arrangement of *Soleirolia soleirolii* (mind your own business), for example, can make the most effective table decoration.

Plants act as humidifiers of dry, centrally-heated air. They make the rooms healthier to live in and even produce minimal amounts of oxygen. However, they also filter out dust, which will settle on the leaves and should be wiped off from time to time.

The recommended humidity level for most houseplants is between 60–70 per cent but in many rooms the humidity falls to around 35 per cent. In the dry atmosphere room humidity can be improved with an electric humidifier, which will also help to protect antique furniture from the effects of central heating.

OPPOSITE: Three plants that can tolerate the dry atmosphere of a centrally heated room: *Bougainvillea* (at the back), *Kalanchoe* (on the right) and *Hibiscus* (at the front). All grow naturally in hot climates where rainfall is light during the summer months

Trailing and climbing plants

One of the best ways to display trailing plants is in hanging baskets either suspended from the ceiling or attached to wall brackets – the glossy leaves falling at eye level or above give an unexpected and attractive dimension to a room.

There are plenty of plants to choose from but they need to be cared for in order to stay attractive and achieve new growth.

Scindapsus aureus or *Epipremnum* (the devil's ivy) is a very vigorous plant with yellow and green variegated leaves, and together with *Scindapsus* 'Marble Queen', which has green and white leaves, gives a superb trailing display.

The *Hedera* family has so many varieties that one could produce a stunning effect using nothing else and the *Chlorophytum* (spider plant) can make a wonderful display, with the creamy stems covered with clusters of plantlets.

Asparagus sprengeri ferns, once seen in butchers' shops, do well in hanging baskets as do the *Tradescantia* family with their variegated leaves. A more delicate hanging plant is *Saxifraga stolonifera* (the mother of thousands). *Syngonium* 'White Butterfly' and *Philodendron scandens* also look beautiful in hanging baskets.

Of the flowering plants, the cascade geraniums, running from mauve through to luminous red, provide a profusion of flowers all through summer. Trailing fuchsias, with varieties such as 'Eva Borg' and 'Marinka', are always popular and the trailing begonias and campanulas can give an unbroken summer of colour.

Aeschynanthus speciosus (the lipstick vine) and *Columnea* (the goldfish plant) make spectacular hanging baskets, their long trails filled with flowers. *Hoya carnosa* (the wax plant) produces clusters of star-shaped flowers which have a very delicate perfume and almost appear to be made of finest porcelain – a really beautiful plant.

The hanging basket itself should be securely fixed. It is important to have one of a good size and I would suggest a minimum diameter of 10cm/4in if you want to produce a very full, bushy plant with plenty of trails. There are many types of plastic baskets available, complete with drip trays. In summer the baskets need to be watered very regularly. Remember – those higher up the wall and nearer to the ceiling or roof of the conservatory can become drier much more quickly since it will be much hotter there than in the room below.

Climbing plants are often simply trailing plants that are supported, hence I will cover them in this section. Their stems are too weak to stand without a framework of some kind. This framework can be simple bamboo, a moss pole, a trellis, wire or even the support of

Stephanotis floribunda is summer-flowering and easily trainable on a wire hoop, trellis or, as here, up a pole. Its sweet-scented white flowers against the dark leaves are a welcome sight, although it is a rather demanding plant

other stronger plants (particularly useful for ones that produce tendrils).

Of the foliage plants, the Swiss cheese plant is popular, and with the thick glossy green of its leaves it can look good against large pieces of furniture – particularly pine. It can be grown on a moss-covered pole, as can the *Philodendron panduriforme* 'Burgundy'. For a variegated climber look for *Syngonium podophyllum*, which has wonderfully deep cut lobes and is equally as good climbing a pole as it is in a hanging basket.

Cissus antarctica (the grape ivy) and *Rhoicissus capensis* (the Cape ivy) are both good climbing or trailing ivies. *Scindapsus aureus*, with its thick bold leaves, can be used in a similar way.

Among the flowering climbers is jasmine, with its clusters or white flowers. The plant is a vigorous grower on a trellis or hoop of thick wire and is easily capable of covering a conservatory wall.

This vigorous climbing plant, *Plumbago auriculata*, provides a beautiful display of light blue flower clusters. It can also be used as a cascading plant over walls

Winter colour

Fortunately, when there are limited supplies of cut flowers from the garden there are plenty of colourful indoor flowering plants to bring cheer to a dull winter's day. Among the most obvious are the poinsettia – we sell over 8 acres of these in their red, orangy-pink and cream varieties through autumn up to Christmas. With good treatment these should keep their coloured bracts for three to four months.

Azalea indica flowers for up to a month during the winter and makes an excellent houseplant. Treat yourself to a miniature standard at Christmas. The versatile *Saintpaulia* (African violet) flowers happily in winter months, as do the primroses, *Primula obconica*, *Primula malacoides* and *Primula acaulis*, each producing a brilliant range of colours.

One of the most commonly sold pot plants is *Cyclamen*, as it is able to tolerate quite cold conditions. It is often seen in window boxes and can withstand a slight frost though a severe one can prove fatal. *Clivia* comes into flower in the late winter months, with its bold orange flower heads strikingly contrasted against the deep green of the leaves. *Kalanchoe* is another plant that flowers freely and lasts well, particularly on a kitchen windowsill. With the advent of special growing lamps in commercial nurseries *Begonia elatior* and *Campanula*, not withstanding the ever-popular *Chrysanthemum indicum* hybrids (the pot chrysanthemums), are freely available. The red 'sails' of *Anthurium* look seasonally cheerful during the winter months and can do much to enliven a dark corner. This plant can also be arranged with the white *Spathiphyllum* to make a highly decorative Christmas display.

Many of the plants you buy at this time of year will have been forced into flower by nursery men. When we force plants into flower we normally have a predetermined date in mind. For example, we know that certain *Azalea* varieties flower around December but to ensure they are ready in the two-week run up to Christmas and not one week late or two weeks early, one has to pay particular attention to detail. Mistakes still occur, but computerization and sophisticated controls, together with the skill of the grower, have helped ensure that the plants arrive in the shops in mint condition.

OPPOSITE: The exotic bright red flowers of *Anthurium* can bloom throughout the year and are set off beautifully by the glossy heart-shaped leaves. Here it is paired with the pot chrysanthemum, which has also been bred to be available in flower all year round

Here *Begonia elatior* provides a splash of winter colour

Fun plants for children

The enthusiasm a child has for a new plant can be short-lived, often to the detriment of the plant. However, there are a few plants that will survive neglect – notably the desert cactus family.

There are also plants for free: it is easy to grow coffee, almonds, avocados, dates or oranges, for example, by planting pips or stones. I have given growing methods for three below.

Avocado: press the rounder end of the stone into a pot filled with a moist multi-purpose compost, and keep in a warm place until the stone splits and the growth spike appears. Keep the compost moist as the leaves develop and pinch out the growing shoots to encourage bushiness. Repot annually. In a few years the plant will be up to 1.5m/5ft. It will not, I'm afraid, bear avocados.

Pineapple: cut off the top 3cm/1in of a ripe fresh fruit. Cut away the flesh to leave the leafy crown and fibrous core. Let this dry out for a couple of days on a sunny windowsill and then plant in a pot filled with moist multi-purpose compost. Place the plant in a sunny spot and allow the root system to develop. Be careful not to overwater.

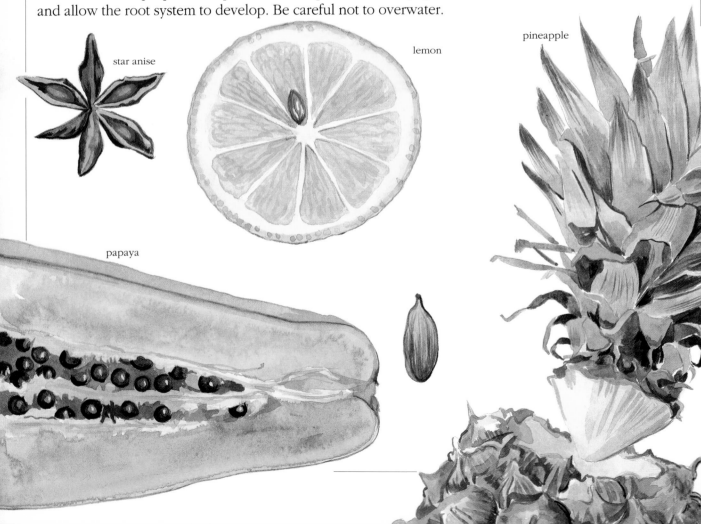

mangosteen

star anise

lemon

pineapple

papaya

Coffee bean: you will be able to grow a good bushy plant up to 1.5m/5ft which will flower but won't, sadly, produce coffee beans. This is an easy plant, provided it is free from draughts and the compost is kept moist at all times. Plant a bean of *Coffea arabica* or *Coffea nana* (from which it is easier to get flowers) in a small 5cm/2in deep pot of moist multi-purpose compost and place in a bright spot without direct sunshine. In a couple of weeks the plant will emerge. It should be repotted once rootbound into a 10cm/4in pot, then every year in spring.

The second category of fun plants for children are those that *do* something, and top in this category is the Venus fly trap (*Dionaea muscipula*): when the insect lands on the hinged leaves they snap shut. It is a demanding plant, requiring a bright, cool, damp position and is at its best if the pot is placed in a small container of water. Of course, finding the insects in winter can be a bit of a problem, but a determined child can keep the Venus fly trap going for years.

The peanut or ground nut (*Arachis hypogaea*) is easy to grow. In early spring, remove the husk and plant the nut 5cm/2in deep in a moist compost. Keep well watered and site the pot in a well-lit, warm position. The plant will grow, bloom for a few hours, then wilt when self-pollination has occurred. The flower stalk then lengthens and bends down to the ground, burrowing into the compost. It is here, underground, that the seed ripens. Make sure you use unsalted peanuts!

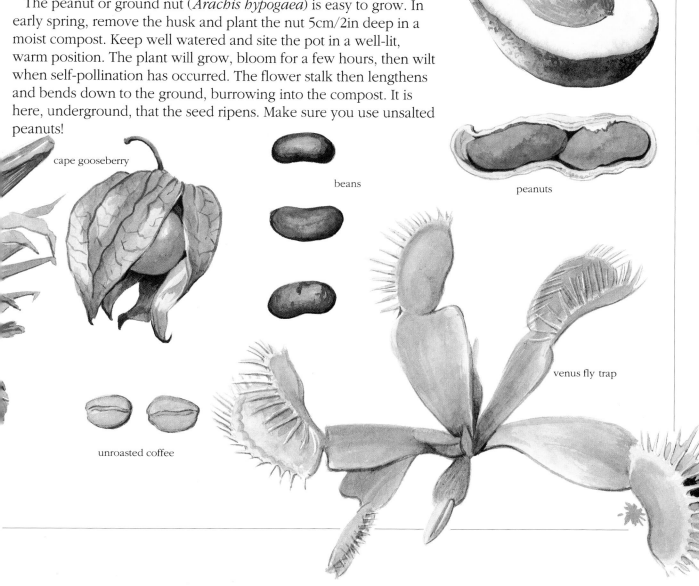

avocado

cape gooseberry

beans

peanuts

unroasted coffee

venus fly trap

Foliage Plants

There is a rich variety of foliage plants to choose from when decorating your house. The leaf forms and patterns are endless, as this is where photosynthesis and respiration are carried out. On the one hand, there is the enchanting pink and cream colour bands on the delicate green leaves of the *Hypoestes* or the *Tradescantia*, on the other the strongly patterned veins of the *Fittonia* or the *Croton*.

There are plants with delicate and graceful fronds, plants that trail and climb, plants that will reach to the ceiling, plants that will form screens – practically an infinite range.

Whilst the plants in this book are divided into foliage and flowering groups, these divisions are artificial as in the main the foliage plants do flower.

The range of foliage plants marketed has grown vastly since the 1950s, and this book aims to include some of the newer varieties you should look out for.

Acalypha hispida (Chenille plant, red hot cattail)

DIFFICULT

Acalypha hispida

A native of the tropical jungle forests of Java and Papua New Guinea, this tall ornamental shrub has bright green oval leaves with hairy undersides. In spring and summer it produces long pendant spikes of bright red flowers that should be removed when they are past their best. The plant can be pruned at the same time.

Acalypha hispida is a quick grower and needs the warm, humid temperatures of its native habitat all year round. Stand the pot over damp gravel or pack it with moist peat and spray every day, avoiding the flowers when they are blooming. It is quite difficult to maintain its humidity requirements in autumn and winter, so if possible put it in a greenhouse or conservatory at this time.

As a houseplant it will grow up to 2m/6ft, but it is advisable to propagate each year from stem cuttings.

Also available is *Acalypha wilksiana*, which has attractive coppery-red leaves, hence its common name 'copperleaf'.

A. hispida 'Balik'

A. wilksiana 'Can Can'

A. wilksiana hybrid 'Harlequin'

CARE

Light and temperature
Bright but indirect light and a constant warm temperature all year, no higher than 26°C/80°F in summer and no lower than 16°C/61°F in winter.

Water and feeding
Water thoroughly in spring and summer, but do not allow the plant to stand in water or the soil to become soggy. Spray the foliage frequently until the flowers start to form, then place the pot over a saucer of pebbles almost covered with water to provide good humidity. Do not spray while in flower. Feed fortnightly with a general liquid fertilizer until after flowering.

Propagation
By 7.5–10cm/3–4in stem cuttings, which should be dusted with rooting powder and established in sandy soil under a plastic cover at a constant temperature of 23°C/75°F.

Repotting
Cut the plant back in early spring to 25cm/10in above a leaf and repot into a 13cm/5in pot using a no. 2 soil-based compost with good drainage.

PROBLEMS

White woolly patches on the stems and leaves indicate mealy bug. Remove with a cloth dipped in methylated spirit.

Webs on the underside of leaves indicate red spider mite. Spray with a systemic insecticide and check humidity level.

Adiantum (Maidenhair fern)

Adiantum fragrans

QUITE EASY

This most delicate of ferns, with dainty, fan-like, pale green triangular leaves on black wiry stalks, comes from the tropical and subtropical areas of Australia, New Zealand and the Americas, where it is to be found growing amongst rocks. Some hardy or nearly hardy varieties grow in the United Kingdom.

It is not difficult to grow indoors, but requires constant monitoring to ensure it does not dry out. This plant needs a steady, humid atmosphere with no direct sunlight, and does well in bathrooms and the shaded parts of a conservatory or greenhouse. Keep the roots moist, but not wet, and spray often, daily if in a heated room.

Adiantum will grow to 60cm/24in across and 30–38cm/12–15in high. There are some 200 varieties, but the most common ones available are *monocolor, fragrans, scuteum roseum* and 'Fritz Lutzii'.

It is a very long-lasting plant.

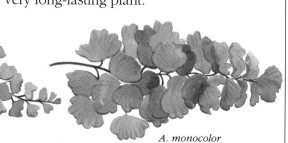

A. scuteum roseum   'Fritz Lutzii'   *A. monocolor*

CARE

Light and temperature
Adiantum grows well in warm, humid and sheltered spots away from direct sunlight. It dislikes both draughts and dry air. The minimum winter temperature is 10°C/50°F and the maximum summer temperature 24°C/75°F.

Water and feeding
The roots must not be allowed to dry out. It is best to submerge the pot in water for 10 minutes, then drain, probably twice weekly in summer and once a week in winter. Feed fortnightly with liquid fertilizer from mid-spring to mid-autumn or use slow-release pellets. These plants love a high degree of humidity in warm temperatures. Spray leaves daily and stand the container on moist pebbles.

Propagation
In spring divide the clumps, leaving a piece of rhizome attached to each clump, and place in a good peat-based compost to which you have added a little fertilizer.

Repotting
Repot in a peat-based compost each spring. Pack the soil lightly as good drainage is essential.

PROBLEMS

Most problems arise from a lack of moisture and humidity.

If the fronds dry up, cut them off and spray daily until new shoots appear.

If the leaves drop, the plant can be cut right back to encourage new growth. Continue watering and spraying while it becomes established.

If the leaves turn pale, the plant has received too much sunlight. Move it out of the sun and into a shadier position.

Aglaonema (Chinese evergreen)

EASY

This group of plants was discovered in the nineteenth century in China and the tropical rainforests and islands of Malaya, Sri Lanka and the Philippines, where they are to be found growing in the shady spots under the tree canopy. There are quite a few varieties, which make good houseplants if kept at a constant temperature and humidity, away from draughts, fires or heaters. They present few problems apart from the occasional yellow leaf if underfed in summer or if allowed to get too cold in winter.

Aglaonema commutatum has decorative variegated foliage – large spear-shaped leaves with silver-green stripes or dots. Sometimes they bloom and, after flowering, develop poisonous red berries.

The plant grows to about 25cm/10in tall and will produce 5–6 new leaves a year. *Aglaonema roebelenii* has thick, leathery, grey-green leaves which grow up to 30cm/1ft long. *Aglaonema crispum* has dark green and silver leaves. The all-green varieties do not require much light, but those with white or variegated yellow foliage need brighter conditions.

The plant will slow down after 2–3 years and should be started again with stem-tip cuttings.

A. roebelenii or
A. crispum
(painted drop tongue)

CARE

Light and temperature
It grows well in constant conditions, without much light, and is fairly tolerant of low temperatures. Ideally temperatures are between 15–24°C/60–75°F – it will withstand 10°C/50°F, but keep the plant on the dry side if the temperature drops this low.

Water and feeding
In summer water thoroughly twice weekly and add liquid fertilizer every 14 days. Do not allow to dry out. Keep much drier in winter. It likes humidity in summer and benefits from spraying twice weekly or being placed over a saucer of wet pebbles. The plant does well in hydroculture.

Propagation
The easiest way to propagate is by division of the root clump. The plant should then be established in a propagator as it will need a high humidity.

Repotting
Repot only as needed, in spring, in a good open compost as the roots like to breathe and good drainage is important.

PROBLEMS

Mealy bug can be a problem, as can red spider mite, if conditions are too light and too dry. Remove them with a cloth soaked in methylated spirit or spray with a systemic insecticide.

Aglaonema commutatum is commonly known as the silver evergreen

Aloe vera (Medicine plant, Barbados aloe, true aloe)

EASY

Aloe vera is sometimes known as *A. barbadensis*

CARE

Light and temperature
Aloe thrives in direct sunlight and a warm temperature, ideally 18°C/64°F. In winter ensure it continues to receive full sunlight and temperatures no lower than 8°C/47°F.

Water and feeding
Immerse the pot in water for 10 minutes, drain well, and allow the compost almost to dry out between waterings. Take care not to let the water settle in the rosette. In winter it will need watering only every 3–4 weeks. Feed monthly in spring and summer with a liquid solution.

Propagation
In spring by removing lateral shoots. The plant yields a sticky pap, so the shoot should be left to dry for 2 days before being planted in a just-damp mixture of no. 2 compost and sand. It should root easily at normal room temperature.

Repotting
Repot young plants annually in spring in a no. 2 potting compost.

PROBLEMS

Take care not to overwater this plant or to let water settle in the rosette as this will cause stem rot, which is recognizable by black marks on the leaves. Allow the compost to dry out completely before watering again and check that the temperature is not too cold.

If the leaves turn brown and dry, the plant has been kept too dry. Soak thoroughly in water for 1 hour and then drain.

If the leaves are a poor colour, the plant does not have enough light. Move to a brighter position.

Aloe vera may be attacked by scale insect. Spray with a systemic insecticide.

This medicinal member of the lily family is a very popular houseplant. Its juice is said to have healing properties for burns, skin and hair, hence its name.

Originally from the semi-arid, subtropical islands of Cape Verde, Canary and Madeira, it is hardy and virtually problem-free. It likes a sunny spot with dry air, the same conditions it enjoys in its native habitat.

Aloe vera grows as a rosette of fleshy, stiff, pointed, grey-green, spotted leaves. It may produce yellow flowers. It is a long-lasting plant and will benefit from a spell outdoors in a sunny, protected spot. There are many new species being marketed.

Ampelopsis (Chinese grape)

EASY

This charming hanging plant resembles a grapevine in the way it trails attractively over a pot or basket. It produces a profusion of long red stems from which grow white or pink marbled leaves.

Originally from the eastern areas of China, *Ampelopsis* grows naturally in the warm temperate rainforests, wrapping itself around the branches and trunks of trees.

It is a good houseplant, easy to look after and a quick grower. It will thrive in both bright and semi-shady conditions as long as it has a reasonable amount of humidity in the form of misting; a conservatory is an ideal spot to grow this plant. It will also benefit from a spell outside in summer.

The plant has a dormant period in winter. It will lose its leaves in late autumn, after which it should be pruned. It can then be reshaped in spring if necessary. Pinch out the new growing tips if you would like a denser plant.

It should live for several years. When the plant is past its best it can be propagated.

Ampelopsis brevipedunculata should be kept in a light position with enough heat to retain its lovely pink-marbled leaves

CARE

Light and temperature
Enjoys indirect sunlight to semi-shady spots in summer with temperatures of 16–18°C/60–64°F. Though deciduous, it also likes bright conditions in winter and a temperature of 5–12°C/41–54°F.

Water and feeding
During spring and summer water thoroughly and do not let the plant dry out. Feed fortnightly with general houseplant fertilizer to manufacturer's recommendations. During winter keep the plant almost dry and prune back hard.

Propagation
From stem-tip cuttings of approximately 10cm/4in in length, making the bottom of the cutting just below a leaf joint with a clean cut. Dip into a rooting hormone and insert it into a peat and sand cutting compost. Water in. Place in a propagator at a temperature of 18°C/64°F.

Repotting
Repot each spring in a no. 2 soil-based compost.

PROBLEMS

Webs on the underside of leaves indicate red spider mite. Spray with a systemic insecticide and keep well watered.

Ananas bracteatus striatus

(Variegated red pineapple)   **EASY**

This spiny-leafed ornamental pineapple is sought after for its spectacular foliage and occasional large brown edible fruits. It forms rosettes of coppery-green pointed leaves which can grow up to 1m/3ft in length, so it needs plenty of space. Always wear gloves when handling it as its leaves are sharp.

Ananas comes from Brazil where it grows naturally and is cultivated in large fields in high temperatures and bright sunlight.

As a houseplant it likes a bright spot but not direct sunlight.

The fruiting spike, usually pink, contrasts attractively with the green and yellow striped leaves. The fruit takes several months to form, usually maturing in spring.

The fruit of the ornamental pineapple needs a lot of space; the rosy-coloured leaves grow up to 1m/40in long and spread as much in width. Dwarf varieties (*Ananas nanus*) are only two-thirds the size.

Ananas bracteatus striatus

CARE

Light and temperature
Ananas requires warm and bright conditions, but not direct sunlight, all year round, with temperatures not below 18°C/64°F in winter. Keep the plant away from cold draughts.

Water and feeding
Water 2–3 times a week in summer and only once a week in winter, allowing the soil to dry out between waterings. Feed every 2 weeks in spring and summer and while the fruit is forming.

Propagation
After fruiting the plant dies down and a small offset grows beside it. When the main plant has begun to shrivel up, separate the offset and its roots with a knife and plant in a 9cm/3.5in pot. Keep moist in a propagator at 20°C/70°F.

Repotting
In spring repot younger plants in a mixture of peat and sand. Older plants will need only the topsoil changed.

PROBLEMS

Ananas is prone to few diseases. It may be attacked by scale insect. Remove these from underneath the leaves with a cloth dipped in methylated spirit.

If the leaves shrivel or the tips are brown, the plant is too dry and hot. Water, spray and move to a cooler position.

If the leaves are a poor colour, move to a brighter spot.

Anthurium scherzerianum

(Flamingo flower)

Anthurium scherzerianum has a spadix that is twisted spirally

QUITE DIFFICULT

This plant is grown for its decorative heart-shaped leaves and pretty bright red or white oval flowers with creamy-coloured spadix that grow throughout the year.

Originally from Central and South America, as a houseplant it is fairly small, growing to 25cm/10in with a slightly wider spread.

It is not a quick grower, and is not recommended for the beginner. It will need careful monitoring to make sure the conditions are right and must be kept away from draughts and temperature variations. The soil should never be allowed to dry out and a constant humidity level is essential. Mist frequently and stand the pot over damp gravel.

It should last for several years.

CARE

Light and temperature
Strong indirect light and a constant temperature of around 18–21°C/64–70°F is ideal. In winter the temperature should not go below 15°C/60°F.

Water and feeding
Water 2–3 times a week in spring and summer, never allowing the compost to dry out. Stand the pot over damp gravel and mist frequently. In winter, it will need less water. In spring and summer fertilize every 2 weeks with a general houseplant solution.

Propagation
Quite difficult. Divide the plant in late winter, ensuring each section has some roots and stems, and plant in a peat-based compost. Establish at a constant temperature of 21°C/70°F.

Repotting
In spring, every second year, in a peat-based compost.

PROBLEMS

This plant can be quite temperamental as it requires the right conditions in order to thrive. If it is too cold and wet or too dry, the leaves will turn yellow. Check the temperature, watering and humidity levels.

Brown spots on the leaves indicate fungus caused by cold and wet conditions. Spray with a systemic fungicide and check temperature and watering.

Prone to mealy bug, red spider mite and aphids. Remove mealy bug and spider mite with a cloth dipped in methylated spirit and spray aphids with a pyrethrum-based insecticide.

Araucaria heterophylla (Norfolk Island pine)

EASY

Discovered in the South Pacific in 1793 by Captain Cook and Sir Joseph Banks, this handsome pine reaches a height of 60m/200ft in its native habitat. As a houseplant it will grow to a much more manageable 1–1.5m/3–6ft. It is a slow grower and after reaching this height is past its best.

The Norfolk Island pine is appealing because of its tiered branches covered with pale green needles. Pruning is not recommended, although this will encourage bushier growth if the plant becomes straggly. The lower branches can be cut off when they become bare.

Araucaria requires a bright, well-lit position, and will enjoy a spell outdoors on mild days. It likes freely circulating air, but not central heating. In summer it needs a lot of moisture, so mist frequently.

Indoors it should last for many years. It can also be used as a Christmas tree.

Araucaria heterophylla has stiff needles, resinous sap and can produce cones

CARE

Light and temperature
A bright, well-ventilated position. In summer it likes temperatures between 18–22°C/64–72°F or a semi-shady spot outdoors with a good breeze. In winter it can withstand cooler temperatures of as low as 5°C/40°F.

Water and feeding
Keep the compost moist in spring, summer and autumn. It will need less water in winter. Mist often. Feed in summer at fortnightly intervals with a general houseplant fertilizer.

Propagation
Difficult to propagate from seed. It is better to buy a small established plant.

Repotting
Repot annually in spring until the plant is 1m/3ft tall, then just replace the topsoil.

PROBLEMS

Dry yellow needles mean conditions are too hot and dry. Water and move to a cooler, well-ventilated spot. Mist frequently.

Mealy bug and greenfly can attack this plant. Treat with a pyrethrum-based insecticide.

Aspidistra (Cast-iron plant)

EASY

Aspidistra comes from China, Japan and the Himalayas, where it grows in poor, marshy soil, and tolerates a range of temperatures, bar frost. It has been a popular houseplant since Victorian times because it flourishes in dark and draughty rooms. It is now enjoying revived popularity because it is attractive, easy to look after and able to withstand most conditions.

A. elatior (also known as *A. lurida*) and *A. elatior* 'Variegata' are the most readily available varieties.

It is a slow grower, each year producing only a few elegant, arched, shiny dark green leaves of between 30–46cm/12–18in. Occasionally small purple, bell-shaped flowers will appear at soil level.

Aspidistra will tolerate periods of dryness, but dislikes sunlight, soggy soil and frequent repotting. Clean the leaves with a damp sponge rather than using leaf shine.

Although it is quite expensive, it is virtually an everlasting houseplant.
It will benefit from a spell outdoors in summer.

Aspidistra elatior

A. elatior 'Variegata' (variegated cast-iron plant)

The yellow or white striped leaves shoot direct from the rhizome

CARE

Light and temperature
A shady position away from bright light or direct sunlight. *Aspidistra* prefers a cool temperature all year of around 13°C/55°F and as low as 7°C/45°F. It will, however, withstand most temperature fluctuations. Variegated species will need a little more light to maintain the leaf colour.

Water and feeding
Immerse the pot in water for 10 minutes and then drain well. Allow the soil almost to dry out between waterings. Never let the plant stand in water. In winter it will need watering less often, especially if the temperature is below 10°C/50°F. Add liquid food monthly and spray occasionally.

Propagation
Divide into small sections in autumn and place in a good potting mixture, ensuring adequate drainage.

Repotting
The plant does not like to be disturbed too often, so repot every 3 or 4 years in a no. 3 compost, ensuring good drainage.

PROBLEMS

If this plant is subjected to sunlight, brown spots will form on the leaves. Move to a shadier position and cut off the damaged leaves.

Aspidistra is susceptible to scale insect, red spider mite and mealy bug. Treat with a systemic insecticide and improve humidity.

Bambusa vulgaris (Bamboo)

EASY

This most exotic-looking houseplant is a relative newcomer. It is grown from a section of bamboo culm which produces a profusion of delicate pale green leafy fronds, giving the appearance of a standard plant.

Bamboo grows freely all over the tropical zones of the Far East, but it has only recently been adapted as a houseplant. It likes bright, sunny conditions and in summer does well outdoors.

A mature plant will grow to about 1m/39in high and the culm is 6–8cm/2–3in in diameter.

It is not particularly long lasting, and will probably have to be replaced after a couple of years.

Bambusa vulgaris

CARE

Light and temperature
This plant likes bright, warm conditions in summer. It will tolerate cooler temperatures in winter, but not below 5°C/40°F.

Water and feeding
Water 2–3 times a week in spring and summer and feed every 3 weeks with a general houseplant fertilizer. Water less in winter, allowing the soil almost to dry out between waterings. Never let the compost get soggy.

Propagation
This plant is difficult to propagate and best left to a professional.

Repotting
This should not be necessary.

PROBLEMS

Bambusa vulgaris is relatively problem free, though it is susceptible to spider mite in winter if the conditions are too warm and dry.

Beaucarnea recurvata (Ponytail plant)

Beaucarnea recurvata

EASY

Originally from the arid desert areas of Mexico, this is a most unusual and eye-catching succulent.

Its bottle-shaped stem serves as a water reservoir and grows several branches from which shoot slim, downward-curving, grey-green leaves of up to 1m/3ft in length. Sometimes it will produce clusters of small white flowers.

As a houseplant it will grow up to 2m/6ft in height and should live for several years.

It likes a bright, sunny position with fresh air and should ideally be positioned near a window. It does not require a lot of attention. Any leaves which fade can be gently peeled off.

Beaucarnea recurvata will benefit from a spell outdoors in summer but must be placed in a protected spot.

CARE

Light and temperature
This plant enjoys bright light and full sun all year round. In winter the temperature should not go below 10°C/50°F.

Water and feeding
Water once a week in summer and less in winter so that the compost stays almost dry. Never let it stand in water. Fertilize with a liquid solution at twice-weekly intervals in summer.

Propagation
By seed or by side shoots in summer. Both will need to be established in greenhouse conditions in a damp compost of peat and sand, covered in plastic and maintained at a temperature of 24°C/75°F.

Repotting
Repot every 2–3 years in a mixture of soil, leaf mould and sand, ensuring good drainage.

PROBLEMS

This plant is relatively problem free as long as it is never left to stand in water.

If its location is too warm and dry it is susceptible to spider mite and scale insect. Treat with a systemic insecticide.

Tips may die back; trim with discretion.

Begonia rex (Leaf begonia)

QUITE EASY

There is an enormous variety of *Begonia rex* hybrids available, and almost all have extremely attractive leaves with beautiful patterns. When choosing, look for good markings and avoid any with damaged leaves or rot on the stem.

Begonia grows in tropical and subtropical areas around the world and specimens from the foothills of the Himalayas were introduced into Europe in Victorian times. It is a most popular houseplant, and will grow to approximately 30cm/12in in height and 46cm/18in in width. It is good as an individual plant or in mixed plantings.

It needs to be kept out of direct sunlight but in a well-lit position and enjoys humidity, but only when the temperature is above 20°C/68°F. It does not like draughts, central heating or varying temperatures.

Begonia leaves are delicate, so treat the plant carefully and do not use leaf shine. Turn the pot regularly to ensure even growth as the plant will tend to grow towards the light.

The plant should last for up to 2 years and is easy to propagate with leaf cuttings.

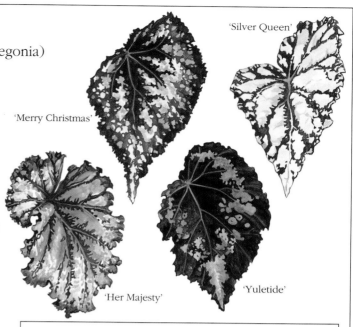

'Merry Christmas'
'Silver Queen'
'Her Majesty'
'Yuletide'

Begonia rex

CARE

Light and temperature
A bright situation but away from direct sunlight. The ideal summer temperature is 21°C/70°F. In winter it can go as low as 10°C/50°F.

Water and feeding
Water twice weekly in summer, with rain water if possible, and spray the leaves regularly. Water only once every 10 days in winter to keep the soil moist. At lower temperatures do not water over the leaves. In spring and summer add liquid fertilizer every 2 weeks.

Propagation
From tip cuttings in late spring. Cut off a shoot below the second pair of leaves. Trim the shoot and remove the lowest pair of leaves. Dip the cut surface in rooting hormone. Insert into compost in a propagator at 21°C/70°F until established.

Repotting
In spring, only when potbound, in a light, open mixture of loam and peat to which a little leaf mould and sand have been added.

PROBLEMS

This is a fragile plant, susceptible to draughts and temperature fluctuations.

If the leaves curl and become brittle, the position is too hot and dry. Water and move to a cooler spot.

If the leaves drop in winter, its position is too cold. Move to a warmer spot.

Red spider mite will cause the leaves to turn dull with webs underneath. Spray with a systemic insecticide.

If there are white or grey powdery patches on the leaves, the plant may have been overwatered and have mildew. Spray with a benomyl-based fungicide and move to a drier area.

Brachychiton rupestris (Queensland bottle tree)

QUITE EASY

This striking plant from Queensland has firm grey-green leaves and a most unusual twisted, bottle-shaped trunk which serves as a water reservoir, necessary in its hot but dry native habitat.

It likes bright, sunny conditions and should spend as much time as possible outdoors. Indoors its ideal location is on a windowsill.

Brachychiton is an undemanding houseplant. It is quite easy to look after and does well in a centrally heated room.

CARE

Light and temperature
In summer *Brachychiton* likes full sun with temperatures between 18–20°C/ 64–68°F. In winter the temperature should not be allowed to go below 10°C/50°F.

Water and feeding
It is important never to overwater this plant or let the compost become soggy, so allow it to dry out between waterings. In summer feed with a weak solution at monthly intervals.

Propagation
By seed, which should be planted in a just damp compost with a little extra sand and kept at a constant temperature of 20°C/71°F until established.

Repotting
Repot in spring each year with a good mixture to which a little sand has been added.

PROBLEMS

Relatively problem free, it may suffer from spider mite or scale insect if its location is too warm and dry.

If the leaves droop it has been overwatered. Allow the compost to dry out between waterings.

Brachychiton rupestris can be bought as a bonsai

Caladium bicolor (Angel wings, mother-in-law plant)

QUITE DIFFICULT

This plant is grown for its distinctive heart-shaped variously coloured leaves which are highlighted with contrasting veins and margins. Originally from Central America and Brazil, in its native tropical habitat *Caladium* grows under shady canopy, as its delicate leaves will burn in direct sunlight.

As a houseplant it should be treated as an annual, except by the expert, as it is very fragile and requires high humidity. The plant produces tubers which can be propagated quite easily.

Caladium grows quickly and may produce a green flower at the end of summer. When the leaves die down in autumn, the compost should be kept just moist and warm. In late winter lay the tubers in a new houseplant mixture, place in a bright spot and keep moist and warm. There are marbled and flecked varieties available.

While growing it likes a bright position out of direct sunlight and away from draughts. It needs plenty of humidity, so stand the pot over damp pebbles and mist frequently. Do not wipe the leaves or use leaf shine. Remove any dead or shrivelled leaves by cutting at the stem base.

Handle this plant carefully as it contains a skin irritant.

CARE

Light and temperature
A bright position, but never direct sunlight. During summer the temperature should be 15–18°C/60–64°F, but can go up to 24°C/75°F if the humidity is increased. In winter, keep the temperature around 13°C/55°F and the compost moist while you are overwintering the tubers.

Water and feeding
Water 2–3 times a week in summer, allowing the compost almost to dry out between waterings. Once the plant has stopped growing, reduce the water gradually until winter when the soil should be kept just moist. Ensure humidity by standing the pot over damp pebbles and spraying with tepid water. Feed with a weak solution of liquid fertilizer every 3 weeks while it is growing.

Propagation
In spring by splitting the overwintered tubers. Establish in a propagator in a mixture of soil, peat and sand at a constant temperature of at least 21°C/70°F.

Repotting
Place tubers in a damp mixture of soil, peat and sand in spring. Keep at a temperature of 24°C/75°F until new leaves appear and mist frequently while the plant becomes established.

PROBLEMS

Greenfly is attracted to this plant. Spray with a systemic insecticide.

Take care not to overwater the plant as this will cause mould on the leaves and the top of the compost. Allow to dry out, ensure there are no draughts and water less often.

The plant needs a certain amount of light to maintain leaf colour. If the leaves fade, conditions are too dark.

Shrivelled leaves mean that the compost is too dry or the temperature too hot. Water immediately and keep the plant moist by standing the pot over damp pebbles and spraying frequently.

Caladium bicolor 'Rhoers Dawn'

Chamaedorea elegans (Parlour palm, good luck palm)

EASY

This showy, shade-loving miniature is one of the best palms for growing indoors, its small but sturdy stem producing a cluster of dark green pinnate leathery leaves.

Originally from the mountainous forests of Mexico and Guatemala, where it grows as a ground-cover plant under very tall trees, it has been a popular houseplant for more than one hundred years.

Indoors it will take several years to grow to its mature height of 120cm/4ft.

Chamaedorea elegans produces pale yellow, ball-like flowers that turn into berries throughout the year. These flowers should be cut off as soon as they appear so that they do not weaken the plant.

This plant likes to be kept moist and in a shady position although it will cope with dry atmospheres for shortish periods.

Clean the foliage with a damp cloth and spray occasionally with tepid water.

Chamaedorea elegans lives for up to 10 years indoors and 2 or more plants may be stored in the same pot

CARE

Light and temperature
A semi-shady position, near a window, will suit this plant. It likes temperatures of up to 20°C/68°F in summer and no lower than 13°C/55°F in winter.

Water and feeding
Water 2 or 3 times a week, and in spring and summer feed with a weak solution of liquid fertilizer every 2–3 weeks. If conditions are dry, stand the pot over damp pebbles. In winter allow the compost to dry out between waterings.

Propagation
By seed in spring at a high temperature. Its propagation is difficult and best left to a professional.

Repotting
Repot each spring into a pot one size larger using a loam-based compost.

PROBLEMS

Red spider mite may attack the plant in dry and centrally heated air. Treat with a systemic insecticide.

Take care not to overwater the plant, indicated by the leaves turning brown. Allow the compost almost to dry out before watering again. Trim any leaves which have turned brown.

Equally it should not be underwatered or the leaves will turn yellow. Immerse the pot in water for 30 minutes, drain well and mist frequently.

Chlorophytum comosum 'Variegatum'

(Spider plant, airplane plant, St Bernard's lily)

Chlorophytum comosum 'Variegatum'

EASY

This rewarding houseplant is graceful, easy and quick to grow (ideal for a beginner), and should last for many years. It is tolerant of most conditions, even occasional neglect, and can be purchased throughout the year.

Originally from the subtropical areas of South Africa, where it grows in semi-shady, rocky outcrops, it was introduced as a houseplant in the mid-nineteenth century.

Chlorophytum has long, narrow, curving bright green leaves with either a cream centre or cream edges. It produces delicate rosettes of white flowers on long stems and these become independent plants with aerial roots that can be potted on. The parent plant will grow up to 46cm/18in in height and width.

Misting should keep the leaves clean as they are too brittle to wipe. Avoid leaf shine.

CARE

Light and temperature
A bright or semi-shady, well-ventilated position, away from direct sunlight, with temperatures not above 18°C/64°F in summer or below freezing point in winter. It can tolerate dark places, although leaves are more strongly coloured with bright light.

Water and feeding
Water 2–3 times a week in summer, allowing the soil almost to dry out between waterings, and once a week in winter. Mist daily. Add liquid food to the water every 2 weeks in summer.

Propagation
Roots and stems can be divided, the old soil carefully removed and smaller plants repotted. As the plantlets produce roots, these can be potted on in a small pot beside the parent. When established with new leaves of their own, these plantlets can be cut away from the parent. Alternatively, plantlets can be rooted in water and then potted at any time during the year.

Repotting
Chlorophytum is quite a quick grower and you may need to repot the parent plant twice a year. Use a loam-based mixture, and try not to break the roots when handling the plant.

PROBLEMS

If the plant is looking out of sorts, it may need feeding or is too warm.

Chlorophytum is sensitive to overwatering. If there are brown, slimy marks in the centre of the plant, allow the compost to dry out more between waterings.

The plant also needs plenty of humidity in the form of daily misting or the leaf tips will turn brown or become shrivelled. These tips can be cut off but will go brown again after a few weeks.

Dry air will also attract red spider mite and aphids. Treat spider mite with a systemic insecticide and aphids with pyrethrum-based insecticide.

Chrysalidocarpus lutescens

QUITE DIFFICULT (Areca palm, yellow palm, butterfly palm)

This slow-growing member of the palm family has graceful yellow-green pinnate fronds of up to 60cm/2ft long and 1.5cm/½in across which curve from a number of slender yellowish stems.

Originally from Madagascar, and bought commercially from Florida, *Chrysalidocarpus* needs bright but indirect light and warmish, humid conditions. It can withstand cool temperatures, but this will hinder growth. Avoid dry air and mist frequently. It does well in a conservatory.

As a houseplant, in the right conditions, it can grow 20cm/8in a year, reaching 2m/6ft as a mature plant. It should last for many years.

CARE

Light and temperature
Good light, but never direct sunlight. It enjoys a warm temperature of between 18–22°C/ 64–71°F all year round with a maximum of 27°C/80°F in summer and a minimum of 10°C/50°F in winter.

Water and feeding
Water thoroughly, but do not allow the compost to become saturated or to dry out. Feed with a liquid solution every 2 weeks in spring and summer.

Propagation
In spring by seed in a propagator with a constant temperature of 18–20°C/64–68°F. Alternatively, remove basal shoots with some roots and place in a mixture of soil, peat and sand. Cover with plastic and leave in a bright position until established.

Repotting
Repot in spring, only as needed, in the mixture recommended above.

PROBLEMS

Scale insect and red spider mite can attack this plant. Spray with a systemic insecticide and increase humidity by misting frequently.

If the air is too dry the leaves will turn yellow or develop brown spots. Improve moisture and humidity. Remove damaged leaves.

Chrysalidocarpus lutescens produces many suckers at the base of the plant, which can be separated and potted up

Cissus antarctica (Kangaroo vine, kangaroo ivy)

EASY

Cissus antarctica is a quick-growing climber, particularly useful for covering large areas quickly. It also looks good in a hanging basket.

This plant comes from Australia where it grows naturally among the protected undergrowth of the bush in the subtropical areas of New South Wales. As a houseplant it likes a cool position with plenty of water in summer and regular misting to prevent the leaves from turning brown at the edges.

Cissus antarctica has a dense, shrubby base with tendrils that grow to about 3m/9ft in length, which grip easily on to a trellis. It has glossy green oval leaves with brown veins and serrated edges. It is a good idea to pinch out new growth occasionally to encourage a dense plant, though it can easily be pruned back if it does become straggly.

The leaves should be cleaned occasionally with rain water. Do not use leaf shine.

Other popular members of the *Cissus* family are the delicately leaved *C. striata* and the interestingly variegated *C. discolor.*

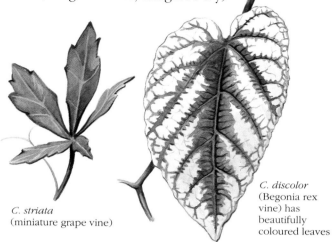

C. striata (miniature grape vine)

C. discolor (Begonia rex vine) has beautifully coloured leaves

CARE

Light and temperature
Keep *Cissus antarctica* in strong but indirect light. The ideal summer temperature is 18–21°C/64–70°F, and in winter no lower than 12°C/54°F.

Water and feeding
Water 2–3 times a week in summer, allowing the compost almost to dry out between waterings. In winter keep the compost just moist and water only every 2 weeks. Add a little liquid fertilizer at fortnightly intervals in summer.

Propagation
In spring using stem-tip cuttings with new growth which will root easily in a mixture of compost and sand. Cover the pot with plastic and put in a warm spot with suffused light until the new plants become established.

Repotting
If the plant is growing vigorously you may need to repot it twice a year. Once it reaches the desired height you can keep it in the same pot and just change the topsoil in spring.

PROBLEMS

If webs appear on the underside of the leaves the plant has been attacked by red spider mite. Spray with systemic insecticide and improve humidity.

Greenfly will cause the leaves to become distorted. Spray with a pyrethrum-based insecticide.

Brown or brittle leaves mean that the plant is too dry and hot. Water and mist well and move to a cooler position.

Take care not to overwater the plant or the leaves will develop brown spots and become mildewy. Check that the drainage is adequate and allow the compost to dry out between waterings. Mildew can be treated with a benomyl-based fungicide.

Cissus antarctica 'Ellen Danica'

Cocos nucifera (Coconut palm)

QUITE DIFFICULT

This exotic, slow-growing plant is a familiar sight along the beaches of South East Asia, the Pacific and Central and Southern America. Its trunk – up to 30m/90ft in height – is topped with feathery fronds which lean out towards the sea. At its base lie large edible nuts contained in brown husks.

Cocos nucifera has been specially cultivated as a houseplant. In the pot the plant is attached to the coconut seed, its glossy palm-like leaves growing from a short stem.

Indoors it can reach up to 3m/9ft, but the first 2–3 years are the most difficult in the plant's life. It does much better in a conservatory than it does in the average room, but once over the first 3 years it can live for a long time.

However the chances of getting any nuts in captivity, so to speak, are remote.

Ensure that the plant has adequate humidity – it does not like dry air – and try to give it a spell outdoors in a protected spot in summer.

Cocos nucifera

CARE

Light and temperature
A bright, warm position, with occasional direct sunlight. The ideal temperature is 18–21°C/64–70°F all year round, and no lower than 15°C/60°F in winter.

Water and feeding
The plant needs regular watering, but allow the compost to dry out between waterings. To ensure adequate humidity, stand the pot over damp pebbles and mist daily with tepid water. Feed with a liquid fertilizer at monthly intervals in spring and summer.

Propagation
This is difficult and best left to a professional.

Repotting
This will be necessary only if the plant outgrows its pot. Use a small container and make sure the nut remains above the surface of the soil. Use a mixture of 3 parts soil, 2 parts peat and 1 part sand.

PROBLEMS

Relatively problem free unless its conditions are too dry, which will cause the leaf tips to turn brown. Water and mist well, and stand the pot over damp gravel. You may have to move it to a better position.

White woolly patches on the leaves and white grubs in the soil indicate mealy bug. Spray malathion on to the leaves and water it into the soil according to the manufacturer's recommendations.

Webs on the underside of the leaves indicate red spider mite. Spray with a systemic insecticide and check watering and humidity is adequate.

Codiaeum (Joseph's coat)

QUITE DIFFICULT

Originally from the tropical areas of Malaysia and Indonesia, this most colourful but fragile houseplant has been popular since it was introduced in the mid-nineteenth century.

Its smooth, laurel-shaped, variegated leaves range in colour from green to yellow, orange and red, with mottled or striped yellow markings. It can grow into quite a large shrub, around 1m/3ft tall and across.

Codiaeum requires constant humid conditions, away from draughts and central heating. Strong light is needed to maintain colour in the leaves; however the plant should not be sprayed while it is in sunlight or the leaves will burn.

The plant rests in winter and loses many of its bottom leaves, so it is often treated as an annual, though the experienced grower can expect it to live for many years and can ensure a bushy plant by removing the growing tips.

Codiaeum 'Gold King'

'Excellent'

'Mrs Iceton'

'Norma'

CARE

Light and temperature
Bright, and occasionally direct, sunlight and a constant temperature all year no lower than 16°C/61°F.

Water and feeding
In summer water 2–3 times a week. Take care never to let the plant dry out. In winter use tepid water every 4–5 days. Spray occasionally to provide humidity and keep the leaves clean. Stand the pot over damp gravel. Feed with a liquid fertilizer every 2 weeks in summer.

Propagation
In spring by stem-tip cuttings using a propagator at a temperature of about 24°C/75°F. The plant yields a milky juice so sprinkle the cuttings in charcoal powder to seal the 'wound' before planting. Use gloves while handling the plant as the juice contains an irritant.

Repotting
In late spring, annually or as needed, in a loam-based compost. Pack tightly, but ensure good drainage.

PROBLEMS

Prone to red spider mite. Spray with a systemic insecticide and improve humidity. Also scale insect and mealy bug. Remove these with a cloth dipped in methylated spirit.

If the bottom leaves drop off, the conditions are too dry or cold or fluctuating. Move to a warmer spot where the conditions are more easily controllable.

Brown tips and shrivelled leaves are caused by hot, dry air or underwatering. Immerse the pot in water for 10 minutes, drain well, and do not allow the compost to dry out. Improve humidity by standing the pot over damp gravel and spraying frequently. The plant may also need to be moved to a cooler position. Damaged leaves can be cut off.

Overwatering will cause stem rot, recognizable by brown patches on the stem and a drooping of the leaves. Allow the compost to dry out and water less.

Coffea arabica (Arabian coffee plant, coffee tree of commerce)

EASY

Coffea arabica is closely related to *Gardenia*

The coffee plant adapts well to indoors and can be expected to grow to 1–2m/3–6ft in height. It has a single stem which in time becomes thick and bushy, especially if the growing tips are removed regularly.

The glossy, oval-shaped, pointed leaves are an attractive dark green and are prominently veined. Mature indoor plants will produce star-shaped white flowers in late summer which turn into green and eventually red berries containing coffee beans.

This plant is originally from the subtropical areas of Ethiopia, where it grows at a high altitude in quite cool temperatures. Indoors it needs a very moist atmosphere, so mist the plant frequently and place the pot over wet gravel. It must never be allowed to dry out completely.

Coffea arabica rests briefly in winter and may lose its leaves. At this time keep it barely damp and well away from central heating and draughts. Prune to keep the plant shapely.

The plant should last for 5–6 years.

CARE

Light and temperature
Bright but indirect light, away from direct sunlight. In summer the ideal temperature is 18–22°C/64–71°F. In winter a minimum of 8°C/45°F will be tolerated if the plant is kept quite dry.

Water and feeding
Water 2–3 times a week in spring and summer, but do not allow the plant to stand in water or to become soggy. Spray frequently. In winter water much less, especially if the surrounding temperature is cold, allowing the compost almost to dry out between waterings. Feed fortnightly with a liquid solution in spring and summer.

Propagation
Specially purchased seeds can be sown in spring and kept at 24°C/75°F in a propagator, in a mixture of loam, peat and sand. Place in a greenhouse or under a plastic cover in diffused light until established.

Repotting
Each spring in a mixture of loam, peat and sand, ensuring good drainage.

PROBLEMS

Relatively problem free, but prone to scale insect and mealy bug, especially if conditions are too dry. Spray with a systemic insecticide and improve humidity.

The leaves will wilt and may go yellow if the plant is overwatered or allowed to become soggy. Let it dry out and then water a little less.

Coleus blumei (Flame nettle)

EASY

This cultivated hybrid is grown for its highly coloured leaves. If the growing tips are pinched out regularly it should become an attractive, bushy plant of 60cm/2ft. It was introduced from Java in 1853.

Indoors it is often grown as an annual because it is quick-growing and easy to propagate. If the plant becomes very tired in winter and you wish to keep it rather than propagate, it can be cut back in spring to within 7.5cm/3in of the compost. *Coleus blumei* likes a moist atmosphere and needs direct light to keep its colours strong and its foliage in good condition.

Coleus blumei

Four of the numerous *Coleus blumei* hybrids

CARE

Light and temperature
Bright, direct sunlight with a warm temperature, ideally around 21°C/70°F. It will withstand temperatures of around 10°C/50°F, but likes slightly higher, preferably not below 13°C/55°F.

Water and feeding
Coleus needs moist, humid conditions so the soil should always be kept damp and the pot stood over wet gravel. Mist often. Keep the compost drier in winter. Feed with a liquid solution every 2 weeks, except in winter.

Propagation
Cut the plant back during winter and keep the compost quite dry. In early spring encourage new growth by watering and fertilizing. Take tip cuttings and place in a damp no. 1 compost. Keep in a shady spot at a temperature of 18°C/64°F.

Repotting
Repot in summertime as the plant outgrows its pot. To check this, remove the plant from the pot and see if it is rootbound.

PROBLEMS

If the temperature is too cool or there is insufficient water or moisture the plant will lose its leaves.

Prone to red spider mite in dry conditions. Remove individually with a cloth soaked in methylated spirit and improve humidity.

Cordyline terminalis (Ti plant, tree of kings, good luck plant)

QUITE DIFFICULT

This plant is sometimes called *Dracaena terminalis* or *Cordyline fruticosa* amongst nursery men.

Originally from the tropical areas of South East Asia and the Pacific, this exotic plant has a short, erect stem from which grow a cluster of slender, sword-shaped leaves up to 50cm/20in long. Its young growth is pink, turning coppery green to red as it matures. The plant will last for many years, though it will shed its lower leaves. As the lower leaves die they should be peeled off gently.

The adult plant will reach up to 3m/9ft, but it will not be easy to get an indoor plant to grow to this height in a pot. The roots will need unrestricted room. It will appreciate being put outdoors in the warm summer months.

Cordyline terminalis is a fragile houseplant and a slow grower. It needs a lot of humidity and a protected position, as it has in its native habitat where it thrives under the tree canopy. It dislikes direct sunlight and temperatures below 12°C/54°F. Mist the plant often, preferably with rain water, and clean the leaves with a damp cloth. Do not use leaf shine.

There are many varieties of *Cordyline terminalis*, including the Hawaiian Ti plant, with an all-green leaf which is used for making hula skirts. Others that are commonly available include the cheerful, broad-leafed 'Kiwi', which grows into a compact plant, the dramatically coloured 'Red Edge', whose leaves are only around 23cm/9in long, and 'Atom', one of the easier varieties both to find on sale and to grow over a long period.

The mature plants produce flowers but it is unlikely that a *Cordyline terminalis* will do so in domestic conditions.

Cordyline australis (the cabbage tree or palm lily) has sword-shaped green leaves from a common point, and was common in Victorian plantings as a centrepiece. It should be grown in full sunlight. *Cordyline indivisa* (the blue dracaena) is bigger altogether, and though sometimes sold as a houseplant, is more suitable for a warm sunny terrace where it will have plenty of room to expand.

Cordyline terminalis 'Lord Robertson'

'Kiwi'

'Red Edge'

'Atom'

C. congesta, sometimes
known as *C. stricta*

CARE

Light and temperature
This plant needs very good light to maintain colour in the leaf, but away from the midday sun which can cause burning in the summer. The ideal temperature is 18–21°C/64–70°F, but it will withstand temperatures of up to 27°C/80°F as long as it receives high humidity in the form of misting 3–4 times daily. In winter it will tolerate temperatures as low as 10°C/50°F.

Water and feeding
Keep the compost damp but never soggy in spring and summer. Reduce the watering considerably in winter, allowing the compost almost to dry out. Feed with a liquid fertilizer at fortnightly intervals in spring and summer. There is plenty of humus in the compost.

Propagation
In spring take tip shoots and pot them in a damp mixture made up of peat and sand. Cover with plastic, place in bright but indirect light and maintain a constant temperature of 18°C/64°F until established, when they can be transferred to a larger pot.

Repotting
In spring in a mixture of leaf mould, peat and sand. Ensure good drainage.

PROBLEMS

Scale insect may attack this plant. Remove with a cloth dipped in methylated spirit.

Webs on the underside of the leaves indicate red spider mite. Spray with a systemic insecticide. The Hawaiian Ti plant is particularly susceptible to this pest.

The leaves may become distorted with greenfly. Spray with a pyrethrum-based insecticide.

If the leaves rot and drop off, the plant may be too cold and wet. Move to a warmer place and if it is too wet allow the compost to dry out before watering.

It the plant gets straggly, cut out the tip to encourage bushiness. This can be used as a cutting (see 'Propagation').

Crassula argentea (Jade tree, money plant)

EASY

Originally from South Africa, this attractive succulent has glossy, dark green, fleshy leaves which grow from a tree-like trunk. It may produce pretty pink or white flowers in spring, which are shortlived.

Crassula makes an ideal houseplant as it likes the warm, dry atmosphere of a centrally heated home and does not require much attention. It should live for a good number of years.

In summer it should be watered regularly, but drained well. Mist occasionally to clean the leaves. In winter it much prefers a cool, dry place to rest.

Crassula is a slow grower, but can be everlasting so it is worthwhile investing in an attractive and sturdy pot. The adult plant should reach 1m/3ft in height. If it is necessary to prune the plant, dust the 'wound' with sulphur to stem the flow of its sap.

It enjoys a spell outside in summer in a sunny but protected position.

CARE

Light and temperature
Crassula needs sunlight. In summer it can withstand almost any amount of heat. In winter the temperature should be cool, but not below 5–7°C/40–45°F. Keep the compost almost dry at this time.

Water and feeding
In summer water 2–3 times a week; in winter once a month should suffice. Feed every 2 weeks in summer with a high-potash fertilizer into the compost or sprayed on the leaves.

Propagation
Usually by seed in a propagator or by stem cuttings, with a growing point and some leaves, which will root easily in a good seeding mixture at room temperature after they have been allowed to dry out for a few days.

Repotting
Only when necessary, probably every 2 years, using a loam-based compost mixed with sand.

PROBLEMS

If the plant does not grow it may need feeding. Also check to see if it is rootbound and needs repotting.

Growth may also be hindered if there are any white woolly patches on the roots, caused by mealy bug. If so, drench the roots with diluted malathion.

If the stems become elongated, the plant is being kept in too shady a place.

If the plant turns black and rotten at the base it has been overwatered and will probably die. Try cutting out the rot and dusting with sulphur.

Crassula will lose its leaves and condition if left in too warm a spot in winter. Move to a cooler, dry place.

Crassula argentea is a succulent cultivated as an indoor plant since the 1830s

Cryptanthus (Starfish plant, earth star)

EASY

Cryptanthus is an ideal houseplant as it thrives in the sun and if treated well is almost problem free.

Originally from Brazil, it grows as an epiphyte in dry thorn forests. It is actually a member of the bromeliad family (see page 119), though atypically it does not store its own water. Its root system is shallow and it can easily be wired on to bark or a log to imitate its native habitat, but care must be taken to ensure it does not dry out.

The plant forms a star-shaped rosette of spiny, arched, pink or brown leaves with wavy cream stripes running across. Small cream flowers may bloom throughout the year. These are concealed within the foliage and account for the plant's genus name, which in Greek means 'hidden flower'.

It is a slow grower, but should last indefinitely.

Top: *Cryptanthus forsterianus*; middle: *Cryptanthus tricolor*; bottom: *Cryptanthus bivattatus*

C. fosterianus (stiff pheasant leaf) is the largest variety

C. bromeliades 'Tricolor' (rainbow star)

CARE

Light and temperature
Bright, sunny conditions throughout the year with warm temperatures of between 20–22°C/68–72°F.

Water and feeding
Provide humidity by standing the pot on damp gravel and misting frequently with rain water. Water the soil sufficiently to keep it moist and allow it to dry out between waterings. Feed every 3–4 weeks in summer with a weak solution.

Propagation
In spring by detaching any well-formed lateral shoots and potting them in a damp mixture of orchid compost. Cover with clear plastic and place in bright but indirect light for about 3 months, then repot in a small container filled with a pure peat mix.

Repotting
Seldom, except for propagation, as the pot only provides support for the plant. They have largish root systems.

PROBLEMS

Leaves will shrivel or turn brown if the atmosphere is too hot or dry. Spray and water regularly as this plant needs a lot of humidity. Trim off the damaged sections of the leaves.

The plant will rot at the base if it is too cold and wet. Allow it to dry out and water less.

Dull leaves indicate lack of light. Spray and move to a warmer position.

Ctenanthe oppenheimiana

QUITE DIFFICULT (Never-never plant)

This Brazilian plant is much sought after for the unusual dark green markings on its pale green foliage. An attractive plant, it has long stalks that produce large pointed elliptical leaves of up to 30cm/12in long which are red underneath.

Its native habitat is the Alto de Sena region in South East Brazil, which has 350–400cm/140–160in of rain per year. It grows along the escarpments of this wet coastal range and is found underneath the low tree canopy of these dripping forests.

Ctenanthe is a good houseplant because it enjoys average room temperatures and has no particular needs. As long as it is not overwatered and has adequate humidity in the form of misting and standing the pot over damp gravel, it should do well. Indoors it should grow to 1m/3ft high and wide.

The plant has a dormant period in winter when it will simply need to be kept warm and the compost prevented from drying out.

It should last for 5–6 years, becoming an attractively bushy plant.

CARE

Light and temperature
Semi-shade during summer at 18–21°C/64–70°F, but it will accept temperatures up to 29°C/85°F. In winter it prefers more light and will withstand temperatures as low as 10°C/50°F if kept almost dry.

Water and feeding
Water thoroughly in spring and summer. Place the pot over pebbles almost covered with water as this plant enjoys high humidity coupled with warm temperatures. Spray daily. Feed every 2 weeks with general houseplant fertilizer from early spring to end of summer. During winter water once a week and less if the temperature drops to 10°C/50°F.

Propagation
In spring from stem cuttings with several leaves. Treat with a rooting powder and pot in a mixture of peat and sand. Cover with plastic or place in a greenhouse at 21°C/70°F until established.

Repotting
In spring in a no. 2 peat-based compost.

PROBLEMS

Mealy bug, scale insect and red spider mite can attack this plant. Spray mealy bug with diluted malathion and scale insect and spider mite with a systemic insecticide.

Hot, dry conditions will cause the leaves to curl. Water well and increase humidity by misting and standing the pot over damp gravel.

If the position is too cold in winter the plant will suffer root rot. Allow to dry out, water less frequently and move to a warmer position.

Ctenanthe lubbersiana has a more upright habit than *C.O. tricolor*

Cupressus (Monterey cypress)

QUITE EASY

This Southern Californian conifer has recently become a popular houseplant. It is quick-growing and can be pruned easily to enhance its natural pyramid shape.

Cupressus can be seen growing along the coastal areas of California, its spreading branches supporting a canopy of bright to dark green needles.

It is easy to grow indoors as long as it has plenty of indirect light and its compost is never allowed to dry out or become soggy. It should be misted occasionally.

The plant should last for many years.

CARE

Light and temperature
Bright but not direct sunlight. The ideal temperature in summer is 18–22°C/64–72°F, with a cooler temperature of 5–10°C/41–50°F in winter.

Water and feeding
Keep moist but never soggy at all times. In winter it will need less water, but must never be allowed to dry out. Feed with a liquid solution every 4 weeks in spring and summer. Mist occasionally.

Propagation
By stem cuttings in spring. Propagating this plant is quite difficult and best left to professionals.

Repotting
As needed, probably every second year, in a mixture of no. 2 soil-based compost.

PROBLEMS

If conditions are too warm and dry, red spider mite will attack the plant. Remove with a cloth soaked in methylated spirit.

Cupressus macrocarpa is rewarding because of its vigorous growth

Cycas revoluta (Sago palm)

EASY

This exotic palm is extremely slow-growing and therefore usually quite expensive.

Originally from South East Asia and Japan, where it grows under canopy, it has a stout pineapple-shaped stem from which project feathery evergreen fronds of up to 1m/3ft in length. The plant will usually produce one of these a year. Its mature height is around 2m/6ft, and it will last 50 or 60 years.

Cycas likes bright, indirect sunlight, thrives in normal room temperatures and does not need much humidity.

Mature plants benefit from a spell outdoors in summer if conditions are warm. Even so it will not flower.

CARE

Light and temperature
Strong but indirect light. It likes average room temperatures – 18–22°C/64–72°F – throughout the year, though it is fairly resistant to occasional cool temperatures and can tolerate as low as 5–10°C/41–50°F.

Water and feeding
Water moderately all year, enough to keep the compost moist but never let it dry out or become soggy. Feed once a month in spring and summer with a weak solution.

Propagation
In spring by seed or by potting basal roots in a seed compost. Establish in a propagator at 30°C/86°F. This process is quite difficult and best left to professionals.

Repotting
Repot every 2–3 years in spring or autumn in a mixture of soil, peat and sand.

PROBLEMS

Red spider mite and scale insect tend to attack this plant. Spray with a systemic insecticide and move to a cooler position.

Cycas revoluta is one of the most primitive flowering plants

Cyperus papyrus (Egyptian paper plant)

DIFFICULT

In ancient Egypt this exotic plant was used for making papyrus.

As a houseplant it grows to 2–3m/6–10ft, with large clusters of long, smooth stems topped with dense thread-like bracts which can produce a large umbrellate flower.

Originally from the marshy river banks of the Mediterranean, it is a demanding houseplant as it needs bright conditions, a lot of moisture and warm winter temperatures. In fact, it is impossible to give this plant too much moisture.

It is long lasting if the conditions are right.

CARE

Light and temperature
Bright light and high temperatures of up to 20–24°C/68–75°F. In winter the temperature should be no lower than 13°C/55°F.

Water and feeding
Cyperus must always be kept very moist and the pot should be stood in a shallow bowl of water so that the compost and roots are always damp. Spray frequently. Use a liquid fertilizer every 2 weeks.

Propagation
Easily by division of clumps. Remove the plant from the pot and break the rootball into sections. Cut off the tips of the leaves on one stem and bend the stem so the leaves are submerged in water. New plants emanate from the old leaf. Change the water every 5 days.

Repotting
In spring, in a mixture if soil, peat and sand, in a smallish pot.

PROBLEMS

The tips of the bracts will turn brown if the plant is too dry. Stand the pot in water. Trim the damaged needles.

Insufficient light will stop growth. Move to a better position.

Prone to whitefly and greenfly. Spray with a pyrethrum-based insecticide.

Cyperus alternifolius 'Zimula'

Dieffenbachia (Dumb cane, leopard lily)

Dieffenbachia picta 'Marianne' is one of the spotted dumb canes

QUITE DIFFICULT

This ornamental houseplant originally came from the tropical rain forests of Colombia, Costa Rica and Venezuela. Growing from a thick stem are elongated dark green leaves which are attractively variegated with creamy yellow in the centre.

As a houseplant it grows up to 1m/3ft. It is a quick grower and can last for a long time, though as the plant becomes older it sheds its lower leaves and is best replaced after 3–4 years.

It requires constant and warm conditions, like those it enjoys in its native habitat, and will do well in central heating as long as it is misted daily and the pot stood over damp gravel. It also benefits from a spell outdoors in summer in a shady spot. It does not like draughts, so make sure it is placed in a protected position.

Dieffenbachia produces a poisonous sap, so always wear gloves when handling the plant.

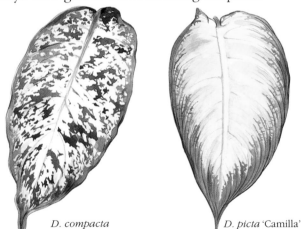

D. compacta   D. picta 'Camilla'

CARE

Light and temperature
This plant thrives in a shady position with a little indirect light. The ideal temperature is around 18°C/64°F. If above 20°C/70°F it will need even more humidity. Do not let the temperature go below 10°C/50°F.

Water and feeding
Water well in summer, probably every second day, as the compost must always be kept moist, but never soggy. In winter water less as the plant will not be growing and soil should be allowed almost to dry out between waterings. Feed every 2 weeks in summer with a liquid fertilizer.

Propagation
By stem-tip cuttings just below a node. Treat the base with a rooting powder and bury the cuttings in a pot filled with damp peat and sand. Place in a greenhouse or wrap in plastic and keep in bright light at a constant temperature of 21–24°C/70–75°F until established. It can also be propagated by cutting the stem into 7–8cm/3in sections and burying in the same medium.

Repotting
In spring, in a mixture of organic soil, peat and sand.

PROBLEMS

Prone to stem rot, indicated by a slimy stem. Do not allow the plant to get too wet. Dust damaged areas with sulphur and take care not to overwater.

Overwatering will also cause the leaves to turn yellow. Allow the compost to dry out and water less.

If the lower leaves droop, the position is too cold. Move to a warmer spot.

Dionaea muscipula (Venus fly trap)

VERY DIFFICULT

A fascinating insectivorous perennial with clusters of dainty rosettes that have spiny leaves hinged in the middle, which close over and kill any insect attracted by its juices. The action is immediate. It has adapted thus, being unable to get nutrition from other sources.

It is a small plant, growing to a maximum height of 7.5–20cm/3–8in. White flowers will appear in summer.

Dionaea muscipula comes from the temperate areas of the Carolinas in North America where it grows in mossy and marshy surroundings. As a houseplant it will require similar conditions to its native habitat – a bright but cool, damp spot with a lot of humidity.

It is a difficult plant to grow indoors and has a dormant period in winter.

Dionaea muscipula

CARE

Light and temperature
Bright but indirect light and a cool, damp position, with temperatures no lower than 10°C/50°F in winter.

Water and feeding
It likes damp conditions and fresh rain water, so the pot should be stood in a shallow container of rain water, and the compost kept moist at all times; never let it dry out. In winter cover the pot with plastic and keep the compost just moist.

Feed occasionally with very small bits of meat or dead insects.

Propagation
In autumn plant seeds in a damp, peaty compost mixed with moss. Cover with plastic until established. Alternatively the rhizome can be divided in spring and each piece placed into its own pot, then covered with plastic until established.

Repotting
Not necessary.

PROBLEMS

Although relatively pest-free, it is difficult to grow as conditions must be as close as possible to its natural habitat in order for the plant to thrive.

It must never be allowed to dry out otherwise the plant will die. Stand in a pot filled with a little water at all times.

In winter, when there are no flies, feed with small pieces of meat.

Dizygotheca elegantissima (False aralia, finger aralia)

QUITE DIFFICULT

A pretty shrub from the tropical islands of the New Hebrides, *Dizygotheca elegantissima* has a slim mottled stem from which grow palm-like, leathery, serrated leaves of around 7.5cm/3in long and 1cm/½in wide. These leaves are reddish-brown when young and dark green when mature.

In its native habitat it grows on the steamy mountainside along with crotons, cycas, cordylines and epipremnums. Indoors it needs similiar conditions, so to ensure plenty of humidity stand the pot over damp pebbles and mist frequently. It will do best in a greenhouse or conservatory.

The plant can be pruned to improve its shape and bushiness.

A mature specimen will grow to 1.5m/4–5ft tall and should last for up to 5 years.

CARE

Light and temperature
Bright but indirect light. The temperature should always be warm, with a summer maximum of 24°C/75°F and a winter minimum of 15°C/60°F when the plant is dormant.

Water and feeding
Immerse the pot in water for 30 minutes and drain well, allowing the compost almost to dry out between waterings. Feed at fortnightly intervals in spring and summer with a liquid solution. In winter water less, but do not allow the plant to dry out completely.

Propagation
Difficult. It is best left to a professional.

Repotting
In spring, as needed, into a pot the next size up. Use a no. 2 peat-based compost.

PROBLEMS

If the plant is overwatered, the foliage will droop, and if it is underwatered, it will lose its leaves. Follow the instructions in 'Water and feeding' carefully.

If the conditions are too dry, the plant will start to look unhealthy. Water well and improve the humidity by standing the pot over damp pebbles and misting daily.

Greenfly tends to attack this plant. Treat with a pyrethrum-based insecticide.

White woolly patches on the leaves and stems indicate mealy bug. Remove with a cloth dipped in methylated spirit.

Dizygotheca elegantissima, sometimes sold as *D. laciniata*, should be planted 2 or 3 to a pot for maximum effect

Dracaena deremensis (Striped dracaena)

QUITE EASY

Originally from the tropical areas of Africa, where its native habitat is under the tree canopy, this elegant shrubby plant has sword-shaped, grey-green striped leaves, with white margins running along the edge, that grow up to 45cm/18in long and 5cm/2in wide.

It likes a protected spot with reasonable light, good humidity and warm temperatures.

Often mistaken for a member of the palm family, *Dracaena deremensis* can grow to 4m/12ft in a relatively dark location. It is a slow grower, but should live for 7–8 years, though the bottom leaves will tend to wither, showing the cane stem.

Dracaena deremensis 'Janet Craig'

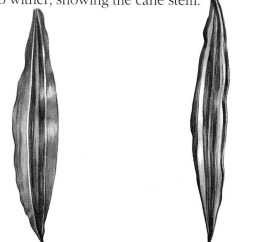

D. d. 'Lemon Lime'   D. d. 'White Stripe'

CARE

Light and temperature
A reasonable amount of light is needed to maintain the colour in the leaves, though it can do well in a shady position. It likes fairly high temperatures, of around 18–24°C/64–75°F, no lower than 12°C/53°F in winter when it has a resting period.

Water and feeding
Water 2–3 times a week while the plant is growing, but do not let the compost get soggy and do not stand the pot in water. When dormant, water sparingly and allow the compost almost to dry out between waterings. Feed at fortnightly intervals in spring and summer with a liquid solution.

Propagation
From basal shoots, tip or stem cuttings. Plant in a mixture of peat and sand, cover with plastic and keep at a constant temperature of around 20–24°C/71–75°F until established.

PROBLEMS

If the lower leaves droop, the plant is too hot and dry. Water well and spray frequently.

If there is no new growth, the plant needs feeding.

Spots on the leaves are caused by a fungal parasite. Treat with a systemic fungicide.

Scale insect and mealy bug are attracted to this plant. Remove with a cloth dipped in methylated spirit.

If the leaves become faded with webbing on the underside, red spider mite has attacked the plant. Spray with a systemic insecticide and improve humidity.

Dracaena deremensis 'Warneckii' has 2 stripes

Dracaena fragrans 'Massangeana' (Dragon tree)

Dracaena fragrans 'Massangeana'

EASY

A popular and hardy house-plant, *Dracaena fragrans* 'Massangeana' will withstand a variety of temperatures and conditions as long as it has adequate humidity. The wide yellow stripe is bordered by narrower yellow lines.

It comes originally from the eastern part of Africa, Sierra Leone and Ethiopia, where it is to be found growing in brick-red soil on the moist slopes and humid valleys of the mountains, especially the Ucambaras. As a houseplant it will reach 1.5m/ 4–5ft in height if given the right conditions.

The plant has rosettes of strong green curving leaves with a central yellow stripe. As it grows it loses its lower leaves, to show a stout bare stem.

Indoors *Dracaena fragrans* likes bright, filtered light, average room temperatures and plenty of humidity, so the pot should be placed over damp pebbles and the plant misted frequently, though not while it is in sunlight.

It does not like draughts so stand in a protected spot.

The plant is a relatively slow grower and should last for several years.

CARE

Light and temperature
It needs plenty of light to bring out the colour in its leaves, but keep the plant out of the midday sun. Ideally it likes warm temperatures of between 18–21°C/ 64–71°F, though it is fairly flexible and will tolerate as low as 13°C/55°F with less frequent watering.

Water and feeding
Water once or twice a week in summer and once a week in winter. Avoid sogginess, but never allow the compost to dry out completely. Feed with a liquid solution every 2 weeks in summer.

Propagation
In spring by stem-tip cuttings or stem sections cut to 8cm/3in long. Establish in a humid propagator at 24°C/75°F.

Repotting
In spring every 2–3 years in a loam- or peat-based compost, ensuring good drainage.

PROBLEMS

It is natural for the plant to lose its lower leaves gradually, but if they are showing signs of drooping generally, the conditions are too dry and hot. Water well and spray.

Brownish spots on the leaves denote botrytis, meaning the plant is possibly too cold and damp. Spray with fungicide, move to a warmer place and allow the surface of the soil to dry out between waterings. You should also remove the damaged leaves.

If the plant is overwatered the leaves and stem will rot. Allow to dry out and water less.

Prone to scale insect and red spider mite. Spray with a systemic insecticide and improve humidity.

Dracaena marginata (Madagascar dragon tree)

QUITE EASY

This exotic-looking plant is the easiest *Dracaena* to grow indoors as it is tolerant of varying room conditions and different degrees of humidity.

The young plant produces leaves from the base. Gradually over the years the lower leaves fall so, as the plant grows, it develops several slender, ringed trunks which produce dense tufts of spiky green leaves with reddish edgings. *D. m.* 'Tricolor', a more recent introduction, has pink, cream and green striped leaves.

In its native habitat, Madagascar, it is quite a substantial specimen, growing to a height of 3m/9ft. Indoors it will reach 2m/6ft, gradually losing its basal leaves, giving the plant its distinctively marked stem.

It should last for several years. In warmer climates it likes a spell outdoors in summer in a sheltered position.

D. m. tricolor was introduced in the 1970s and is a splendidly coloured plant

Dracaena marginata

CARE

Light and temperature
The plant needs a reasonable amount of light to keep the colour in its leaves and requires temperatures of 18–21°C/64–71°F all year, though it will withstand temperatures as low as 13°C/55°F in winter.

Water and feeding
Water 2–3 times a week in summer and spray frequently. In winter, when the plant is dormant, water less and allow the soil almost to dry out between waterings. Feed at fortnightly intervals with a liquid solution in spring and summer.

Propagation
By stem-tip cuttings or stem sections cut to 8cm/3in lengths. Place in a no. 2 peat-based compost and establish in a propagator at 24°C/75°F.

Repotting
For the first 2 years repot each spring in a no. 2 peat-based compost. Thereafter every other year, finishing up in a 20–25cm/8–10in pot, replacing the top 7.5cm/3in of compost annually.

PROBLEMS

If conditions are too dry, the lower leaves will droop. Water and spray more often.

If the position is too cold the plant will lose its leaves and stop growing. Move to a better location.

If there is no new growth in spring the plant needs feeding.

White woolly patches on the leaves and stems indicate mealy bug. Remove with a cloth dipped in methylated spirit or spray with diluted malathion.

D. m. colorama is a more recent introduction and equally adaptable and easy to grow

Dracaena reflexa (Song of India)

QUITE DIFFICULT

This ornamental *Dracaena* comes from the monsoon forests and mangrove swamps of India and Sri Lanka, where it is found under the tree canopy growing to 4m/12ft if given support.

It has beautiful, broad, creamy-yellow arched leaves, with a central green stripe, that grow up to 15cm/6in long.

It is a sensitive houseplant and a slow grower. A mature specimen will reach 1m/3ft in height with a spread of 50cm/18in. It should last for many years, though it will shed its lower leaves.

Although it likes plenty of humidity, take care not to overwater the plant and do not repot it too often. Stand the pot over a saucer of damp pebbles.

Dracaena reflexa

CARE

Light and temperature
Bright but indirect light and warm temperatures, not below 18°C/64°F, all year.

Water and feeding
Keep just moist, avoiding sogginess and never letting the compost dry out. Feed every 2 weeks in spring and summer with a liquid solution.

Propagation
By top cuttings. Establish in a propagator at a constant temperature of 25°C/77°F.

Repotting
Do not repot this plant very often, every 3 years is recommended.

PROBLEMS

The plant will shed its lower leaves naturally as it grows.

Take care to ensure good humidity as dry conditions, especially central heating, will cause browned edges on the leaves. Water carefully and mist frequently.

Watch for mealy bugs and treat with a swab dipped in methylated spirit.

Epipremnum aureum (Devil's ivy)

EASY

This plant is also commonly known as *Scindapsus aureus*.
A vigorous climber, it comes from the humid tropical Solomon and South East Asian islands, where it attaches itself to the bark of host tree trunks.

It is easy to grow indoors and as a houseplant its aerial roots can be trained to cover a moss pole to a height of 1–1.5m/3–5ft, or its tendrils can look good trailing over a hanging basket. The plant can also be grown in water.

Epipremnum has glossy green leaves covered with yellow patches or spots. These will gradually fade and should be removed from the stem. Pinch out new shoots occasionally to ensure dense growth. It needs warm, humid conditions and should be sprayed frequently with tepid water.

Wash your hands after handling the plant as the leaves contain an irritant.

Epipremnum aureum
'Marble Queen'

Epipremnum aureum

CARE

Light and temperature
Bright indirect light with temperatures around 18–24°C/64–75°F all year, and never below 13°C/55°F.

Water and feeding
In spring and summer water 2–3 times a week, allowing the soil to dry out between waterings. Good drainage is essential for this plant. Water less in winter. Spray frequently. Use a liquid fertilizer every 2 weeks in spring and summer.

Propagation
In spring from stem-tip cuttings 10cm/4in long. Allow to root in water and then plant in the mixture recommended below.

Repotting
Every other year in a peat-based no. 2 compost.

PROBLEMS

Ensure good drainage and avoid overwatering as the plant can develop stem rot. Allow the compost to dry out and water less frequently.

If the position is too damp or dark there may be root rot and leaf drop. Move to a brighter position.

White woolly patches on the leaves indicate mealy bug. Remove with a cloth dipped in methylated spirit or spray with diluted malathion.

Euonymus japonica (Japanese spindle tree)

QUITE DIFFICULT

Originally from Japan, where it is found by the sea and is often used for hedges, *Euonymus japonica* is a multiple-branched evergreen with either fine leathery leaves with white edges or dark green glossy leaves 3–5cm/1–2in long which have central yellow patches. In late spring it may develop small white flowers.

As a houseplant it will grow up to 1m/3ft. It can be made into quite a bushy specimen if the growing shoots are regularly pinched out.

It is a hardy houseplant. It likes good light, but tolerates very cold rooms. If kept in a heated room it will probably shed its leaves in winter.

Place the plant outdoors for a spell in early summer. After it has passed its best indoors it can be moved into the garden in summer where it will make an attractive shrub.

Euonymus japonica 'Argenteo', the silver queen

CARE

Light and temperature
Bright but indirect light and cool temperatures suit this plant. In winter it benefits from 3–4 hours of sunshine daily. The ideal temperature is between 13–16°C/55–61°F, a little higher if it is stood over a bowl of wet pebbles.

Water and feeding
Water well in summer, letting the topsoil dry out between waterings. In winter water sparingly, but ensure it doesn't dry out completely. Mist leaves occasionally. Feed with liquid fertilizer at fortnightly intervals in spring and summer.

Propagation
In spring take tip cuttings 7.5cm/3in long, dust with rooting hormone, place in a mixture of soil, peat and sand, and keep at between 21–24°C/70–75°F in filtered light until established.

Repotting
In spring using a mixture of soil, peat and sand, but only when the plant has outgrown its container.

PROBLEMS

Cobwebs underneath the leaves indicate red spider mite. It can also be attacked by aphids and scale insect. Spray with a systemic insecticide.

Leaf drop may occur if the plant is kept in too warm a spot during winter.

Mildew is a common problems with this plant. If it appears on the leaves, spray with a fungicide.

Euphorbia trigona (Spurge)

EASY

This cactus-like succulent grows upright stout stems which produce lateral rows of thorny leaves.

Originally from the arid areas of Africa, it is a most undemanding houseplant, requiring only good light and a little water in order to thrive indoors. It does, however, benefit from a spell outside in summer on a warm patio.

The plant produces a poisonous juice so it should be handled with care and kept out of the reach of children·and animals.

CARE

Light and temperature
Bright, even direct, sunlight with temperatures between 15–18°C/60–64°F all year.

Water and feeding
This plant does not need a lot of water. In spring and summer water only once a week and in winter only occasionally by submerging the pot in water for 15 minutes and then allowing it to drain. The top of the compost should dry out between waterings. In spring and summer feed monthly with a weak solution.

Propagation
By cuttings. Run tepid water over the cutting until the sap has stopped flowing. Allow to dry and plant in a compost for cactus.

Repotting
Only as necessary in a cactus potting mixture.

PROBLEMS

This plant is relatively problem free.

Always use gloves when handling.

Euphorbia trigona 'Hermentiona'

Fatshedera lizei (Ivy tree)

'Variegata'

'Anna Michels'

EASY

This hybrid, a cross between *Fatsia japonica* and *Hedera helix*, was created in France in 1910 and retains the best features of both species. It is a climber, up to a height of 1–1.5m/3–5ft, and usually needs support in the form of a stake or moss pole.

It has glossy dark green leaves with five lobes, and mature plants may produce small green flowers.

Fatshedera is quite a hardy plant, but it must not be overwatered or allowed to dry out. Spray regularly and if it is in a centrally heated room stand the pot over damp pebbles. Indoors it will tolerate quite dark conditions, though it prefers good light, which will improve the appearance of the plant. Pinch out the new growth to encourage bushiness and wash the leaves occasionally with a damp cloth. Do not use leaf shine.

It should last for several years, at which point you may wish to propagate a new plant.

Fatshedera lizei 'Pia'

CARE

Light and temperature
A well-lit room and quite cool temperatures – as low as 7°C/45°F in winter and not above 18°C/64°F in summer.

Water and feeding
Water 2–3 times a week in summer, but do not allow the pot to stand in water or the compost to become soggy. Water less in winter, especially if the temperature is low, but take care not to let it dry out. Use a houseplant fertilizer every 2 weeks in spring and summer.

Propagation
In spring root stem-tip cuttings of 10–15cm/4–6in in water. Cover with plastic and establish at a minimum temperature of 13°C/55°F in filtered light.

Repotting
A young plant should be repotted in spring in a no. 2 peat-based compost, and a mature plant only when potbound.

PROBLEMS

If the leaves turn yellow, the plant has been overwatered. Allow to dry out and water less.

If the plant becomes spindly it needs to be moved to a lighter place to encourage denser growth.

Red spider mite and aphids can attack this plant. Spray with a systemic or pyrethrum-based insecticide respectively and increase humidity.

Fatsia japonica (Japanese aralia, false castor oil plant)

EASY

An attractive evergreen shrub with dark, shiny, lobed and pointed leaves, *Fatsia japonica* will grow up to 2m/6ft as a mature houseplant and may produce creamy white flowers in autumn.

Originally from the temperate zones of Japan, where it grows in the rainforests, it is easy to look after indoors.

A quick grower, it prefers a cool spot and a protected position away from draughts, yet it is very tolerant of both high and low temperatures and can be planted outdoors in summer where it will soon acclimatize. It will not, however, withstand heavy frosts.

To encourage a denser plant, pinch out the new growth occasionally. It can also be pruned to improve its shape. Clean the leaves with a damp cloth and do not use leaf shine.

Fatsia japonica should last for many years.

PROBLEMS

If the temperature is too warm, the leaves will turn yellow and fall off. Mist and move to a cooler spot.

Overwatering will cause the leaves to droop. Allow the compost to dry out and follow the instructions in 'Water and feeding'.

Susceptible to aphids. Treat with a pyrethrum-based insecticide.

Cobwebs on the underside of leaves indicate red spider mite, encouraged by dry conditions. Water well and spray with systemic insecticide.

CARE

Light and temperature
A bright, even sunny, spot will suit this plant. The temperature should never go above 21°C/72°F in summer but can go as low as zero in winter.

Water and feeding
Immerse the pot in water for 30 minutes, drain well and allow to dry out before watering again. You may need to do this 2–3 times a week in summer, but less in winter. Mist frequently. Feed with a liquid solution at fortnightly intervals in spring and summer.

Propagation
Take basal shoots and plant in a mixture of peat and sand. Establish in a cool greenhouse or under a plastic cover in indirect light at 15°C/60°F.

Repotting
In spring, as necessary, in a no. 2 compost.

Fatsia japonica was a favourite with the Victorians, having been discovered in 1838.

Ficus benjamina 'Starlight' (Weeping fig)

EASY

This relatively recent introduction from Israel is a very much improved version of *Ficus benjamina* 'Variegata', the much sought-after tropical tree also known as the 'weeping fig'.

In good conditions 'Starlight' will grow to a densely foliaged 3m/9ft, its leaves very much whiter than the original plant and dappled with green blotches.

As a houseplant it should last for many years.

CARE

Light and temperature
Being variegated it is important that it is in a very good light situation, but away from the midday sun where the leaves could burn. It enjoys temperatures up to 24°C/75°F in summer and no lower than 13°C/55°F in winter.

Water and feeding
Water thoroughly in spring and summer, but allow the surface of the compost to dry out between waterings. Do not let the plant stand in water or the leaves will drop. During summer spray daily, particularly during high temperatures. Feed at fortnightly intervals during spring and summer with a general houseplant liquid fertilizer. In winter, depending on the temperature, 1 good watering per week should suffice.

Propagation
By stem-tip cuttings taken in spring and placed in a compost of peat and sand and maintained in a propagator at 24°C/75°F. Water the cuttings thoroughly.

Repotting
Annually in spring into a no. 2 peat-based compost. When the plant is mature, you will only need to change the topsoil in the container.

PROBLEMS

If the leaves drip, the plant is receiving insufficient light or too much water.

Brown scaly insects on the underside of the leaves will cause leaf discoloration. Remove the insects with a cloth dipped in methylated spirit.

Cobwebs on the underside of the leaves indicates red spider mite. Spray with a systemic insecticide, check watering and spray more often.

Opposite: *Ficus benjamina* 'Starlight'

F. benjamina 'Reginald'

F. benjamina 'Natasha'

F. nitida (Indian laurel) is a sun-lover and greedy for light. Its leaves are a rich dark green and the plant has an erect habit. It is used as an outdoor tub plant in the southwest of America. It does well, even in dry atmospheres.

F. longifolium likes similar conditions to *F. benjamina* but has elongated dark green leaves of up to 14cm/6in; they look dramatic displayed against white walls.

F. 'Curly' is a colourful variety of weeping fig. Keep it in a very light position so that the leaves are well variegated.

Ficus diversifolia (Mistletoe fig)

QUITE EASY

This is the hardiest and also the most slow-growing of the fig family.
It grows to around 2.5m/8ft tall and has small, firm, almost round, dull
green leaves which grow sparsely on a well-branched stem.

Originally from the tropical areas of India and Malaya, it produces
inedible green berries which turn yellow-orange.

It is important not to overwater this plant. Mist now and again with
tepid rain water and clean the leaves occasionally using a sponge.

Ficus diversifolia has a good life-expectancy as a houseplant and
should live for 10–15 years.

F. diversifolia

CARE

Light and temperature
Bright but indirect light with a few hours
of morning sunshine will help stimulate
growth. It likes average room
temperatures, but no lower than
13°C/55°F in winter.

Water and feeding
Always use tepid water for this plant.
Water 2–3 times a week in summer only
when the compost has dried out. Water
less in winter. Feed at fortnightly
intervals with a liquid solution in
summer.

Propagation
From stem-tip cuttings in summer,
ensuring the stems are fleshy not
woody. Use a rooting hormone and
provide bottom heat while the new
plants are becoming established.

Repotting
Repot every 2 years, in the spring, into a
loam-based no. 2 compost. For mature
plants it is necessary only to change the
topsoil in the pot.

PROBLEMS

Sudden loss of leaves is usually caused
by overwatering or by moving the plant
to a different environment.

Ficus diversifolia

Ficus elastica robusta (Indian rubber plant)

EASY

This sturdy old favourite with glossy, deep green foliage is possibly the most common houseplant of all.

Originally from the moist tropical areas of India and Malaysia, where it grows as a large tree up to 30m/90ft in height, this relatively new commercial variety is an improved version of the original, *Ficus decora*.

It is easy to grow, but is susceptible to root rot if its soil is allowed to become soggy, so take care not to overwater it.

Ficus elastica robusta can grow up to 10m/30ft indoors in a warm situation with good light. It will live to a ripe old age and can acclimatize itself to a wide range of conditions. But do remember to keep it out of dark corners and draughts.

To develop a strong, bushy plant pinch out the growing tips occasionally. The plant will 'bleed' a white sticky substance when cut, so seal the wound with petroleum jelly.

CARE

Light and temperature
Bright conditions with some direct sunlight each day. It prefers a minimum temperature of 13°C/55°F throughout the year.

Water and feeding
Water thoroughly but allow the compost to dry out between waterings. Rain water is recommended since tap water may cause lime deposits on the roots which slows down the growth. Never allow the plant to stand in water for more than an hour. In winter water once a week at the most – the lower the temperature the less water is required. Feed weekly with a liquid fertilizer in spring and summer.

Propagation
Take a 7.5cm/3in length of fleshy, not woody, stem with a leaf attached. Treat it with a rooting hormone and provide bottom heat while the new plant becomes established.

Repotting
Once a year in spring in a no. 2 compost. The plant needs a large pot and probably a stake to keep it stable. For mature plants it is only necessary to change the topsoil in the pot.

PROBLEMS

If root rot occurs, indicated by leaf drop and a straggly plant, treat it immediately by completely removing the soggy compost to expose the roots. Cut away the infected roots and dust with charcoal. Repot in fresh compost.

Brown areas on the leaves mean the plant has been scorched by the sun or is too close to a heater.

Scale insect and red spider mite can attack this plant. Treat with systemic insecticide.

Ficus elastica robusta

Ficus lyrata (Banjo fig, fiddle-leaf fig)

EASY

This imposing fig has a single stem with large, glossy, bright green violin-shaped leaves of up to 30cm/ 12in in length. It looks striking in a large room, though it will need to be firmly staked while growing.

Originally from the tropical rainforests of West Africa, where it grows as a close-headed tree around 12m/36ft in height, as a houseplant it will reach a substantial 6m/20ft if it has good light and warm conditions, similar to those it enjoys in its native habitat. It will withstand central heating, but does not like draughts.

The foliage must be kept dust-free and leaves should be sponged individually with tepid water. Trim the new shoots occasionally to thicken the plant. It should not need pruning except to reduce growth.

It is a sensitive plant, so if a leaf or stem is damaged or torn, cover the 'wound' with petroleum jelly or a tissue to seal it.

Ficus lyrata has been a popular houseplant since the seventies and should live for up to 12 years.

Ficus lyrata

CARE

Light and temperature
Bright but indirect light and no draughts. It likes normal room temperatures and warm conditions, but no lower than 15–18°C/60–64°F in winter.

Water and feeding
In summer immerse the pot in water for 30 minutes, drain well, and allow to dry out before watering again. In winter it will need watering less. Feed fortnightly in spring and summer with a liquid fertilizer.

Propagation
From cuttings, but this is not easy and best left to professionals.

Repotting
Each spring in a mixture of soil, peat and sand.

PROBLEMS

Drooping leaves indicate that the plant needs water. Soak well and allow to drain. It may need watering more often.

If the lower leaves turn yellow and drop, the plant has been overwatered. Allow to dry out and water less.

Brown patches may appear on the leaves, indicating that the plant needs to be moved to a warmer spot. If the brown patches become too big, snip off the leaf.

Watch for mealy bug and red spider mite. Treat with a systemic insecticide.

Ficus pumila (Creeping fig)

QUITE EASY

An elegant creeper which can also be kept in a hanging basket or trained to grow up a moss-covered pole.

Originally from the temperate areas of Indo-China and Japan, where it grows like ivy climbing over walls, *Ficus pumila* has a many-branched stem and thin, slightly crinkled, heart-shaped, dark green leaves which become larger and more oblong as the plant matures. It should grow several trails a year. There are variegated varieties, such as 'Sonny' and 'Bellis'.

This plant withstands quite cool temperatures and likes a rest period in winter at 7–10°C/44–50°F. Spray daily in summer and every second day in winter (daily if it is in a centrally heated room). This should also keep the leaves clean. Do not use leaf shine.

Ficus pumila is a long-living plant provided it is kept moist and humid, but never soggy. Cut back occasionally to encourage a dense and bushy plant.

CARE

Light and temperature
Good indirect light and a warm, shady position. In summer it will tolerate up to 30°C/84°F but the plant requires plenty of humidity at this temperature. Spray frequently. It will withstand a temperature as low as 6°C/43°F in winter as long as it is kept very much on the dry side.

Water and feeding
Water carefully, allowing the top of the compost to dry out between waterings. Never let it dry out completely, even in winter, or become soggy. Mist often. Feed every 2 weeks in spring and summer with a liquid fertilizer.

Propagation
In spring with stem-tip cuttings potted in a mixture of peat and sand. Remove lower leaves, cover with plastic and place in indirect light until new shoots appear. Repot after 4 months.

Repotting
In spring as necessary in a good house-plant mixture.

PROBLEMS

If the leaves fall off, the plant has either been allowed to dry out or its winter position is too cool and damp.

Scale insect and red spider mite may attack this plant. Spray with a systemic insecticide and improve humidity.

'Bellis'

'Sonny'

Ficus pumila

Ficus radicans 'Variegata' (Rooting fig)

QUITE DIFFICULT

This sturdy climber produces long, elegant stems with largish pointed green and creamy-white variegated leaves. It also looks good in a hanging basket.

Originally from Indonesia, where its natural habitat is the floor of the forests and lower slopes of the mountainous areas, *Ficus radicans* was first introduced as a houseplant in Victorian times.

It needs good light to maintain its leaf colour, and a humid atmosphere to do well indoors. Stand the pot over damp pebbles and spray daily in summer and every second day in winter unless it is in a centrally heated room (when it should be sprayed daily).

It is a fairly slow grower. A mature plant should have an approximate height and spread of 1m/3ft. Growing tips can be pinched out to encourage density.

It will have a long life if the conditions are sufficiently moist. Do not use leaf shine.

F. radicans

Ficus radicans 'Variegata'

CARE

Light and temperature
It needs bright but indirect light and fairly cool temperatures – as low as 12°C/55°F.

Water and feeding
Water 2–3 times a week in summer, never letting the compost dry out. Once a week should be sufficient in winter. Feed with a liquid fertilizer every 2 weeks when it is growing. Mist daily.

Propagation
In spring with 10cm/4in stem-tip cuttings. Place in a mixture of compost and sand and establish in a propagator or under a plastic cover at 16–18°C/61–64°F.

Repotting
For younger plants, once a year in spring in a loam- or peat-based compost. For mature plants it is necessary only to change the topsoil.

PROBLEMS

If conditions are too dry the leaves will shrivel and become papery. Soak for 1 hour in a container of water, drain well, and water more often.

If the plant is overwatered or allowed to stand in water the leaves will turn yellow and fall off. Allow it almost to dry out and water more sparingly.

Scale insect can trouble this plant. Remove with a cloth dipped in methylated spirit.

Cobwebs underneath indicate red spider mite. Spray with a systemic insecticide and improve humidity.

Fittonia (Snakeskin plant, mosaic plant, painted net leaf, silver net leaf)

DIFFICULT

This pretty foliage plant has delicate veined oval leaves about 7.5cm/3in long. There are two varieties: *F. argyroneura*, which has olive-green leaves with a distinct white veining, and *F. verschaffeltii*, with slightly darker green leaves and a red veining. There are also miniature versions of each. Green flowers may appear in summer and should be cut off immediately so as not to impede the plant's growth.

Originally from the tropical rainforests of Peru, where it grows as a low ground-cover creeper, it was introduced as a houseplant in the mid-nineteenth century.

Fittonia is an attractive and popular specimen that flourishes in shady situations, but it is quite difficult to grow because it needs a constant, humid temperature never below 18°C/64°F. Draughts, dry air and direct sunlight must be avoided at all costs. The plant is ideal in bottle gardens and terrariums and good in mixed bowls.

Fittonia tends to become straggly, so the new growth should be pinched out regularly to encourage density.

For the expert, this plant will have a long life.

F. verschaffeltii
(painted net leaf)

Fittonia argyroneura nana (silver net leaf)

CARE

Light and temperature
A bright to semi-shady position, but no direct sunlight. A warm temperature all year, never below 18°C/64°F.

Water and feeding
Keep the compost damp but never soggy using tepid water. Dry air will kill the plant so mist often and stand the pot over wet gravel or surround with damp peat. Feed monthly in summer with a liquid fertilizer.

Propagation
In spring using stem-tip cuttings. They will need to be established in a heated propagator at around 24°C/75°F.

Repotting
Annually in spring, in a half pot as the plant has a very shallow root system. Use a no. 2 potting compost or a no. 2 peat-based compost.

PROBLEMS

Draughts or a cold surrounding temperature will cause the leaves to drop. Move to a warmer, more protected position and improve humidity.

Dry air and direct sunlight will cause shrivelled leaves. Soak the plant in water for 30 minutes, drain well and place in a semi-shady position. Never let the compost dry out.

Yellow leaves are caused by overwatering. Remove the damaged leaves, check the drainage and allow the compost almost to dry out before watering again. Water less often.

Greenfly can attack this plant. Spray with a systemic insecticide.

Grevillea robusta (Silky oak)

EASY

This most attractive small tree has feathery, fern-like downy leaves which are silvery brown as they shoot, turning to grey-green when mature.

In the warm and temperate zones of Australia, its native habitat, it is often seen as a feature tree in gardens and along streets, growing to 30m/90ft. As a houseplant it will grow quickly to 2m/6ft.

Grevillea robusta likes to be outdoors in spring and summer, though it does well indoors if the temperature is around 18°C/64°F and the light is good. The pot should be stood over damp gravel to increase humidity.

If you would like a dense, bushy plant, pinch out the central growing shoots.

Grevillea robusta is usually past its best after 2–3 years.

Grevillea robusta will reach the ceiling given half a chance; cut back severely in late winter

PROBLEMS

Relatively problem free.

Old leaves may turn brown and should be removed. Check that the roots are not too dry.

Watch for aphids and whitefly. Spray with a pyrethrum-based insecticide.

CARE

Light and temperature
A well-lit position, quite sunny in winter, and average to warm conditions – around 18°C/64°F. In winter it can go as low as 6°C/43°F.

Water and feeding
Water once or twice a week in spring and summer, allowing the surface of the compost to dry out between waterings. In winter water less, just enough to ensure it doesn't dry out completely. Feed every 2 weeks in spring and summer with a liquid fertilizer.

Propagation
By seed in spring at a constant temperature of 13–16°C/55–61°F. It is quite difficult.

Repotting
In spring in an equal mixture of lime-free soil, peat and sand.

Gynura x. sarmentosa (Purple passion vine, velvet plant)

QUITE EASY

This unusual plant is a native of the mountainous forests of Java, where it climbs to a height of 1m/3ft, having attached itself to a tree.

For indoors it has been specially cultivated as a quick-growing perennial, producing trailing stems of up to 1.5m/4–5ft, which are also suitable for climbing.

Gynura x. sarmentosa has soft, irregularly shaped, lobed leaves that are deep red underneath and covered with a violet down. Clusters of orange flowers may appear in spring; they should be removed immediately as they have an unpleasant smell.

To maintain its colour, the plant needs direct sunlight for several hours a day, especially in winter, though in general it will tolerate average light and room temperature conditions. If the temperature is warm, stand the pot over damp gravel to ensure adequate humidity. Do not spray the foliage.

Past its best after 2 years, *Gynura* should be replaced by propagation.

CARE

Light and temperature
Several hours of sunlight each day throughout the year. In summer *Gynura* likes temperatures around 18–20°C/64–70°F and in winter between 12–14°C/53–57°F, with no lower than 10°C/50°F.

Water and feeding
Water once or twice a week, allowing the surface of the compost to dry out between waterings. If the temperature is below 15°C/59°F reduce the amount of water. Feed with a liquid solution every month all year round.

Propagation
By stem-tip cuttings of 10cm/4in, potted in a mixture of peat and sand. Stand in a well-lit position, away from direct sunlight, and when the plants are well established repot in a no. 2 loam-based compost.

Repotting
Every spring in the mixture recommended above.

PROBLEMS

If the leaves are green rather than purple, the plant needs more light.

Black marks on the leaves are caused by careless watering. Do not mist this plant and do not let water settle on the leaves.

Susceptible to greenfly, whitefly and aphids. Treat with a pyrethrum-based insecticide.

If the plant starts to look past its best, replace by propagation.

Gynura x. sarmentosa is a hybrid of *G. aurantiaca* (velvet plant) and *G. bicolor* (oak-leaved velvet plant)

Hedera helix (Common ivy, English ivy)

EASY

In ancient times ivy was the plant associated with Bacchus, the god of wine. Today there are many varieties available, but *Hedera helix* is among the most popular, as it is a quick grower and will cling easily to almost all surfaces. It also looks good in a hanging basket or as a standard.

Hedera helix grows freely in Europe, Asia and North Africa. Its lobed leaves are a glossy dark green with cream veins, growing up to 6cm/2in long.

Ivy is quite difficult to cultivate indoors because it likes a cool temperature and does not fare well in a centrally heated room. It will need frequent misting to ensure adequate humidity.

The plant will soon become straggly unless new growth is regularly pinched out. These cuttings can be propagated.

Hedera helix will have a long life, and can be moved outdoors where it will continue to grow well albeit more slowly.

Hedera helix 'Golden Child'

CARE

Light and temperature
Bright to semi-shady conditions. Variegated plants will need light to maintain leaf colour. The temperature should be cool, ideally 15°C/60°F, and preferably unheated in winter.

Water and feeding
Do not overwater – 2–3 times a week should be sufficient in summer to keep the compost moist. In winter water less, although if it is in a heated room it will need more watering and misting. Wipe the leaves occasionally with a damp cloth. In summer feed every 2 weeks with a liquid solution.

Propagation
Easily done from stem tips or aerial roots which root easily in water or a potting mixture.

Repotting
In spring every 2 years in a good houseplant mixture. Cut the plant back at the same time to encourage bushiness.

PROBLEMS

If the plant is located in a dry position, the leaf tips will turn brown and attract spider mite and scale insect. Treat with a systemic insecticide and mist frequently to improve humidity.

If the leaf edges are brown, conditions are too warm. Cut back and move to a cooler spot.

If the veining becomes slight move to a brighter position.

Fine holes in the leaves may indicate that the plant is infested with thrips. Treat with a pyrethrum-based insecticide.

Hedera helix 'Pittsburgh'

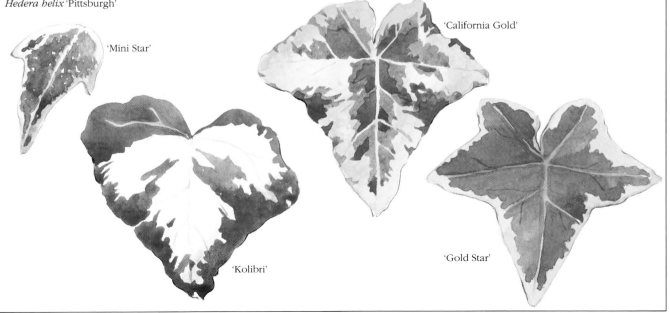

'Mini Star'

'California Gold'

'Kolibri'

'Gold Star'

Hedera canariensis (Canary Islands ivy)

EASY

This is one of the most popular varieties of ivy for the house. It is tolerant of most conditions and is easy to grow – an ideal plant for a beginner and the neglectful.

A native of the Canary Islands, where it grows freely on lower slopes, it has largish, slightly leathery, all-green leaves, but there are variegated varieties available which have silver, grey or white markings. The variety 'Gloire de Marengo' is recommended.

H. canariensis is long-lasting and a fairly quick grower that will attach itself easily to a stake, pillar or wall. It can also be grown outdoors if it is not too cold. If you do move the plant outside, do so in summer to allow it to establish itself before winter.

Pinch out the growing tips regularly to encourage a dense and bushy specimen.

Regular spraying should keep the leaves clean; if not, wipe with a damp cloth. Do not use leaf shine.

As a houseplant, it likes cool, humid conditions and will not do well if it is too hot or dry. Also take care not to overwater this plant.

Hedera canariensis 'Gloire de Marengo' has been cultivated in Europe for over 200 years

CARE

Light and temperature
Bright light is essential, especially for a variegated plant. It can tolerate most temperatures, but prefers to be kept cool, the ideal being between 7–15°C/45–60°F. If the temperature is warmer, increase the humidity.

Water and feeding
Water once or twice a week in spring and summer and less in winter. Mist frequently for humidity and stand the pot over damp pebbles. In summer feed fortnightly with a liquid fertilizer.

Propagation
By stem-tip cuttings which are most easily rooted in water. Plant 2 or 3 together when established.

Repotting
Repot younger plants in spring. If the plant is growing vigorously, you may need to do this twice a year. For mature plants it is only necessary to change the topsoil.

PROBLEMS

The edges of the leaves will turn brown if the position is too dry or hot. Move to a cooler spot and improve humidity.

Black spots on the leaves mean that the plant has been overwatered. Allow to dry out and water less.

Prone to red spider mite and greenfly. Spray with a systemic insecticide and improve the humidity level.

Thrip can be sprayed with a pyrethrum-based insecticide.

Scale insect will discolour the leaves. Remove with a cloth dipped in methylated spirit.

Howea (Paradise palm, kentia palm, sentry palm)

QUITE DIFFICULT

This palm is native to Lord Howe Island off the east coast of Australia, where it lives in subtropical, seaside conditions. It has only recently become a sought-after houseplant.

The differences between the two species – *H. forsteriana* (paradise palm or kentia palm) and *H. belmoreana* (sentry palm) – are sometimes hard to distinguish. In its native habitat, *H. forsteriana* will grow up to 20m/60ft, its fronds well spaced and durable. *H. belmoreana* is more slow-growing and its fronds are thinner and more upright.

Both varieties have a single, robust trunk from which grow dark green pinnate fronds which should be cleaned regularly with a damp cloth. The plants may also produce clusters of yellow-green fruit.

Avoid direct sunlight which will turn the leaf tips brown. *Howea* can withstand almost completely shady conditions, but the plant will not grow unless there is some light. Good drainage is essential.

Howea is extremely long-lasting – up to 80 years.

CARE

Light and temperature
Light to semi-shady conditions, always avoiding direct sunlight. Average to warm temperatures throughout the year, and no lower than 10°C/50°F in winter.

Water and feeding
Water well in spring and summer, and always keep the compost moist. In winter it will need watering less often. Avoid saturation and never allow the compost to dry out. Mist often. Feed fortnightly in spring and summer with a general houseplant fertilizer.

Propagation
From seed in a propagator at 27°C/80°F. This is difficult to do, and best left to professionals.

Repotting
Only when potbound as the plant does not like to be disturbed. Use a good soil- and peat-based mixture.

PROBLEMS

Howea adapts well as a houseplant as long as it has a warm, humid and protected spot and is neither overwatered nor underwatered.

Overwatering will make the leaves turn brown. Allow to dry out and water less.

Underwatering will make the leaves turn yellow. Immerse the pot in water for 30 minutes, drain well, and never allow the compost to dry out.

The lower leaves will die naturally, and should be cut off.

Red spider mite will attack the plant if conditions are too dry. Spray with a systemic insecticide and improve humidity.

Howea forsteriana

Hypoestes sanguinolenta (Polka dot plant, freckle face)

QUITE DIFFICULT

Clockwise from the top: *H. s.* 'Bettina', *H. s.* 'Rose', *H. s.* 'White', *H. s.* 'Ruby'

A showy houseplant originating from Madagascar, where it grows in humid, tropical conditions as a ground-cover plant. It has small, downy, oblong green leaves with coloured veins and splashes of pink spots. New varieties have been bred to include white, ruby and rose colourings and these are much more compact in habit. There are often several plants in a small pot.

Hypoestes is a very good ground-cover plant for mixed bowls and bottle gardens, but it needs adequate light to keep its colouring bright and vibrant. It also tends to become very straggly and it is best to replace it annually. Pinch out the growing tips in young plants.

This plant is quite particular about its position. Do not put it in a dry atmosphere or near a heater or gas fire. Do not use leaf shine.

CARE

Light and temperature
It likes bright, indirect sunlight, with plenty of warmth and humidity. Place the pot over damp pebbles and maintain a temperature of 18–24°C/64–75°F all year round if possible.

Water and feeding
Water 2–3 times a week in summer, and possibly only once a week in winter using tepid water. Feed with half the recommended dose of liquid fertilizer at fortnightly intervals.

Propagation
It is best to raise a new plant from seed each spring. Cuttings can also be rooted in spring and summer in a mixture of soil, peat and sand. Either place them in a propagator or cover the pot with plastic and keep at a constant temperature of not less than 21°C/70°F while they become established.

Repotting
If growing fast, pot on during the first season. Discard when plant becomes leggy.

PROBLEMS

This plant is sensitive to the cold and to being overwatered in winter, causing it to droop. Allow the soil to dry out in a warmer position and then water less.

Discoloured leaves indicate the plant has been attacked by scale insect. Remove these with a cloth dipped in methylated spirit.

Leea coccinea

QUITE DIFFICULT

This striking shrub-like plant is grown for its most attractive burgundy-coloured, multi-pointed leaves, which will turn green as the plant matures. It may produce small grape-like flowers.

Originally a low-growing shrub from the dense tropical forests of Cambodia, it was introduced into England during the 1880s and owes its name to the famous Scottish gardener James Lee. It is now enjoying a revival in popularity – and deservedly so.

Indoors it requires a high level of humidity and moisture and a warm temperature all year round, but will not tolerate draughts. It should last for 5–6 years.

A healthy plant will produce droplets on the leaves, which is natural.

L. c. 'Burgundy' will only keep its red colour in good light

Leea coccinea 'Green'

CARE

Light and temperature
Bright but indirect light is necessary to maintain the colour of its foliage. It likes warm temperatures all year, preferably no lower than 16°C/61°F in winter.

Water and feeding
Keep quite moist at all times, but never soggy. The compost must not be allowed to dry out. Provide plenty of humidity and mist often. Feed with a weak solution every 2 weeks in spring and summer.

Propagation
From seed or stem cuttings in a warm propagator. This is difficult and best left to a professional.

Repotting
In spring, as necessary, in a good houseplant mixture, ensuring adequate drainage.

PROBLEMS

If the air is too dry the plant will be attacked by aphids and red spider mite. Spray aphids with a pyrethrum-based insecticide and remove spider mites with a cloth dipped in methylated spirit.

Leea is sensitive to overwatering and underwatering, both of which will cause the leaves to drop. Follow the instructions in 'Water and feeding' carefully.

Licuala grandis

QUITE EASY

A native of the New Britain Islands near New Guinea, this very attractive small fan palm has a slim trunk, around 2m/6ft tall, topped with almost round green leaves that are plaited and toothed along the edge.

Recently commercialized species are available from 60cm/24in, though you will need to hunt for them as production is relatively small.

Licuala grandis

CARE

Light and temperature
Diffused sunlight, but will take quite low light conditions. The plant must be kept warm all year round with a minimum temperature of 15°C/60°F. It loves warmth and will take temperatures up to 30°C/85°F.

Water and feeding
Being a stove plant it enjoys high humidity. During spring and summer place on a saucer of wet pebbles. Water thoroughly, but do not allow it to stand in water and become waterlogged. Spray leaves daily when the temperature rises above 18°C/64°F. During winter water weekly but do not allow the soil to dry out. Feed with general houseplant fertilizer at fortnightly intervals during spring and summer.

Propagation
Difficult. Best left to a professional.

Repotting
In spring, but only if rootbound, in a no.2 loam-based compost.

PROBLEMS

Webs on the underside of leaves indicate red spider mite, caused by the plant becoming too dry. Spray with diluted malathion at fortnightly intervals. Raise humidity and water the plant thoroughly.

Maranta leuconeura (Prayer plant, rabbit's tracks, red herringbone plant)

QUITE DIFFICULT

M. l. 'Kerchoveana' and *M. l.* 'Erythrophylla' (also known as *M. tricolor*) are two of the most popular varieties of this family of plants renowned for its beautiful leaf markings, some almost appearing as if they are hand-painted.

Both are known as prayer plants as their leaves curl up at night.

Maranta is quite a difficult houseplant to maintain because of its humidity requirements, but worth persevering with. It should last for many years, but it is usually best to divide the plant after 3 or 4 years.

Originally from the tropical rainforests of South America, where it grows as a small plant with spreading branches under the protection of the tree canopy, *Maranta* likes warm conditions with plenty of humidity. Use soft and tepid water at all times. Spray daily and stand the pot on wet pebbles or surround with moist peat to ensure good humidity. If spraying doesn't keep the leaves clean, wipe gently with a damp cloth. Do not use leaf shine.

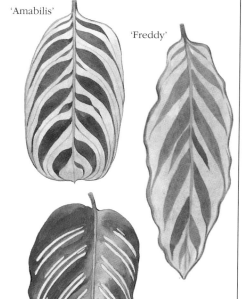

'Amabilis'
'Freddy'
M. ornata

CARE

Light and temperature
Bright light but never direct sun. It likes warm temperatures, ideally 16–18°C/60–64°F all year, and as high as 28°C/83°F if there is good humidity. Avoid draughts.

Water and feeding
Keep the compost moist at all times with tepid water, never allowing it to dry out between waterings. It will need less water in winter. Mist leaves regularly. Feed every 2 weeks in late spring and early summer with a weak liquid solution.

Propagation
Divide the plant in early spring as new growth emerges, ensuring each division has both roots and stems, and transfer to individual 9cm/4in pots. Cover with plastic and keep warm – 18°C/64°F – until established.

Repotting
In spring every 2–3 years in a peat-based compost. Ensure adequate drainage.

PROBLEMS

This is a delicate plant. Falling leaves or brown leaf tips may be caused by the air being too dry. Remove dead growth and improve the humidity. Also check for red spider mite and remove with a cloth dipped in methylated spirit.

Underwatering is indicated by curled or spotted leaves and yellow lower leaves. Remove the damaged leaves and keep the compost moist at all times.

Maranta leuconeura 'Erythrophylla'

Monsteria deliciosa (Swiss cheese plant, Mexican breadfruit plant)

EASY

This attractive old favourite has beautiful glossy dark green perforated leaves which can grow as large as 60cm/2ft across.

A mature plant produces a hard green edible fruit that smells like a pineapple.

Originally from Mexico and Guatemala, where it grows as a tree climber in tropical conditions, it does well as a houseplant in most warm and humid conditions, except direct sunlight. Indoors it can grow up to 2.5m/8ft. It requires plenty of room and will need a stake for support as it grows.

Wash the leaves occasionally with a damp sponge and mist often. You can use leaf shine.

Monsteria deliciosa produces many aerial roots which are used to anchor the plant. These should be wound around the plant and placed on top of the pot and pegged.

This plant should live indefinitely.

CARE

Light and temperature
Bright to semi-shady conditions, but no direct sunlight. In winter the plant needs a little extra brightness. The ideal temperature is 18–22°C/64–72°F all year.

Water and feeding
Keep slightly moist, but never soggy, all year round and mist often – it needs a lot of humidity. Never allow the compost to dry out between waterings. Feed fortnightly with a weak solution in spring and summer.

Propagation
In spring from leaf tip cuttings which must be established in a propagator at 24°C/75°F in a peat and sand mixture.

Repotting
As necessary, probably every 2 years, into a slightly larger pot. Use a mixture of peat and sand and ensure adequate drainage.

PROBLEMS

Overwatering is the major cause of problems for this plant and manifests itself in root rot, yellowed leaves or leaves weeping at the edges. Allow the plant to dry out and then take care not to water so often.

Stem rot, indicated by slimy patches on the stem, is also caused by overwatering and should be treated by repotting the plant in a dry and warm compost.

If the leaves turn brown and develop papery edges or black patches, the surroundings are too dry or cold. Mist the leaves and surround the pot with damp peat.

This plant is susceptible to red spider mite. Treat with a systemic insecticide and improve humidity.

Monsteria deliciosa thrives if given good humidity – up to 60 per cent or more

Pellionia pulchra (Satin pellionia)

EASY

This exotic creeper grows throughout the tropical forests of Vietnam and adapts well as a houseplant. It looks especially good in a hanging basket.

It produces a profusion of pretty pink stems which have light grey-green oblong leaves marked with brown-black veins. Underneath, the leaves are light purple.

As in its natural habitat, where it grows as a ground cover under the tree canopy, it enjoys warmth, a lot of humidity and a protected position. It should be sprayed daily.

The plant should live for several years, but it does tend to become spindly and it is best to divide the plant at this point to produce a fresher specimen.

CARE

Light and temperature
A well-lit position, though not direct sunlight, but it also adapts to a shady situation. It likes warm temperatures of up to 28°C/82°F in summer with good humidity. The temperature should not go below 16°C/61°F in winter.

Water and feeding
Water well throughout the year, allowing the compost to stay moist but never soggy. To ensure good humidity, stand the pot over damp pebbles and spray daily.

Propagation
In summer, by division, ensuring each section has roots. Pot individually in a no. 2 peat-based compost. Alternatively, by 5cm/2in stem cuttings, which will establish easily in the same mixture.

Repotting
Each year in spring in a no. 2 peat-based compost.

PROBLEMS

If the leaves start to droop, the plant is too dry. Place in a bucket of water for 30 minutes.

If scorch marks appear on the leaves or the leaves turn crisp and start to drop, conditions are too hot. Move to a cooler situation.

Grey mould on the base of the stems indicates botrytis caused by the plant being too wet and cold. Move to a warmer place and spray with fungicide.

Pellionia pulchra

Peperomia caperata

EASY

There are several hundred members of this small, bushy, herbaceous family which is characterized by a great variety of attractive and unusual leaves and colours.

Originally from tropical areas of Brazil, where it is found under the tree canopy, *Peperomia* grows to 10–15cm/4–6in high and often produces creamy white flower spikes. It also looks good in a hanging basket.

It likes warm, humid conditions, as in its native habitat, with bright but indirect sunlight. Spray the foliage daily and stand the pot over damp gravel to ensure adequate humidity.

This plant is past its best after 2–3 years when it becomes quite straggly. It can then be propagated.

PROBLEMS

Overwatering will cause leaf and stem rot, particularly in winter. Allow the compost almost to dry out between waterings.

Dry air will cause the leaves to turn brown and fall. Improve humidity by standing the pot over damp gravel and misting frequently.

Red spider mite will cause the leaves to go yellow with cobwebbing on the underside. Spray with systemic insecticide.

CARE

Light and temperature
Bright to semi-shady conditions with a temperature of around 21°C/70°F. It will tolerate temperatures as low as 10°C/50°F in winter if the compost is kept fairly dry.

Water and feeding
Keep moist all year round, but do not allow the compost to get soggy, especially in winter, or the roots and stem will rot. Ensure good humidity all year. Feed at monthly intervals in summer with a liquid solution.

Propagation
In spring or summer with leaf bud or stem cuttings into a good houseplant mixture.

Repotting
Only when potbound, in a soil-based compost.

Peperomia caperata 'Emerald Ripple' one of the small-leaved species

Peperomia caperata 'Nigra' and 'Lilium'

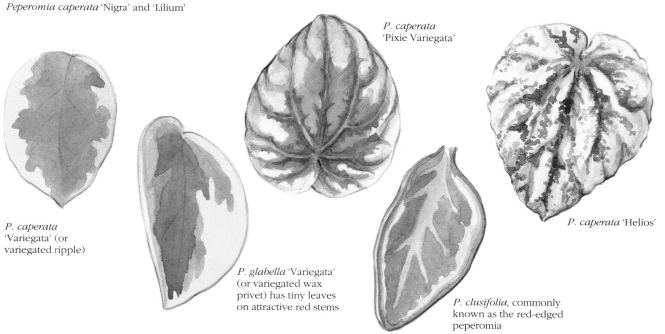

P. caperata
'Pixie Variegata'

P. caperata 'Helios'

P. caperata
'Variegata' (or
variegated ripple)

P. glabella 'Variegata'
(or variegated wax
privet) has tiny leaves
on attractive red stems

P. clusifolia, commonly
known as the red-edged
peperomia

Peperomia obtusifolia (Pepper face, baby rubber plant)

QUITE DIFFICULT

This ornamental herbaceous shrub comes from Mexico and Central America, where it can be found at the base of trees and as an epiphyte.

As a houseplant it will grow to about 30cm/1ft, producing long stems of fleshy oval leaves with green and gold markings. It is a good plant for a hanging basket. Short spikes of white flowers will bloom from early summer to late autumn and both plain green and variegated varieties are common.

A robust plant, it should be watered sparingly as it stores water in its leaves. However it likes moisture in the form of humidity, so spray frequently and stand the pot over damp gravel. It is a good plant for the bathroom.

Spraying should also keep the leaves clean. Do not use leaf shine.

Peperomia obtusifolia is not an easy plant to maintain and it is probably best to propagate every 2 years.

Peperomia obtusifolia is sometimes labelled *P. variegata*

PROBLEMS

This plant is extremely sensitive to overwatering, which will cause damage to the leaves and stem rot. Remove the damaged parts and dust with sulphur. Check drainage and allow to dry out until recovered.

Susceptible to scale insect and red spider mite. Spray with systemic insecticide and improve humidity.

CARE

Light and temperature
Bright but indirect light, and occasionally full sun, is needed to maintain the leaf colour. It likes quite warm temperatures, no higher than 24°C/75°F in summer and no lower than 10°C/50°F in winter.

Water and feeding
Water carefully, allowing the compost to dry out between waterings. Provide good humidity by spraying and by standing the pot over damp gravel. Feed with a weak solution at monthly intervals in spring and summer.

Propagation
By 7.5cm/3in stem-tip cuttings, several of which can be planted together in a damp mixture of peat and sand. Use a rooting powder and cover with plastic. Establish in good light at 18°C/64°F, then move to a larger pot.

Repotting
Young plants should be repotted each spring in fairly shallow pots in a mixture of peat and sand.

Philodendron

EASY

The *Philodendron* family is versatile and far ranging. Few of the many trailing and climbing species will present problems either for the beginner or for the neglectful plant owner.

Until the beginning of the twentieth century, philodendrons were unknown outside their native habitat of tropical South America. There, the plants scramble over tree trunks in dense jungle, their roots attaching themselves to the tree bark. The plants bloom wonderfully here, but it is rare for the indoor philodendron to produce a decent flower. On average you can expect a lifespan of 5 years.

Philodendron scandens (the sweetheart plant, parlour ivy or heart-leafed philodendron) is an easy and popular small-leafed species. Its constant growth and glossy, waxy leaves make it a durable indoor plant in a group arrangement. It will climb willingly, and is particularly suited to moss-covered supports. Equally it can be used effectively in hanging basket arrangements.

Pinch out the growing shoots regularly to keep the bushy shape of the plant.

P. melanochrysum (black-gold philodendron) is exquisitely delicate and comes from Colombia and Costa Rica. At first the leaves are heart-shaped and have prominent veining; by the time the plant's leaves reach maturity they are velvety and elongated.

CARE

Light and temperature
Some, like *P. scandens*, will grow happily in shade. Most, however, like bright light. Average warmth, with temperatures not less than 12–18°C/55–64°F in winter, and not more than 24°C/75°F in summer. High humidity is important so if possible stand plants on a tray of moist pebbles.

Watering and feeding
Water twice weekly during summer, once a week during winter. Spray the leaves with tepid rain water to help humidity. A weak solution of liquid food should be added to the watering once a fortnight during the summer months.

Repotting
Only when the plant becomes top-heavy. Once the plant has matured, in an 18cm/7in pot, just change the topsoil each spring. If the leaves look poor and growth is not apparent repot in spring.

Propagation
Not easy, as they are normally propagated from seed grown in the tropics. Stem cuttings can be taken, but again not easy. Try in early summer: dip in rooting hormone powder and then into fresh compost at a temperature of 24°C/75°F.

PROBLEMS

If the leaves at the base of the plant turn yellow and fall, the plant is probably being overwatered. Reduce watering and allow soil to dry out between applications.

If the philodendron does not develop, ensure the plant is given the right conditions in both summer and winter. These plants need a contrast between seasons.

Brown tips may develop on the leathery leaves. Make sure the plant is out of strong direct sunlight.

P. selloum (lacy tree philodendron). Its leaves can be up to 60cm/2ft long

P. panduraeforme (fiddle-leaf) can be trained to grow up a pole

P. 'Emerald Queen' is an F1 hybrid

Phoenix canariensis (Canary Islands date palm)

EASY

This imposing palm, a native of the subtropical Canary Islands, has a thick, upright trunk with arching pinnate, shiny green leaves.

In its native habitat it grows to 15m/45ft high, with leaves up to 6m/18ft long. As a houseplant, it will reach a more modest 3m/9ft, with leaves of up to 1m/3ft in length, growing from a short stem. It may produce long clusters of small yellowy flowers in spring, and subsequently small, date-like fruit.

Phoenix canariensis will live indefinitely and benefits from a spell outdoors in summer.

Clean the leaves with a damp cloth. Do not use leaf shine. The leaves will gradually die off and should be trimmed close to the trunk.

CARE

Light and temperature
Prefers indirect light when young, but once it is more than 3 years old it will take full sunlight. It likes quite warm temperatures in the summer, up to a maximum of 27°C/80°F, and no lower than 10°C/50°F in winter.

Water and feeding
In spring and summer water frequently, ensuring that the compost does not dry out, but do not allow it to become soggy either. Mist frequently, particularly in very warm weather. In winter water when the surface of the compost dries out. Feed with a liquid fertilizer at fortnightly intervals in spring and summer.

Propagation
By seed. This is difficult and best left to a professional.

Repotting
Repot younger plants every second year, in spring, in a loam-based no. 3 compost. Mature plants will need only the topsoil changed.

PROBLEMS

Prone to scale insect and mealy bug. Remove with a cloth dipped in methylated spirit, but be careful as the spines are very spiteful.

Red spider mite is indicated by cobwebs on the leaves. Spray with a systemic insecticide.

If the leaves develop brown tips, the air is probably too dry. Cut off the damaged parts, water well, and mist the plant regularly.

If the plant has been overwatered, or the conditions are too cold, it may develop brown spots on the leaves. Cut off the damaged parts and allow the compost to dry out a little more between waterings. Check the drainage and move to a warmer spot.

Phoenix canariensis

Pilea cadieri (Aluminium plant, artillery plant, water melon pilea)

QUITE EASY

This small herbaceous plant has pretty, light green oval or pointed leaves and grows to a maximum height of 15cm/6in.

Pilea grows freely as a native in tropical areas around the world. It is a quick-growing succulent, and makes an attractive small house-plant or a good ground cover for a mixed indoor or window garden.

It is quite easy to grow as long as conditions do not become too cold in winter or too wet. As in its native habitat, it likes a protected position, away from any cold draughts.

Pilea will last for years, but does tend to become straggly, so it is better to treat it as an annual and propagate from cuttings each spring.

'Norfolk'

'Ellen'

Pilea cadieri

'Bronze'

CARE

Light and temperature
Bright to semi-shady conditions. The temperatures should be no higher than 21°C/70°F in summer, and no lower than 10°C/50°F in winter.

Water and feeding
Water thoroughly in spring and summer, allowing the compost to dry out between waterings. In winter it will need less water. Mist regularly with tepid water to ensure adequate humidity. Feed each week in spring and summer with a liquid fertilizer.

Propagation
Easily from stem cuttings 7.5cm/3in long in spring which should be treated with rooting hormone and then placed in a mixture of peat and sand, and kept just warm until established.

Repotting
In spring in a mixture of peat and sand if you are not propagating.

PROBLEMS

Prone to red spider mite if conditions are too dry. Spray with a systemic insecticide and improve humidity.

If conditions are too cold and wet the plant will lose its leaves in winter or develop stem rot. Cut back in spring to encourage new growth.

If the leaves turn brown on the tips and edges the plant may need more light or the temperature is too cold.

Radermachera (Emerald tree, Asian bell tree)

EASY

This is a recently introduced houseplant which has become popular because of its attractive appearance and resistance to the dry atmosphere of most homes.

A native of China and Taiwan, where it grows as a tiny evergreen tree, it has small, shiny, veined leaves with long points. As a houseplant it has the appearance of a small tree and may produce yellow bells.

Although quite easy to look after, *Radermachera* will not do well near fires or smokers, as smoke will cause it to lose its leaves.

Radermachera needs bright conditions with plenty of humidity, so spray often. The plant also benefits from a spell outdoors in summer in a protected spot.

It should last for several years.

CARE

Light and temperature
Bright indirect light and average room temperatures all year, no lower than 15°C/60°F in winter.

Water and feeding
Water regularly to keep the compost moist at all times. In winter water more sparingly. Avoid sogginess, but never let the compost dry out. Feed each week in spring and summer with a liquid fertilizer.

Propagation
In summer by stem cuttings. Establish in a propagator at a temperature of 21°C/71°F.

Repotting
As necessary, in spring, in a no. 2 peat-based compost.

PROBLEMS

Dry or overly warm conditions in winter may cause the plant to be attacked by red spider mite or scale insect. Remove with a cloth dipped in methylated spirit.

Susceptible to aphids and thrips. Spray with a pyrethrum-based insecticide.

Radermachera

Raphis (Lady palm)

EASY

One of the most popular palms in America, there are many varieties of *Raphis*, which has delicate heads of fan-shaped leaves topping thin stems of unbranching 'bamboo'. Like many of the palms, *Raphis* comes from Southern China, where it grows in the tropical and shady rainforests, receiving little or no sunlight. It was introduced into Europe in the 1890s.

There are dwarf varieties available, growing to 60cm/2ft, and also varieties with variegated leaves that can occasionally be found for sale as indoor plants. The most commonly available are *Raphis excelsa*, which reaches 2m/80cm, and the somewhat smaller, more delicate, *Raphis humilis*.

The lady palm likes good air circulation and can look very decorative in a stairwell during the winter months, appreciating a spell on a warm patio outside in summer, providing it receives little sun. It makes an excellent conservatory plant.

Raphis excelsa can be bought in dwarf forms which have variegated leaves

CARE

Light and temperature
A semi-sunny location and good light. It will cope with cooler temperatures, 10°C/50°F in winter and average temperatures in summer. Avoid temperature fluctuations and draughts.

Water and feeding
Keep the compost evenly moist, watering freely in summer and less so in winter. It needs good humidity and the palmate fronds should be misted regularly. In summer feed every 7 days with a weak solution of liquid fertilizer.

Propagation
Shoots can be carefully separated from the main plant and potted up into loam-based compost. Nursery men propagate from seed at high temperatures, but as a houseplant *Raphis* will not flower or produce seed.

Repotting
Necessary only when the plant outgrows its pot. Use well-draining loam-based soil and move to a pot one size larger in spring.

PROBLEMS

Red spider mite can attack this plant. Spray with a systemic insecticide.

If the leaf tips of the fronds become brown, move the plant to a slightly cooler position and increase the humidity. Stand on a tray of pebbles.

Rhoeo discolor (Moses in the basket)

QUITE DIFFICULT

This striking plant has a short stem from which radiate a number of firm pointed dark green leaves that are purple underneath. It may produce spikes of white flowers.

Originally from the Central Americas, where its native habitat is along the Pacific coastline from Mexico into Central America, *Rhoeo* is quite a delicate houseplant. It likes a warm, humid position, away from draughts, and should be misted often with tepid soft water. The compost must never be allowed to get soggy, especially in winter.

Clean the leaves occasionally with a damp cloth and do not use leaf shine.

It should last for 2–3 years.

CARE

Light and temperature
Indirect light and a warm, constant temperature, ideally 18°C/64°F, all year, and no lower than 15°C/60°F in winter.

Water and feeding
Water carefully and ensure the compost is never soggy, especially in winter. Provide good humidity and mist often. Feed once a week in spring and summer with a liquid solution.

Propagation
In spring from side shoots or stem cuttings. Allow cuttings to dry out for a couple of days, then pot in a mixture of peat and sand.

Repotting
Each spring in a no. 2 peat-based compost.

PROBLEMS

This plant needs good humidity but is sensitive to overwatering. If the air is too dry the leaves will curl and turn brown, and if overwatered it will suffer stem rot. Allow to dry out before watering again.

Rhoeo discolor is also known as *R. bermudensis*, and the variegated form has pale creamy vertical stripes on the upper side of the leaf

Rhoicissus rhomboidea (Grape ivy, Natal vine)

EASY

This very versatile climbing plant has pretty dark green and glossy leaves that are made up of three smaller leaflets. Its native habitat is Cape Province, South Africa, where it grows almost anywhere in light shade. It was introduced into Europe in the 1940s and has become one of the most popular indoor plants.

Rhoicissus rhomboidea is the most commonly available variety, but *R. r.* 'Ellen Danica' is more unusual because its leaflets have lobes. *R. capensis* (Cape or evergreen grape) has large brown-edged leaves with brown and velvety undersides. It will, in exceptional circumstances, produce red berries.

All varieties can grow into large plants, up to 3m/10ft tall, and they are tuberous-rooted. They develop new growth freely and climb by using tendrils. They normally have a life expectancy of up to 10 years, but are susceptible to sudden wilt.

R. capensis has leaves up to 20cm/8in across

CARE

Light and temperature
A north- or east-facing window is best, as these plants do not like direct sunlight. In winter, temperatures should not fall below 15°C/60°F. Normal room temperature is fine in summer but the plants will not thrive if the room becomes stuffy.

Water and feeding
Keep the compost moist in summer, taking care not to overwater or the plant's leaves will go limp and rot. In winter, water every fortnight. Feed every 2 weeks with liquid plant food in summer. Moisten the leaves in summer and stand the plant on a tray of moist pebbles if possible.

Repotting
Once a year in spring, using fresh compost, until the plant reaches maturity. Then change the 5cm/2in of topsoil each year.

Propagation
Take stem-tip cuttings with 2 leaves, and root them in a mixture of half compost and half sand at a temperature of 18°C/64°. Repot into potting compost when cuttings have taken, in 21–28 days.

PROBLEMS

If signs of mildew fungus disease become obvious, reduce watering immediately and water less frequently.

Red spider mite or greenfly may attack this plant. Treat with a systemic insecticide.

Brown patches may develop on the leaves which will eventually drop off. Remove affected leaves. Improve the humidity if the atmosphere is dry.

If the leaves look drab, consider if the temperature is high enough. Overwatering may also be a cause.

Rhoicissus rhomboidea grows either as a pot plant or can be trained as a climber on a moss pole

Sansevieria trifasciata (Mother-in-law's tongue, snake plant)

EASY

'Golden Hahnii'

One of the hardiest of all indoor plants, this succulent member of the lily family needs little attention. Originally from the arid zones of Zaire, the former Belgian Congo, it thrives on good light, normal room temperatures and fairly dry conditions with good drainage.

There are several varieties widely available, all of which form rosettes of firm green leaves with yellow margins of varying lengths. The slow-growing *S. trifasciata laurentii* has elegant upright leaves of 1m/3ft in length. The varieties *S. trifasciata* 'Hahnii' are miniatures growing to 15cm/6in in height in compact rosettes.

The plant should produce a spike covered with tiny yellow flowers. Remove this when it has finished flowering.

Wipe the leaves occasionally with a damp cloth and do not use leaf shine.

This plant should be long-lasting.

CARE

Light and temperature
Tolerant of most conditions, *Sansevieria* prefers bright light, even direct sunlight, to encourage growth. It likes warm temperatures all year, but in winter will withstand as low as 6°C/43°F.

Water and feeding
Water carefully and allow the soil to dry out between waterings. Never let water accumulate on the rosette. Feed with a liquid solution at monthly intervals in spring and summer.

Propagation
By leaf cuttings. Cut the leaf acrossways into 2.5cm/1in sections. Make a small nick with the knife into the edge nearest the base of the leaf. Insert, nick downwards, into a peat and sand seeding compost. Water well, place in a propagator and establish at 21°C/70°F. Propagation can also be done by removing mature side shoots and potting up into a peat and sand compost.

Repotting
This plant likes to be potbound, so repot only as necessary in a mixture of peat and sand, ensuring good drainage.

PROBLEMS

Most problems will be caused by overwatering. Brown patches on the leaves, or at the base of the leaves, are caused by overwatering. Allow to dry out and reduce amount of water.

Leaves that are damaged on the edges may be caused by unstable potting. Check that the plant is firmly positioned.

Susceptible to vine weevils. Treat with a pyrethrum-based insecticide.

Mealy bug may attack the plant. Remove with a cloth dipped in methylated spirit.

Sansevieria trifasciata grows either in a compact form or, as here, with erect, stiff leaves

Saxifraga stolonifera (Strawberry geranium)

QUITE EASY

This quite hardy plant comes from the temperate zones of China and Japan.

It is a small, dense plant with attractive round or kidney-shaped olive-green veined leaves which are pale purple underneath. It forms a number of runners with tiny plantlets on the end which trail over the edge of the pot, so it is best grown in a hanging basket. Small white star-shaped flowers are produced in summer. There is also a variegated version, 'Tricolor', with red, green and cream leaves which, being a little more fragile, requires a higher temperature.

S. stolonifera likes cool, bright conditions. A relatively quick grower when young it is best to propagate every 2–3 years as the plant can become straggly.

CARE

Light and temperature
Bright conditions, but not direct sunlight. The temperature should be quite cool all year round, and can go as low as 7°C/ 45°F in winter.

Water and feeding
Water 2–3 times a week in spring and summer and less in winter. In summer, feed every 2 weeks with a liquid solution and spray every 3 weeks to clean the leaves.

Propagation
It will produce small offshoots which often have roots. Plant several together in a mixture of soil, peat and sand and trim the stems.

Repotting
Each year in spring in a mixture of soil, peat and sand.

PROBLEMS

Take care not to overwater as this will cause stem rot. Allow to dry out and then water a little less.

If conditions are too warm, greenfly or aphids will be a problem. Spray with a systemic insecticide and move to a cooler position.

'Tricolor'

Saxifraga stolonifera bears its flowers in clusters on tall thin stalks

Schefflera (Umbrella tree, parasol plant)

EASY

The umbrella tree, so called as its leaves look like the spokes of an umbrella, is a sturdy and impressive houseplant with glossy palmate clusters of long-stemmed green leaves, sometimes variegated.

It is a quick grower, to a height of up to 3m/10ft, and benefits from frequent pruning to encourage a bushier plant.

Originally from the subtropical areas of Asia and Australia, *Schefflera actinophylla* grows into a substantial tree in its native habitat. Indoors it adapts to a range of temperatures all year round, and benefits from a spell outside in summer in a protected spot.

S. arboricola (Hawaiian elf) has an erect habit and clusters of blackish berries; it is a popular house plant.

Clean the leaves regularly with a damp cloth.

As a houseplant it is almost indestructible, and with good conditions should be everlasting.

CARE

Light and temperature
Bright or lightly shaded conditions with temperatures of 10–18°C/50–64°F throughout the year. It will withstand up to 27°C/80°F in summer.

Water and feeding
Water regularly in spring and summer, keeping the compost moist at all times. In temperatures above 18°C/64°F spray regularly. Feed with a liquid fertilizer at fortnightly intervals during summer. In winter water thoroughly but allow to dry out between waterings.

Propagation
By seed in spring or by root cuttings, both of which need to be established in a propagator at 21–24°C/70–75°F. This is quite difficult and best left to a professional.

Repotting
Pot on every year or two, as the plant becomes rootbound, in a rich soil- or peat-based compost.

PROBLEMS

Virtually problem free.

The foliage will turn brown if the plant is underwatered.

S. arboricola 'Trinette' has dainty leaves

S. 'Nora' is sometimes known as the octopus plant

S. arboricola comes in several variegated forms, here *S.a. capello*

Scirpus cernuus (Dougal plant, mini bulrush)

EASY

This plant resembles a miniature bulrush, hence its common name. It has glossy green rounded stems which arch gracefully over the pot. In summer it produces small green-white flowers on the ends of the blades. It is often sold, as below, in a tube to show it off better.

As a mature plant its height will be 15cm/6in and its width up to 30cm/1ft, so it grows well in a hanging basket and is good for confined spaces in the house. In its native habitat – the tropical and subtropical Mediterranean area – it grows more erect.

In the house it needs a humid condition, so stand the pot in a small container at all times and mist around the plant (but not on it). It should last for many years so long as it is not allowed to dry out.

CARE

Light and temperature
Prefers indirect sunlight but will withstand full sun. It will take low temperatures, down to 7°C/46°F, but prefers 10°C/55°F. The higher the temperature, the more humidity is needed.

Water and feeding
Water well, never letting the soil dry out. In spring and summer feed every 2 weeks with a weak solution.

Propagation
Remove the plant from the pot and divide the rootball into 2 or 3 sections by cutting through from top to bottom. Plant each section in its own pot in a loam-based mixture. It will establish easily.

Repotting
It is best to divide the plant as for propagation.

PROBLEMS

The leaves will lose their colour if there is not enough light. Move to a position with good light.

Outside leaves can go brown in summer if it is too hot. Remove damaged leaves and put the plant in a cooler place.

Scirpus cernuus may attract greenfly. Spray with a pyrethrum-based insecticide.

Scirpus cernuus is a more upright plant in its native habitat where it gets enough hours of daylight.

Selaginella apoda (Basket selaginella, creeping moss)

QUITE EASY

This member of the *Selaginella* family has pale green moss-like leaves which form a dense mat of foliage. A favourite in Victorian times, it is only now enjoying a revival in popularity.

Originally from the warm temperate zones of the East Coast of North America, it does well in a terrarium as it dislikes dry air and draughty rooms.

Selaginella apoda should be grown in a shallow pot, away from direct light. The pot should be surrounded by damp peat and misted often. Use fresh tepid water for watering and misting and do not use leaf shine. It can grow quite quickly and can easily be cut back, by half if necessary.

It should last for 2 or 3 years.

Selaginella apoda can look effective in a mixed planting

CARE

Light and temperature
A shady to semi-shady position with warm constant temperatures, ideally 18–24°C/64–75°F all year.

Water and feeding
Water freely throughout the year and mist daily to ensure adequate humidity. Keep the soil moist but not soggy, and never let the compost dry out. Feed every 3 weeks in spring and summer with a liquid fertilizer.

Propagation
In spring, with cuttings planted in a growing mixture for 3–4 weeks. Once established move to its adult pot.

Repotting
In spring, in the same container, using a no. 2 peat-based compost with added leafmould.

PROBLEMS

Ensure adequate humidity otherwise the plant will not last.

Prone to aphids and spider mites. Treat aphids with a pyrethrum-based insecticide and mites with a systemic insecticide.

S. rubra is the red-leafed species

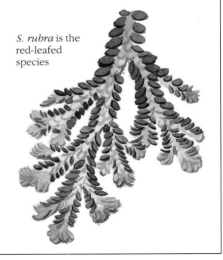

Selaginella kraussiana (Spreading clubmoss, trailing selaginella)

QUITE EASY

This fern-like plant is a quick-growing creeper which produces graceful trailing golden stems that look particularly good in a hanging basket or in a terrarium.

Originally from South Africa and Cameroon, where it is a ground-cover plant, it is quite easy to grow indoors as long as its surroundings are warm, damp and humid. It does not like dry air or draughts. Mist the leaves regularly and stand the pot over wet gravel to ensure good humidity.

Although it is not a fern, it produces spores on the tip of its leaves instead of seeds. Do not use leaf shine.

As a mature plant its spread will be approximately 30cm/12in and it should last for 2–3 years.

CARE

Light and temperature
A shady to semi-shady spot, with warm temperatures between 18–24°C/64–75°F all year.

Water and feeding
Water well all year, ensuring that the compost stays moist but never soggy. Use a liquid fertilizer every 3 weeks.

Propagation
In spring take 7.5cm/3in cuttings and plant in damp no. 2 peat-based compost. The cuttings will take a few weeks to root and can then be transferred to a larger pot.

Repotting
Each spring, in a no. 2 peat-based compost with added leafmould.

PROBLEMS

Relatively problem free as long as the atmosphere is sufficiently humid – aphids and spider mites can attack a dry plant. Spray aphids with a pyrethrum-based insecticide and mites with a systemic insecticide.

Selaginella kraussiana likes protection from draughts

Selaginella martensii (Resurrection plant, rose of Jericho)

QUITE EASY

This pretty compact plant has fleshy light green feathery leaves which hang down in rows from small upright stems. As a houseplant it will grow to approximately 30cm/1ft high with a spread of 15cm/6in.

Its native habitat, among the undergrowth of the mountainous forests of Mexico, is damp and protected, and indoors it needs similar conditions – moderately warm and shady with good humidity. It is ideal for a terrarium. Spray daily and stand the pot over damp gravel. Avoid dry and draughty conditions and do not use leaf shine.

It should last for 2–3 years.

'Variegata'

PROBLEMS

If conditions are too dry, the leaves will turn yellow and die. Cut off the affected ones, submerge the pot in water for a short time and drain well. Mist frequently.

Susceptible to aphids and red spider mite. Spray aphids with a pyrethrum-based insecticide and mites with a systemic insecticide.

CARE

Light and temperature
Shady or indirect light and warm temperatures, preferably 18–24°C/64–75°F in summer, down to 12°C/55°F in winter.

Water and feeding
Water well all year, keeping the compost moist but not soggy. Spray with tepid water every day. Use a weak liquid fertilizer every 3 weeks in spring and summer.

Propagation
In spring by taking 7.5cm/3in cuttings and planting in a moist no. 2 peat-based compost. Keep warm and in indirect light. It will not take long to establish and can then be planted in another pot.

Repotting
Every spring, in the same pot, in a mixture of no. 2 peat-based compost

Selaginella martensii is one of the more erect forms

Senecio rowleyanus (String of pearls)

QUITE EASY

This trailing plant with succulent pea-like leaves hails from Southern Namibia where it can be found growing from the rocky outcrops in full sun. The plant will form dense mats.

It is best used in a hanging basket, either indoors or in a good sunny situation in a conservatory. There the beadlike leaves, which are marbled in greens and whites, can be seen to good advantage.

The common name of the plant is obvious once it is seen.

Good air circulation is important as these plants have been adapted from a naturally airy growing site.

CARE

Light and temperature
In summer in a sunny position. It will withstand a temperature up to 30°C/85°F. In winter keep in good light but the temperature may go down to 10°C/50°F.

Water and feeding
Allow the surface of the compost to dry out between waterings. Feed at monthly intervals during spring and summer with a general houseplant fertilizer at half strength.

Propagation
Break off 10cm/4in pieces of stem, allow to dry for 48 hours and pot into cactus compost at a temperature of 21°C/71°F.

Repotting
Every second year in a cactus compost.

PROBLEMS

Aphids may attack this plant. Spray with a systemic insecticide.

Senecio rowleyanus

Soleirolia soleirolii (Baby's tears, mind your own business)

QUITE EASY

This tiny-leaved ground-cover plant grows freely throughout the Mediterranean area in moist spots between paving stones or cracks in rocks. Despite its delicate appearance, it is a tenacious grower and can easily take over if not watched carefully. In the last few years it has become extremely popular.

As a houseplant it is particularly useful for hanging baskets or among a mixed arrangement.

It is a good idea to propagate new plants as the older ones pass their best. This is very easy to do.

CARE

Light and temperature
Bright, indirect light or semi-shady conditions with cool temperatures never above 21°C/70°F.

Water and feeding
Always keep the compost moist and never let it dry out, even in winter. Spray frequently if the temperature exceeds 21°C/70°F, otherwise at weekly intervals during spring and summer. Feed monthly in spring and summer with a liquid fertilizer.

Propagation
Any time of the year by dividing the plant into small sections which can be put into a good houseplant mixture – they will establish very quickly.

Repotting
In spring in a soil- or peat-based compost.

PROBLEMS

Virtually problem free.

The foliage will turn brown if the plant is underwatered.

Soleirolia soleirolii 'Helxine'

Sparmannia africana (African hemp, house lime)

QUITE EASY

CARE

Light and temperature
A bright or semi-shady position with no direct sunlight. The ideal temperature is 15°C/60°F all year, and no lower than 7°C/45°F in winter.

Water and feeding
Water profusely in the summer, possibly up to 4 times weekly, depending on the conditions. Mist frequently. In winter probably only once a week, but do not allow the compost to dry out completely. Feed with a liquid solution at fortnightly intervals in spring and summer.

Propagation
In spring, with 15cm/6in tip cuttings, which should be planted in a moist mixture of peat and sand. Place in a light position and maintain a constant temperature of 18°C/64°F until established.

Repotting
Every year, in spring, in a no. 3 compost. If the plant is growing quickly it may need to be repotted twice a year.

PROBLEMS

A dry, hot atmosphere will cause the leaves to turn yellow. Improve the humidity by standing the pot over damp gravel and misting frequently.

Dry conditions will also encourage aphids and red spider mite. Treat aphids with a pyrethrum-based insecticide, and spider mite with a systemic insecticide.

Sparmannia africana – pruning can encourage it to flower more than once during the same season

This subtropical plant is similar in appearance to a linden tree and, in Germany where it is very popular, it is even known as Zimmer-linde. It has large, lobed, light green leaves covered with white hair. In its native habitat, the boggy marshes of South Africa, it grows to a height of 6m/18ft.

It is very quick-growing in conservatory conditions, and should be pruned back to around 2m/6–7ft. It will flower after 3 years (as long as it is kept in a pot slightly too small for the rootball), producing clusters of white flowers with purple stamens. Prune it before its winter resting period to improve the plant for the following year.

It should last for 3–4 years. Cuttings take root easily.

Syngonium (Goosefoot plant)

QUITE EASY

Syngonium 'White Butterfly'

CARE

Light and temperature
Bright but indirect light and temperatures around 17–21°C/64–70°F are ideal. In winter the temperature should not go below 15°C/60°F.

Water and feeding
In spring and summer do not let the plant dry out, so water 3–4 times a week. Stand the plant on pebbles almost covered with water to provide good humidity, which the plant thrives upon. Feed every 2 weeks with a general houseplant fertilizer. In winter water less and allow the plant to dry out between waterings.

Propagation
Take stem-tip cuttings approximately 10cm/4in in length. Dip them in a rooting hormone and place in a cutting compost in a propagator at 21°C/70°F.

Repotting
Each spring in a peat-based compost.

PROBLEMS

Scale insect and red spider mite trouble this plant. Remove scale insect with a cloth dipped in methylated spirit and spider mite with a systemic insecticide.

If the plant becomes straggly, it needs more light.

There are several commercial varieties of this plant available, but the most popular is 'White Butterfly', which has large white leaves with green edges. An unusual feature of *Syngonium* is the changing shape of its leaves, which are oval, becoming lobed as they mature.

This pretty climber from Central America can be found growing in trees, using its aerial roots to cling on to whatever it is climbing. Indoors, it will do well if it is trained up a damp moss pole, from which it will also gather moisture. A vigorous grower, it needs repotting often.

As in its native habitat, it needs a good humidity level, so mist frequently and place the pot over damp gravel. There it has beautiful white flowers but these do not appear in the pot plant.

As a houseplant it will grow up to 1.5m/4–5ft and should last for several years, at which point it can easily be propagated.

Syngonium is often sold under the name *Nephthytis.*

Tolmiea menziesii (Piggyback plant)

EASY

This perennial herb, with soft green heart-shaped leaves covered with white bristles, grows identical miniature plants which can be cut off and rooted. In spring it may also produce small greenish flowers.

It was originally from the warm temperate Pacific coast of America where it grows as far north as Alaska. It is good for hanging baskets or as a ground cover and will reach an average height of 15cm/6in with a spread of 30cm/1ft.

It is easy to grow indoors because it likes a cool, well-ventilated spot out of the sun. Avoid warm, dry air. Mist the leaves occasionally and do not let the compost dry out. Do not use leaf shine.

After 2–3 years it can become straggly so it is best to propagate. It can eventually be planted outdoors.

CARE

Light and temperature
A bright to semi-shady, well-ventilated position. In summer it does well outdoors; indoors keep the temperature around 18°C/64°F. In winter it likes a cool position, between 5–10°C/40–50°F. An unheated room is ideal, but ensure it has good light.

Water and feeding
Water 2–3 times a week in spring and summer. In winter it will need less water –
just enough to keep the compost moist. Feed at fortnightly intervals in spring and summer with a weak liquid fertilizer.

Propagation
Easily done by taking an offshoot and planting it in a soil- or peat-based compost.

Repotting
Repot annually in spring using a soil- or peat-based compost.

T. menziesii

PROBLEMS

Direct sunlight can damage the leaves. Make sure the plant is in a bright position, away from the sun.

If the leaves turn brown the plant is too hot and should be moved to a cooler position.

Overwatering and a cold temperature may cause stem rot, which can be recognized by brown slimy marks on the stem. Move to a warmer position and allow the compost to dry out. Water more sparingly, especially in winter.

Red spider mite can attack this plant. Spray with a systemic insecticide.

Tolmiea menziesii is very hardy

Tradescantia (Wandering Jew, inch plant)

EASY

Originally from Central America, Argentina and Brazil, this energetic creeper has smallish, shiny, oval green leaves with creamy yellow stripes and banks. In its native habitat it is found as a ground-cover and trailing plant. Its fast-growing stems, with their profusion of leaves, make it ideal for a hanging basket. New growth can be pinched out to encourage a denser plant.

Tradescantia is a good plant for the beginner as it accommodates a reasonable range of conditions and will not die if it misses out on the occasional watering. Its only disadvantage is that it tends to become straggly after a year or two and should be replaced by propagation, which is very easy.

It only needs to be misted occasionally, which should keep the leaves sufficiently clean.

From the same group as *Tradescantia* is the species *Zebrina*, which comes from Mexico. Strong direct light intensifies its leaf colours.

CARE

Light and temperature
Bright but indirect light, especially for variegated varieties, which need light to maintain their leaf colour. The ideal temperature is 18°C/64°F all year.

Water and feeding
Water 2–3 times a week in spring and summer and once a week in winter, allowing the soil almost to dry out between waterings. Mist occasionally. Fertilize every 2 weeks in spring and summer with a general houseplant solution.

Propagation
It is best to propagate each year in spring. Stem-tip cuttings will root easily in a mixture of loam and sand or in water, and have no special temperature requirements.

Repotting
Propagation is recommended.

PROBLEMS

If the leaves turn brown, the plant is either too dry or in too much light. Water more frequently and make sure it does not have direct sunlight.

Straggly growth means that the plant needs lighter conditions or that it is past its best and should be replaced by propagation.

Red spider mite and greenfly tend to attack this plant. Spray spider mite with a systemic insecticide and greenfly with a pyrethrum-based insecticide.

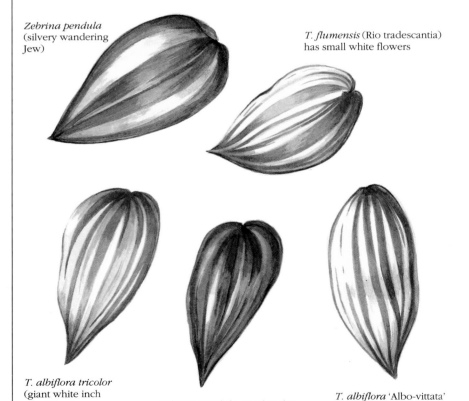

Zebrina pendula (silvery wandering Jew)

T. flumensis (Rio tradescantia) has small white flowers

T. albiflora tricolor (giant white inch plant) has large fleshy leaves

Zebrina pendula quadricolor (happy wandering Jew)

T. albiflora 'Albo-vittata'

Opposite: *Tradescantia*

Yucca elephantipes (Spineless yucca, pine lily)

EASY

This most exotic member of the lily family comes from the subtropical areas of Mexico and Guatemala, where it grows to a height of 15m/45ft in sunny, arid conditions.

The sturdy trunk is swollen at the base and from the top grow numerous rosettes of firm, glossy green, pointed leaves. It can also produce clusters of creamy white flowers.

Canes of 30cm–2m/1–6ft are now imported from the West Indies and Central America and quite often different stem lengths are potted together.

As a houseplant *Yucca elephantipes* is hardy and not at all temperamental, preferring a dry, sunny position, but also able to adapt to semi-shade. Mist occasionally. Wipe the leaves with a damp cloth from time to time but do not use leaf shine. The plant will benefit from a spell outdoors in summer.

It should live for many years.

Yucca elephantipes flowers after a number of years

CARE

Light and temperature
Bright light, even direct sunlight, especially in winter, though it will also be happy in a semi-shady position. It likes a temperature of 18–22°C/64–71°F all year, and no lower than 7°C/45°F in winter.

Water and feeding
Water thoroughly, but allow the compost almost to dry out between waterings. It will need less water in winter. Spray occasionally. Feed at fortnightly intervals in spring and summer.

Propagation
Side shoots will appear in spring that can be planted on individually in small pots in a mixture of no. 2 compost and sand. Maintain a constant temperature of 24°C/75°F until established.

Repotting
For young plants, repot every second year in a no. 2 compost mixed with sand. For mature plants it is necessary only to change the topsoil.

PROBLEMS

If the leaves turn yellow, the plant probably needs more light. Cut off the damaged leaves and move to a sunnier position.

Scale insect can attack this plant. Spray with a systemic insecticide.

Bromeliads

The glorious leaf colours of bromeliads are unforgettable and dramatic; they are showy plants and well worth having for the sharp colours of their flowers alone. Imagine a South American jungle filled with orchids and bromeliads, in all their brilliant colours, on the floor of the forest and attached to the trunks of trees.

There are over 1400 known species of bromeliad; in this book we have covered some of those most adaptable to cultivation as indoor plants. They should be watered through the natural well in the centre of the plant for, in their native habitat, the rain falls on the leaves and runs down into this well.

The mother plant of the bromeliad dies after flowering, leaving behind it 2 or 3 plantlets to grow on and replace it. Plants should ideally be purchased when the flower spathe is just beginning to emerge from the well.

Aechmea fasciata (Urn plant, Greek vase plant, bottle brush plant)

EASY

This plant, also known as *Billbergia rhodocynea*, comes from Brazil, where it was discovered in 1826. Naturally epiphytic, its natural habitat is on the floor of the jungle.

The name *Aechmea* derives from the Greek for lance tip – a reference to the sharply pointed central pink bract that is surrounded by long strap-shaped leaves. The actual flowers are small and blue, blooming on the edges of the spike in summer and lasting for up to 6 weeks. The plant forms a natural well that holds water in its centre.

After the flowers die, the pink spike slowly shrivels and at the same time replaces itself with 2 or 3 baby spikes or rosettes. Eventually these baby spikes can be repotted as individual plants, but the main plant will not bloom again for another year.

Aechmea will grow to 60cm/2ft across with leaves up to 30cm/1ft long. It will be 3 or 4 years old before the pink bract spikes appear and the plant flowers for the first time. There is a very striking variety called 'Purpurea' that has maroon-coloured leaves with silver markings.

CARE

Light and temperature
Aechmea is a very tolerant plant and can take either direct or indirect sunlight. The temperature should be no lower than 12°C/55°F and no higher than 27°C/80°F.

Water and feeding
Water twice a week and keep 2.5cm/½in water in the central spike. If possible, use rain water. Do not feed. Misting the leaves with weak solutions of fertilizer helps.

Propagation
The amateur finds offsets easier than raising seed. In springtime remove the offsets at the base of the plant once they look to be viable (after 4–6 months). Pot them on into a rich, barely moist potting compost. Do not separate the new rosette until the parent has completely shrivelled up.

Repotting
This is rarely required, but if needs be should be done at the onset of the growing period.

PROBLEMS

The flower stem may rot through overwatering at too low temperatures. Empty the rosette and allow the compost to dry out.

If the leaves develop brown tips and shrivel before flowering, the plant is getting too hot and dry. Increase watering.

If greenfly infests the plant, spray with diluted malathion.

Aechmea is also prone to scale insect and mealy bug, which should be treated with methylated spirit.

If bract spikes and flowers fail to appear move the plant to a sunnier situation.

Aechmea fasciata

Guzmania lingulata major (Scarlet star)

EASY

Guzmania lingulata 'Empire'

'Orangeade'

This is a striking houseplant, with strappy green leaves and a bright red or orange star-shaped bract that produces small white or yellow flowers, which soon fade away.

There are almost 90 species of *Guzmania*, their native habitat the West Indies and South America. The plant is named after the Spanish chemist, Antonino Guzman, and was introduced into Europe at the beginning of the nineteenth century. It grows naturally on the forest floor under deep-shade leaf canopy.

Although it is an epiphyte, in the house it is usually grown in a pot, but can do well if tied on to pieces of bark with its roots bound into sphagnum moss.

Guzmania dies after it has produced its flowers in summer but a new plant can easily be propagated from the offsets which appear as the parent plant dies.

It can grow to 30–38cm/12–15in tall and 25cm/10in across with a life expectancy of 2–3 years.

New hybrids are constantly being introduced by nursery men. *G. lingulata major* from Ecuador does well with its scarlet star, and *G. l.* 'Orangeade' and *G. l.* 'Empire' are just two of the dramatic new plants now available.

CARE

Light and temperature
A bright situation, but protect the plant from strong direct sun in the middle of the day. Keep between 15–18°C/60–64°F in summer and ensure the humidity level is high.

Water and feeding
Water up to 3 times weekly, keeping the potting compost moist. In winter, water only once a week. Do not feed. If possible, spray with rain water and keep about 2.5cm/1in water in the central funnel of the bract. Refill this every 3 weeks or so.

Propagation
The young shoots, which should be 9cm/3in long, appear as the parent plant is in flower. Wait until these offshoots have roots of their own before separating them, preferably in spring. Then use potting soil suitable for orchids.

Repotting
Not necessary.

PROBLEMS

If the lower leaves go brown, water the plant more often. It is normal for bromeliads to die back after flowering, but new offshoots will appear.

Rot at the base of the plant may have been caused by overwatering. Reduce watering immediately. The plant may well not recover.

Neoregelia carolinae (Blushing bromeliad, cartwheel plant)

EASY

This is one of the most spectacular bromeliads. It has stiff strap-shaped leaves, which turn a brilliant red colour near the centre of the plant, usually in spring towards flowering time.

The plant has a central funnel with small purple summer flowers, which are far less dramatic than the surrounding red leaves. *Neoregelia carolinae* 'Tricolor' is an even more striking variety, as it has yellow striped leaves as well as the central red ones.

This plant can grow to a span of 60cm/2ft, but is more often only 38–46cm/15–18in across.

As an indoor plant it can live for up to 5 years.

Neoregelia carolinae 'Marechalli'. Its red centre can spread to over half the plant.

CARE

Light and temperature
Strong light, which enhances the colour of the foliage, is needed, but avoid scorching midday sun, as the symmetry of the plant is ruined by the removal of sun-scorched leaves. Keep temperatures at 15°C/60°F all year, never below 13°C/55°F in winter or above 21°C/70°F in summer.

Water and feeding
Keep the central funnel full of water at all times, as this is from where the plant draws most of its nourishment. About once a month, drain the cup and refill with fresh water. In summer, water the compost as well, once or twice a week, always keeping it moist. Feed each fortnight in summer with a half-strength dose of liquid food.

Propagation
After flowering, the mother plant produces plantlets. Wait for them to grow to half the size of the parent, then cut free and plant into a sandy compost containing perlite. Keep humidity high and pot on after 3 months into 12cm/5in pots filled with a good draining and light compost, including grit and charcoal if possible.

Repotting
Each May, into a pot one size larger.

PROBLEMS

If the leaves lose their glorious colour, put the plant on a window ledge where its foliage will brighten up quickly. But beware of leaves becoming scorched.

Brown leaf tips may be caused by allowing the compost to dry out. Water frequently, particularly in summer months.

If the leaves become motley, check the lime content in the water as lime deposits can cause stain marks.

Nidularium (Bird's nest)

EASY

This bromeliad, from tropical South America, is rarely seen. Like the *Neoregelia*, it has a central rosette of very short leaves. This 'bird's nest' turns bright red in summer during flowering time – the plant's name derives from the Latin word *nidus*, meaning nest. The stiff strappy leaves can grow to about 30cm/12in long. The white flowers are uninteresting and short-lived.

There are many varieties of this plant. *N. innocentii* has saw-edged leaves which are coloured purple above and wine-red underneath. *N innocentii striatum* has variegated leaves while *N. fulgens* (blushing cap) has spotted ones.

Nidularium innocentii

CARE

Light and temperature
Bright light, but away from direct midday sun. Again keep temperatures at about 15°C/60°F all year round.

Water and feeding
Ensure the central funnel is full of water at all times. During the summer months, keep the compost moist by watering once or twice a week. It requires high humidity so place it on a tray of wet pebbles.

Propagation
By offsets, which appear at the base of the plant. Wait until the mother plant has shrivelled completely after flowering, then separate the rosettes and pot them on into a sandy, well-draining compost. Keep them moist, at temperatures of 15°C/60°F.

Repotting
Only when separating plantlets or when seriously pot bound.

PROBLEMS

Overwatering will cause the plant to rot and die. Water the compost less often.

If the leaves develop brown tips, either the air is too dry or the plant is receiving insufficient water. Increase watering, using rain water if possible, and mist during summer.

Tillandsia lindenii (Blue-flowered torch)

EASY

This dramatic bromeliad has grass-like leaves and an eye-catching central pink bract with a flower head up to 30cm/12in long. The bracts bear deep blue flowers with white throats 5cm/2in across.

Like all bromeliads, its native habitat is in the tropical and subtropical areas of South America and it is an epiphyte, growing on rocks or on the trunks and in hollows of other trees and plants, which give it support. The plant can also thrive in arid desert.

Tillandsia cyanea (pink quill) has similar leaves but a more compact and smaller flower head, which is again coloured pink with plain blue flowers.

Both *Tillandsia cyanea* and *Tillandsia lindenii* are green-leaved bromeliads.

The tillandsias sold as pot plants are often either attached to a stone or growing from the branch of a tree. They have practically no roots, and feed and nourish themselves through their leaves. *Tillandsia usneoides* (air plant or Spanish moss) is the most commonly purchased of the grey tillandsias.

CARE

Light and temperature
Bright filtered light suits *Tillandsia*, but keep it away from direct midday sun. Average room temperatures should be maintained throughout the year.

Water and feeding
Keep the central funnel full of water at all times. As well, during the summer, keep the compost moist by watering once or twice a week. The plant should be stood on a tray of damp pebbles to increase humidity. Mist the leaves frequently. Do not feed.

Propagation
By offshoots which appear at the base of the plant as the spike starts to die back. Wait until the mother plant has completely shrivelled up after flowering before separating and potting on the new plantlets. Use a bromeliad soil or sandy compost. Keep moist, at a temperature of 15°C/60°F.

Repotting
Only when absolutely necessary.

PROBLEMS

If the flowers fail to appear in spring, move the plant to a lighter position.

Insufficient water or dry atmospheres can cause the leaf tips to brown. Increase watering, using rain water if possible, and mist the leaves often.

Rot can be caused by overwatering.

Opposite: *Tillandsia cyanea*

Vriesea splendens (Flame sword)

DIFFICULT

There are around 100 known species of *Vriesea*, one of the showiest of the bromeliads. It is named after the Dutch botanist, W. H. de Vriese and is a native of tropical Guyana.

V. splendens 'Major' is the most readily available variety. It has stiff strappy dark green leaves, with purple- or chocolate-coloured bands running across them, which grow up to 45cm/18in long.

The central bright orange bract gives the plant its common name of flaming sword. It may appear at anytime throughout the year and can last for months. In summer small yellow flowers develop, but only after the plant has been potted up for several years.

CARE

Light and temperature
3–4 hours a day of direct sunlight will force the bromeliad into flower. Hot midday sun should be avoided. Keep the temperature at around 15°C/60°F throughout the year.

Water and feeding
As for all bromeliads, liquid fertilizer should not be given. Keep the potting compost moist by watering once or twice a week in summer months and less frequently during the cooler times. Mist the leaves and stand the plant on a tray of moist pebbles to increase humidity.

Propagation
Offsets are formed in spring and can be separated from the parent plant after the plant spike has shrivelled completely. They should be cut away with a sharp knife and potted on into a well-drained sandy compost. Keep the temperature on the warm side and avoid draughts.

Repotting
Only when absolutely essential, if the plant is potbound.

PROBLEMS

Overwatering can cause the plant to rot. It will be difficult to rescue, but try cutting down on watering immediately.

If the bract spikes do not appear, move the plant to a sunnier situation in early spring.

If the atmosphere is too dry brown tips may develop at the end of the leaves. Increase humidity by placing the plant on a tray of moist pebbles.

The spathe of *Vriesea splendens* 'Major' should be removed after the flowers die

Ferns

Among the oldest plants known, there are some 250 species of fern found all over the world. They were fashionable in Victorian times and today their delicate and attractive leaves make them popular as indoor plants, particularly in mixed groupings.

Ferns reproduce themselves through spores and do not flower. Many of them grow naturally in deep shade in tropical forests; others are epiphytic, found attached high up on tree trunks or colonizing cliff tops in full sunshine. They are mostly rhizomes.

As indoor plants, all ferns will do well if given high humidity. Standing the plant on a tray of damp pebbles is essential for success, but plants do not like spray-misting on their leaves.

Asparagus falcatus (Sicklethorn)

EASY

This showy, fern-like plant is actually a member of the lily family. It comes from South Africa, where it grows in protected and shady subtropical conditions.

It is a tolerant plant, with sturdy prickly stems from which grow delicate needle-shaped leaves. It will sometimes produce white flowers and then attractive but poisonous red berries.

Asparagus falcatus is not particularly fussy about its conditions, except it will not do well in temperatures above 21°C/ 70°F. The fronds will gradually die and should be cut off when they are past their best.

The plant will usually live for 3 years, after which time it should be propagated from seed.

Do not use leaf shine.

CARE

Light and temperature
Quite cool and shady conditions away from bright light. In summer the ideal temperature is 12–15°C/55–60°F. In winter it can go as low as 8°C/45°F.

Water and feeding
In summer water 2–3 times a week, never allowing the compost to dry out completely. In winter water once a week, or less if the temperature is very low. To ensure good humidity the pot can be stood over damp pebbles and the plant misted frequently.

Propagation
By seed in spring. Establish in a damp soil-based compost under a plastic cover. Or the parent plant can be divided into several smaller plants which should be repotted separately.

Repotting
This plant does not like to be moved and should only be repotted when it has outgrown its container.

PROBLEMS

If conditions are too dry the plant will be attacked by scale insect and red spider mite. Spray with a systemic insecticide and improve humidity.

The plant must never be allowed to dry out. If it does, cut back almost to soil level, immerse the pot in water for 1 hour, drain well, and keep at about 12°C/53°F until it starts to rejuvenate.

If the leaves turn yellow, the conditions may be too warm and dry. Water well, move to a cooler spot and mist frequently.

A. densiflorus meyerii
(plume asparagus)

A. sprengeri
(emerald fern)

A. falcatus

Asparagus plumosus, sometimes known as *A. setaceus*, is frequently used in floral bouquets

Asparagus plumosus (Asparagus fern)

EASY

Another from South Africa, this is a climber and can make a fresh and impressive show on a trellis, preferably made of wood, displaying its bright green, somewhat flattened, branches borne on wiry stems. As a room divider it can look extremely attractive, and is also seen climbing up around pictures and mirrors. It is frequently used in bridal bouquets.

The needle-like foliage may turn yellow and fall, either because of age or because the plant has been allowed to dry out. Red berries may form on the plant and are extremely attractive.

Care is as for other asparagus ferns outlined opposite.

Asplenium nidus (Bird's nest fern)

EASY

This exotic forest fern comes from the humid tropical areas of South East Asia and Australia, where it grows as an epiphyte in protected but constantly damp positions.

It forms a handsome rosette of lance-shaped, bright green leaves with dark central veins which will grow to almost 1m/3ft in length. These leaves are very delicate and should be cleaned carefully with a damp cloth from time to time. Do not use leaf shine.

Asplenium does well as a houseplant. It is a relatively quick grower and is at its best for 3 years, after which it should be propagated (which is difficult to do at home).

It likes a warm, humid and partly shady spot, away from draughts, but can tolerate central heating if there is sufficient humidity.

A. nidus

Asplenium nidus

CARE

Light and temperature
A semi-shady position, away from direct sunlight. The ideal temperature is 20°C/ 68°F all year, and no lower than 16°C/ 61°F in winter.

Water and feeding
Water 2–3 times a week in summer to keep the compost moist at all times. In winter water less, allowing the top of the compost almost to dry out between waterings. To ensure adequate humidity, stand the pot over damp pebbles. In spring and summer fertilize with a general houseplant solution at fortnightly intervals.

Propagation
By spore. This is difficult and best left to a professional.

Repotting
This plant does not like to be moved unnecessarily so pot on in summer only when it has become rootbound.

PROBLEMS

Prone to scale insect, which should be treated with a systemic insecticide.

Damaged or dried fronds can be cut off at the stem.

Brown spots on the leaves mean that the position is too cold and draughty. Move to a warmer, more protected spot.

Blechnum gibbum

QUITE DIFFICULT

An expansive palm-like fern with a spread of up to 1m/3ft, *Blechnum* will need a reasonable amount of space indoors. Originally from New Caledonia, it has a sturdy black trunk which grows to 1m/3ft. From this it produces a broad spread of arching pinnate fronds, some of which are fertile.

Indoors, it prefers coolish, dry conditions, though it also accommodates warm temperatures of up to 24°C/75°F as long as it has a high humidity level in the form of frequent misting and standing the pot over damp gravel. Once established, it should last for many years. Misting should keep the leaves clean.

The other common *Blechnum* is the Brazilian tree fern, *B. braziliense.*

CARE

Light and temperature
Bright but indirect light with temperatures ranging from 18–24°C/64–75°F, and no lower than 10°C/50°F in winter.

Water and feeding
Water carefully, allowing the top of the compost to dry out between waterings. As the temperature rises, increase the humidity. Use a general houseplant fertilizer at fortnightly intervals in spring and summer.

Propagation
From spores. This is difficult and best left to a professional.

Repotting
In spring, every second year, in a no. 2 peat-based compost, ensuring good drainage.

PROBLEMS

Mealy bug, scale insect and aphids can attack this plant. Remove mealy bug and scale insect with a cloth dipped in methylated spirit and spray aphids with a pyrethrum-based insecticide.

If the pinnas start to fall, the humidity must be increased. Ensure the plant stands over damp pebbles at all times and improve air circulation.

Blechnum gibbum is available in both narrow-leaved and wide-leaved varieties

Cyrtomium falcatum (Holly fern)

EASY

A handsome fern, *Cyrtomium falcatum* grows in the relatively cool foothills of China, Japan, Hawaii and the Celebes, in areas where the temperature seldom exceeds 18°C/64°F.

It produces a number of dark, scaly stalks which bear shiny dark green pointed leaflets (like holly). Its fronds will grow up to 60cm/2ft in length.

It is a very tolerant houseplant and does not have any special requirements, even accommodating central heating and draughts. It will live for many years.

Occasional misting should keep the leaves clean; otherwise wipe with a damp cloth. Do not use leaf shine.

The leaves of *Cyrtomium falcatum* look more like those of a holly bush and are up to 10cm/4in long

PROBLEMS

Prone to scale insect and aphids. Remove scale insect with a cloth dipped in methylated spirit and spray aphids with a pyrethrum-based insecticide.

CARE

Light and temperature
Bright indirect light is best, though it will tolerate semi-shady conditions. The ideal temperature is 18°C/64°F. If it goes above 21°C/70°F, stand the pot over damp gravel. In winter it should be no lower than 13°C/55°F.

Water and feeding
Water carefully all year, allowing the compost almost to dry out between waterings. It will need less water in winter. Feed at fortnightly intervals in spring and summer with a general houseplant fertilizer.

Propagation
In spring, by rhizomes. When dividing up the rhizome ensure each section has an active growing point. One can also collect the spores that, when ripe, will drop off from the underside of the leaves. Place these on to a tray of damp peat and put in a propagator at a temperature of 21°C/70°F. This can be quite a difficult process and is best left to a professional.

Repotting
Each year in spring, in a no. 2 peat-based compost, until the plant is mature, when it will only be necessary to replace the top 5cm/2in of soil in the container.

Davallia canariensis (Hare's foot fern, rabbit's foot fern)

QUITE EASY

An unusual creeping rhizome that grows over the edge of the pot, rather like a rabbit or hare's foot, is the main feature of this plant. For some reason, however, it will not grow over the edge of a plastic pot.

The rhizome is brown and covered with hair-like scales which are white on the tips. Dark wiry stalks produce light green leathery pinnate fronds of up to 30cm/1ft long. The plant also looks good in a hanging basket. It does well indoors as it does not require a humidity level as high as most ferns.

Davallia canariensis is originally from the Canary Islands, Spain and North Africa, where it grows as an epiphyte fern under the tree canopy of the humid subtropical forests.

It should last for 5–6 years.

CARE

Light and temperature
Bright but indirect light and temperatures around 18–21°C/64–70°F. In winter the temperature should not go below 13°C/55°F.

Water and feeding
Water thoroughly during spring and summer, but do not allow to become waterlogged. Place the pot on pebbles almost covered with water to provide humidity, and feed with a general houseplant fertilizer at fortnightly intervals. During winter allow the top of the compost to dry out between waterings.

Propagation
In spring, by dividing the rhizome into several sections, each with roots and fronds. Plant in a mixture of peat and sand, cover with plastic and place in bright but indirect light until established.

Repotting
Young plants will need repotting each spring in a no. 2 peat-based compost. For mature plants it is necessary only to change the topsoil.

PROBLEMS

Scale insect and aphids tend to attack this plant. Remove scale insect with a cloth dipped in methylated spirit and spray aphids with a pyrethrum-based insecticide.

If the fronds turn brown the conditions are too hot or too dry. Give it more water and raise the humidity.

Davallia canariensis

Didymochlaena truncatula (Cloak fern)

QUITE DIFFICULT

This attractive ground fern is to be found in all the tropical areas of the world, where it flourishes in spots protected by its taller neighbours.

Its leaves are slightly leathery, growing from coppery-coloured stems in a herringbone pattern.

Didymochlaena truncatula does not like central heating and needs a moist, warm and protected position in order to thrive. Mist frequently with fresh tepid water and never allow the compost to dry out completely.

If the conditions are right, it will last for a long time as a houseplant.

CARE

Light and temperature
This plant will grow in a quite shady position, but it needs warmth and humidity in order to thrive. The temperature should never be below 16°C/61°F even in winter.

Water and feeding
Use fresh tepid water at all times for misting and to keep the compost moist. Never allow the plant to dry out completely. Feed every 2 weeks in spring and summer with a weak liquid solution.

Propagation
By division in spring. Spores produced by the plant in autumn need to be sown in early spring, in a propagator at a temperature of 18–21°C/64–71°F in a seed compost.

Repotting
In spring, as necessary, using a good houseplant mixture.

PROBLEMS

This plant will survive only in very humid conditions. If it is too dry and the leaves start to wither, cut back all the leaves to the base of the plant and place in a bucket of water for 30 minutes. Remove, and place the plant in a warm position out of direct sunlight. Do not allow the plant to dry out, and when shoots start to appear, mist frequently.

Dryness will also encourage scale insect to attack the plant. Remove with a cloth dipped in methylated spirit.

Microlepia strigosa

QUITE EASY

A very popular fern, *Microlepia* has been in demand as a houseplant since its introduction from Assam more than 100 years ago. It was discovered in Northern India by the British botanist, Thomas Moore.

A ground plant which thrives in moist, protected tropical and subtropical areas throughout the world, *Microlepia* has delicate pale green bipinnate fronds which can grow up to 1m/3ft long. It needs plenty of space as it develops.

This plant likes a warm temperature with good humidity, so stand the pot on damp pebbles and mist frequently. If these conditions are maintained you should have a problem-free plant that is very long- lasting.

Microlepia strigosa is robust and grows from a creeping rhizome

CARE

Light and temperature
Bright but indirect light. This plant must never be in direct sunlight. Warm temperatures all year, and not below 16°C/61°F in winter.

Water and feeding
Water 2–3 times a week, enough to keep the compost moist, and mist frequently with tepid water. In winter water a little less. Feed monthly in spring and summer with a weak solution.

Propagation
In spring by division of the rhizome (make sure each section has good growth on it), or by sowing spores in a moist bed and maintaining the temperature at 20°C/71°F until the new plants are established.

Repotting
Each spring in a peat-based compost.

PROBLEMS

If the conditions or the compost are too dry the fronds will shrivel and die. Cut back for new growth to commence.

Nephrolepis (Sword fern, Boston fern, fishbone fern)

EASY

This common fern, with long tapering fronds that can grow up to 1m/3ft, was a favourite in Victorian times.

It grows freely in all tropical regions of the world, from Africa to the Americas and the Far East. A good humidity is essential, and it likes warm, bright, but semi-shady conditions (as it enjoys in its native habitat) all year round.

Spray each day with tepid rain water and stand the pot over wet gravel. Never allow the compost to dry out or to become water-logged.

It is a good houseplant as it will tolerate a fairly dark position, but it does not always do well in a centrally heated room or close to a gas fire. In the right conditions *Nephrolepis* will last a long time.

Do not use insecticides or leaf shine on this plant.

PROBLEMS

Sometimes the fern will deteriorate for no apparent reason. Cut it down to just above soil level and keep warm and humid until it begins to grow again.

Dry and dropping leaves are caused by dry air. Immerse the pot in water, drain, surround the pot with damp peat, and spray daily. If it does not recover, cut it right back and treat as above.

Scale insect and mealy bug can be attracted to this plant. Remove with a cloth dipped in methylated spirit. Do not use an insecticide.

CARE

Light and temperature
Bright to semi-shady conditions, but no direct sunlight and no dry air. In summer temperatures should be 18–24°C/64–75°F and in winter 13–16°C/55–61°F.

Water and feeding
Water 2–3 times a week with room temperature water in spring and summer, and feed each week with a weak liquid fertilizer. For the rest of the year water a little less, but never allow the compost to dry out.

Propagation
From plantlets that form on runners coming out of the crown of the plant. Pot these in a peaty mixture and keep at a constant temperature of 20°C/68°F until established.

Repotting
Repot in a peat-based mixture in spring as it becomes rootbound. The plant can be divided into smaller sections at the same time.

N. cordata

'Teddy Junior'

Nephrolepis exaltata bostoniensis (the Boston fern) was, surprisingly enough, discovered in that city in 1894 and will tolerate air-conditioning

Pellaea rotundifolia (Button fern, cliff brake)

QUITE EASY

Although a fern, this native of the temperate forests of New Zealand produces a profusion of thin black stems from which grow small, arched fronds of dark green leathery leaflets. The fronds reach 20cm/8in in length and will trail over the pot, making the plant ideal for a hanging basket.

Unusually, *Pellaea* prefers fairly dry conditions. The compost must never be allowed to become waterlogged or the plant will die. It does not appreciate misting either.

If conditions are right the plant will not have a rest period and should continue to grow all year round.

CARE

Light and temperature
Fairly bright but indirect light with constant temperatures, preferably not above 21°C/71°F. Increase humidity as the temperature rises. In winter it will tolerate as low as 6°C/43°F.

Water and feeding
Keep the compost moist, but never soggy, taking care not to let the plant dry out completely. Feed with a liquid solution of general houseplant fertilizer once a week during summer.

Propagation
Divide the rhizome into 2 or 3 sections, each with roots and some growth, and establish in a mixture of loam, peat and sand.

Repotting
Pot on as needed in a shallow pot, ensuring good drainage.

PROBLEMS

Never allow the compost to get soggy or the plant will die.

Susceptible to scale insect, mealy bug and aphids. Remove scale insect and mealy bug with a cloth dipped in methylated spirit. Spray aphids with a pyrethrum-based insecticide.

Pellaea rotundifolia bears little resemblance to the commonly perceived fern

Platycerium (Staghorn fern, elkhorn fern)

EASY

This exotic fern comes from the tropical areas of Australia and Papua New Guinea, where it grows in rainforests as an epiphyte, though it does adapt quite well to indoor conditions.

As a houseplant it likes to be attached to wood, as it often is in its native habitat. It does well surrounded by peat and moss and hung from a wall or pillar and thrives well in a basket, its main fronds – up to 1m/3ft long – arching over the pot and dividing into several antler-like shapes. These fronds produce spores on their undersides, and gradually turn brown and papery before being replaced by new ones. At the back are sterile leaves which grow upright and act as a support for the plant.

Platycerium will tolerate central heating as long as it has plenty of humidity. Spray with rain water daily and this should also keep the fronds clean. Do not use leaf shine.

It should last for many years.

Platycerium alcicorne

CARE

Light and temperature
Bright light or weak direct light. The ideal temperature is 21°C/71°F all year, with plenty of humidity, and no lower than 13°C/55°F in winter.

Water and feeding
In spring and summer submerge the pot in water for 15 minutes to make the compost moist. Allow the soil to dry out between waterings. In winter, when the plant is dormant, submerge for only 5 minutes. Add a weak solution to the water 2 or 3 times during spring and summer to encourage growth.

Propagation
From spores, which is difficult and best left to a professional, or from offsets with roots removed from the base and planted in a damp compost. Cover with plastic until established.

Repotting
Not necessary.

PROBLEMS

If conditions are too dry the plant will look limp. Submerge the pot in water. Spray and water more often.

If the leaves rot, conditions are too wet and cold. Water less and move to a warmer position.

If the plant is attacked by scale insect, remove with a cloth dipped in methylated spirit.

Pteris (Ribbon fern)

QUITE EASY

One of the largest groups of fern available as a houseplant – there are more than 150 varieties – *Pteris* has adapted well to the dry atmosphere of most homes. As long as it is never allowed to dry out, this native of the temperate and subtropical areas of Australia and New Zealand should thrive, growing to 1m/3ft tall.

There are several varieties readily available, most having compact fronds with elegant ribbon-shaped leaves that may carry a cream stripe. Some species have 2 types of frond – short sterile ones which grow close to the rhizome and long fertile ones which produce spores. It is natural for the fronds to die – cut back and new ones will form. Do not use leaf shine.

It should be a long-lasting houseplant.

PROBLEMS

If the fronds turn brown the plant is too dry. Cut off the damaged fronds, submerge the pot in water then drain well. Spray daily.

If the plant has too much light the fronds will shrivel. Move to a shadier position.

It is susceptible to aphids. Spray with a pyrethrum-based insecticide.

Mealy bug and scale insect should be removed with a cloth dipped in methylated spirit.

CARE

Light and temperature
Bright but indirect light. Average room temperatures of up to 22°C/74°F will suit this plant, and not below 13°C/55°F in winter.

Water and feeding
Water plentifully in summer but ensure good drainage as the compost should never be allowed to become soggy. In winter let the soil almost dry out between waterings. Mist daily to provide humidity and place the pot over damp gravel. Feed every week in spring and summer with a general houseplant liquid fertilizer.

Propagation
Best done by spores collected from the plant in autumn and sown in early March, on a peat and sand compost in a propagator at 21°C/71°F.

Repotting
As needed, when the root system has filled the pot, using a mixture of loam, peat and sand.

Pteris cretica 'Parkeri'

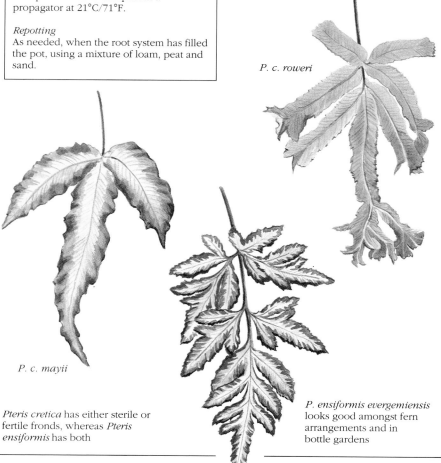

P. c. roweri

P. c. mayii

Pteris cretica has either sterile or fertile fronds, whereas *Pteris ensiformis* has both

P. ensiformis evergemiensis looks good amongst fern arrangements and in bottle gardens

Flowering Plants

Nursery men the world over are constantly
seeking to improve the quality of our
flowering plants: producing bigger blooms,
lasting for longer periods, with new colours
and greater readiness to flower.

None the less we have a wealth of beautiful
and fragrant flowering plants to choose from
throughout every season of the year. There
are plants with richly fragrant flowers such as
Gardenia and *Stephanotis*. There are those
that are easy to grow like *Chrysanthemum* or
Clivia, which has dramatic orange flower
heads. And there are the challenging plants,
such as *Columnea* or *Medinilla* – growing
these successfully can be enormously
rewarding.

The overriding factor for that success is the
correct amount of light. After all, the
flowering plants we propagate and you
purchase have been adapted from ones that
grow in the wild in the subtropical and
tropical regions of the world. In this book,
I have described these conditions so that
cultivation at home can emulate them as
closely as possible.

Achimenes (Hot water plant, nut orchid)

QUITE EASY

Achimenes, a member of the gesneriad family, has been popular for some 100 years

There are many folk myths associated with *Achimenes*, a plant early settlers in the United States took on their travels. Originally from Guatemala, it grows in high humidity in semi-shaded conditions.

A weak-stemmed plant, it bears masses of white, pink, blue, purple or yellow flowers throughout summer. Because its stems are weak, it is ideal for a hanging basket, where the flowers can trail downwards. It has hairy heart-shaped, jagged-edged leaves and grows up to 30cm/1ft high. After 2 or 3 years discard the plant.

There are several varieties. *Achimenes erecta* is a trailer, bearing bright red flowers. *Achimenes longiflora* has purple flowers, and there is a white variety as well. The tallest species is *Achimenes grandiflora*, which can grow to 60cm/2ft, but this is hard to find. More easily available are the *Achimenes* hybrids, which include 'Master Ingram', 'Rose Little Beauty' and 'Pink Beauty' (or 'Charm'), 'Purple King' and 'Paul Arnold'. These hybrids have been popular since the 1840s. Their flowering season is from early summer through to autumn.

Never place *Achimenes* in direct sun.

CARE

Light and temperature
Bright light away from direct summer sun. Warm humid conditions with an average temperature of 13°C/55°F throughout the growing season.

Water and feeding
Never let this plant dry out, even for a single day. Spray occasionally. Feed once a fortnight with a weak liquid fertilizer during the flowering season. After blooms have finished, allow the plant to rest. Stimulate growth the following spring by watering with tepid water or else remove the rhizomes from the soil in autumn, and allow to dry off throughout the winter.

Propagation
Divide the peculiarly scaly rhizomes in early spring and plant up to 6 together in a pot about 15cm/6in across, or take cuttings in late spring in seed-raising compost and place in a propagator at a temperature of 21°C/70°F.

Repotting
The rhizomes need repotting in early spring, with the top 2.5cm/1in of soil being replaced with rich humus compost. It is easy to divide rhizomes when repotting.

PROBLEMS

Cobwebs forming on the underside of leaves indicate red spider mite. Spray with a systemic insecticide and do not allow the plant to dry out.

Leaves may become discoloured – spray less often.

If flowers do not form increase humidity and place in a lighter position, but avoiding direct sunlight.

Aphelandra squarrosa (Zebra plant, saffron spike)

DIFFICULT

There are many species of this plant, but only 2 have been hybridized as houseplants. By far the most commonly found is *Aphelandra squarrosa*, known as the zebra plant because of its distinctive leaf markings. Originally from tropical South America, this plant is greedy when it comes to humidity. Try to site it in a spot where it can stand on a tray of pebbles.

In domestic circumstances *Aphelandra* will be difficult to keep going for more than a year – leaves will fall from the base upwards and it usually becomes leggy. The stems are almost black, in stark contrast to the handsome yellow bract which appears for a month or more in autumn.

Aphelandra squarrosa 'Dania' has a striking golden bract, from which stem insignificant white flowers (though breeding by nursery men has improved this variety), and *Aphelandra squarrosa* 'Louisae' has bracts with deep orange tops. Both form reasonably bushy plants of up to 45cm/½in high and wide.

CARE

Light and temperature
Aphelandra likes bright light but no direct sun. The leaves burn easily. In summer keep at 18–27°C/64–80°F. After flowering has taken place in autumn, temperatures can drop to 12°C/55°F. Cold air will cause it to drop its leaves, as will too much sun and any hint of draughts.

Water and feeding
Always use soft warm water and never let the compost dry out. – waterlogging is fatal. Spray the leaves each day with warm water and cut off all faded bracts above a good pair of leaves. From early spring to early autumn feed on a weekly basis, and twice a week when the plant is in flower.

Propagation
In early spring take stem cuttings from leaf axils, preferably with 2 pairs of leaves, and pot up using a rooting hormone. A heated propagator must be used, and once new leaves signal the cutting has taken, pot on into a 15cm/6in container. Acclimatize the young plant carefully.

Repotting
If you have a sufficiently good specimen, repot it in spring in good compost.

PROBLEMS

Major leaf loss and brown leaf tips can be caused by dryness at the roots, even for a very short time. Other possible causes are too much sun, draughts or cold air and lack of humidity.

Cobwebs may form on the underside of leaves, indicating red spider mites caused by dryness. Use a systemic insecticide.

White woolly patches in the axils of leaves are caused by mealy bug. Spray with diluted malathion.

Aphelandra squarrosa 'Dania' has most dramatic creamy veining on its leaves

Ardisia crenata (Coral berry, spice berry)

EASY

This small and erect shrub, which grows up to 1m/3ft high, bears shiny red berries at Christmas time.

Its original habitat is the subtropical areas of Japan, where it reaches double the height it can attain as an indoor plant. It has waxy deep green leathery leaves, with tiny white or pale pink flowers that are really rather insignificant. The berries which follow are by far the most attractive feature of the plant and will last until the onset of flowering the following season. They form on almost horizontal stalks at the lower end of the plant foliage.

Ardisia will last for 3–4 years – and indeed go on for more, though it easily loses its vigour. Prune back each spring before flowering.

CARE

Light and temperature
Bright light, and some direct sun each day. Keep cool in winter and always away from draughts. It needs a minimum 9°C/45°F in winter. Never let the compost dry out and prune in spring.

Water and feeding
Always keep the compost moist, watering less often in winter than in summer. Spray often and feed each fortnight. Stand over damp pebbles if possible.

Propagation
Through stem cuttings taken in spring or summer, or seeds sown in early spring. Neither method is easy.

Repotting
When potbound, move on to a pot one size larger.

PROBLEMS

If there are few berries, use a brush to pollinate the flowers the following season.

If the plant is reluctant to flower, ensure it has high humidity during spring when the buds are forming.

Leaves become mottled with webs on the underside, indicating red spider mite. Spray with insecticide and raise humidity.

If white woolly patches appear on and in axils of leaves the plant has been infested with mealy bug. Remove with a swab dipped in methylated spirit.

If the flowers drop before the fruit is set the plant is too cold. Move to a warmer position.

Ardisia crenata should never be positioned in a draughty place

Azalea indica (Indian azalea)

QUITE DIFFICULT

Azaleas bring a sunburst of colour into the house, from scarlet to apricot to white. A member of the *Rhododendron* family and originating from China and Thailand, they are dwarf shrubs that can grow up to 45cm/1.5ft in height.

Azalea indica, or the Indian azalea, is by far the most popular. It has rich green leaves of up to 4cm/1.5in long with hairy undersides and the flowers are open and bell-shaped. It is forced into flower for winter colour but will suffer thereafter, and should not be neglected if the plant is to last until the following season.

Azaleas are usually bought when in flower. Pick one with a mass of buds, rather than blooms, so you can enjoy the spectacular show of flowers, either single or double, on top of the little flat bush. It should be watered by the immersion method (see page 232) perhaps every day when in flower.

After flowering, keep watering and place it outside during the summer. This variety is not frost-hardy, so the plant must be brought into the house when summer is over.

Azalea indica

'Osta'

'Indica'

'Inga'

CARE

Light and temperature
A pot-grown azalea loves cool temperatures. It likes good light but not direct sunshine, so a north-facing window is ideal.

Water and feeding
Keep the compost wet but not soggy at all times, using rain water. Remember azaleas hate lime. An occasional spray with rain water helps to prolong the life of the blooms. Pick off faded flowers promptly.

If you feed the plant each fortnight it should flower again the next autumn. In spring, after the danger of frost has passed, take the pot outside and place it in a light but cool place. Keep the compost wet all season before bringing it indoors in autumn.

Propagation
Cuttings of healthy young shoots around 7cm/3in can be taken in summer and rooted in a heated propagator in the middle of summer at temperatures of 21–24°C/70–75°F. Use only lime-free compost and keep moist with rain water.

Repotting
After the first season and when the plant has outgrown the pot, repot in spring, always using lime-free compost and keep in the garden throughout summer.

PROBLEMS

Shrivelled or yellowing leaves, or a short flowering period are the most common complaints. Always water azaleas thoroughly, if possible soaking the entire pot each week at least. Water with soft water and always use lime-free compost.

Lime in the water causes yellowing leaves. This indicates chlorosis, caused by a lack of iron if grown in lime soil. Treat with multi-tonic and pick off the affected leaves.

Too much sun will cause the flowers to wither and brown and then drop off, as will too little humidity and too much hot dry air. Keep azaleas well away from radiators.

Begonia elatior

EASY

There are around 900 different species of *Begonia*, which is named after the Frenchman Michel Begon (1638–1710), who was a patron of botanical science.

Some species are grown for their leaf colour; others, including *Begonia elatior*, for their flowers. Two English nursery men – Veitch in the 1880s and Clibrans in the 1900s – developed *B. elatior*, which is a native of Brazil, and Dutch specialists began marketing it just after World War II.

The plant is covered by a mass of single or double flowers in cheerful colours. It can be bought in flower at any time of year and indoors will last for about 3 months.

The German *Begonia elatior* 'Reiger' strain is among the most reliable varieties, with a long-lasting flowering period, and *Begonia elatior* 'Reigers Schwabenland' is particularly recommended.

Pinching out the growing tips when the plant is young will keep it bushy. It is normally discarded after flowering, though it is possible to keep it going through 2 or 3 flowerings.

Begonia tuberosa

Begonia elatior 'Reiger'

The flower head of *Begonia elatior*

Begonia elatior

Begonia elatior in its varied colours

B. tuber-hybrida 'Harlequin'

CARE

Light and temperature
Begonia prefers a light position, but not direct sunlight, which will scorch the leaves and flowers. Temperatures above 20°C/70°F are best avoided.

Water and feeding
When the plant is in flower, water often, but do not allow the soil to become soggy. Spray the foliage and flowers to keep moist air around the plant, but do not do this when the plant is in direct sunlight. Feeding is not strictly necessary, as the plant is usually discarded after flowering.

Propagation
Some varieties, like the double orange 'Charisma', can be raised from seed. Otherwise, new shoots can be used as cuttings.

Repotting
If raising from seed, pot on the seedlings only once after they reach flowering size.

PROBLEMS

Begonia is prone to powdery mildew. Cut off the diseased leaves and spray with a systemic fungicide. Improving ventilation and cutting back on watering often helps.

Botrytis causes brown, grey and mouldy patches and can be avoided by the same treatments as for powdery mildew.

Aphids and red spider mites need to be sprayed with appropriate insecticides.

Too little light and too little or too much water can cause yellowing of the leaves. If stems become long and leggy, there is inadequate light. Leaves will curl up if there is too much heat and they will rot and droop if the plant is overwatered.

The leaves will need to be sprayed with water if they develop brown tips.

If the plant collapses, the causes are most often stem rot disease (caused by overwatering), swollen bumps on the tubers (known as root knot), eelworm or vine weevil, which causes tunnels in the tuberous stems.

Beloperone guttata (Shrimp plant)

EASY

Beloperone guttata is sometimes listed as *Justicia brandegeana*

CARE

Light and temperature
The stems of the shrimp plant become quite woody and if there is too much heat they will become softened and the plant will grow straggly. Temperatures of 20°C/71°F in summer and 18°C/64°F in winter will suit this plant. To produce colourful bracts it will need direct sunlight. This should be for relatively short periods in summer on a windowsill.

Water and feeding
Keep moist but not wet from spring to autumn, but drier in the winter months. Feed each fortnight during summer with a weak solution of houseplant fertilizer.

Propagation
In spring cut back the stems to 10cm/3in above the soil and repot at the same time. Tips of shoots can be rooted in a propagator at 18°C/64°F.

Repotting
In spring, prune back plants to around half their size and repot in good compost.

PROBLEMS

The plant will lose leaves if it becomes rootbound. Repot if necessary.

If leaves turn yellow, the plant has been overwatered. Allow the compost to dry out thoroughly before watering again.

Spray the plant with insecticide if it is attacked by aphids during hot weather; this is all too common.

If bracts do not develop, prune especially hard at the onset of the dormant period, and in early spring place the plant on an extremely sunny windowsill.

This small oval-leafed plant can survive for many years and grows up to 90cm/3ft square. Keep pruning out the stem tips to make the plant bushier and disregard those who tell you it is an annual.

The reddy-orange flower bracts are like overlapping Tuscan roof tiles and support a white flower which emerges at the end. The bracts appear almost all year round but the white flowers are insignificant and short-lived.

Beloperone guttata's native habitat is the tropical areas of Mexico, where it grows under tall trees. As an indoor plant it is very adaptable and cuttings can be rooted easily. There is a yellow form called 'Yellow Queen', which may be found on supermarket shelves from time to time.

Clever use can be made of this plant in hanging baskets.

Bougainvillea glabra (Paper flower)

'White Dania'

'Amethyst'

'Afterglow'

DIFFICULT

This is a glorious tropical climber, with dazzling purplish-pink bracts in groups of three which develop in spring and summer and last a long time. It is not an easy houseplant to grow or to make bloom again the next season. The stems are woody with spines and the leaves are narrow and smooth. In its native habitat of Brazil, it will grow to 9m/30ft but reaches considerably less when kept in a pot.

There are many different species, but I would say the most successful is *Bougainvillea glabra* 'Alexandra'. *Bougainvillea spectabilis* is altogether larger with stout spines. Its bracts measure up to 5cm/2in square and the plant has a spreading habit. Commonly found varieties include the American 'Crimson Lake' or 'Scarlett O'Hara' and the European 'Amethyst' and 'White Dania'.

This plant needs to be pruned in autumn and kept cool throughout the winter. Many bougainvilleas are available trained on hoops but they can also be found as standards or bushes.

Bougainvillea glabra 'Alexandra'

CARE

Light and temperature
Keep the plant warm in summer; it will appreciate a spell outdoors baking in the sun. Maintain a minimum winter temperature of 7°C/45°F.

Water and feeding
When spring arrives, increase watering from once a fortnight to 2–3 times a week and feed the plant every 2 weeks with a weak solution of liquid fertilizer. It will need doses of potassium fertilizer each spring. Spray with tepid water on warm days and keep the compost moist in spring and summer, but almost dry in winter.

Propagation
In spring. Use 8–10cm/3–4in cuttings dipped in hormone rooting powder. Place in a propagator at a constant temperature of 21–24°C/70–75°F with high humidity. Many of the leaves may drop. This is, however, a difficult plant to root and propagation is best left to professionals.

Repotting
Repot in spring, and only when the existing pot has been outgrown. Use standard compost to which has been added some woodash. Sphagnum peat moss also helps.

PROBLEMS

Bad ventilation and a humidity level that is too high will cause mealy bugs. Spray with an insecticide.

Cobwebs underneath the leaves are caused by red spider mite due to the plant becoming dry. Use a systemic insecticide.

Yellowing of leaves is caused by the plant being too wet. Always ensure the compost has very good drainage.

Bouvardia (Sweet bouvardia, scarlet trompetilla)

DIFFICULT

This is a gloriously scented plant with trusses of pink or white 4-lobed flowers which come out from summer through to midwinter. Originally from Mexico, it is similar to *Ixora* as both of these species belong to the madder family.

Bouvardia lasts for only a couple of years, even when it has had the most expert and loving attention. It is valued for the time of year it blooms and for its scent as much as anything else.

Prune it vigorously in early spring and keep it on the dry side through a good period of rest during the early summer months.

CARE

Light and temperature
Bright light, but keep shaded from direct summer sun. Minimum temperatures of 10°C/50°F in autumn help to set flower buds. Room temperature in summer.

Water and feeding
Water freely while the plant is flowering and feed each fortnight. After flowering, allow compost to dry out between waterings.

Propagation
Through stem cuttings taken in spring.

Repotting
Should be repotted each spring in a mixture of general purpose soil, perlite and peat.

B. longifolia has the most delightful scented white flowers

Bouvardia 'Bridesmaid'

B. ternifolia can bear its scarlet blossoms for much of the year

PROBLEMS

Webs on the underside of leaves indicate red spider mite. Spray with a systemic insecticide and raise humidity.

If the plant droops it is too cold or too dry.

If the leaves dry out move the plant to a cooler spot.

Browallia (Bush violet, amethyst flower, sapphire flower)

EASY

With proper care and attention, this dainty, simple plant can bloom for weeks. In fact it is often bought for its long flowering period and then thrown out. *Browallia speciosa* flowers naturally during the second half of the year, depending on the time of sowing, and looks particularly effective when massed with others as a group.

From tropical Colombia, the plant grows up to 50cm/20in in height and has dark green leaves with blue, lavender and white flowers. Some plants need stakes to support the stems. The more the plant is pinched out in its early growing days the better. You should pick off the dead flowers regularly and discard the plant when the flowering season is over.

The variety 'Major' produces large blue flowers, while 'Alba' has white blooms. The only other *Browallia* found as an indoor plant is *Browallia viscosa*, which is smaller than the bush violet and has white-throated flowers that are more subtle.

The bush violet, being a member of the deadly nightshade family, and therefore poisonous, should be kept well out of the reach of children and animals.

Browallia speciosa can look extremely effective in a hanging basket

CARE

Light and temperature
Browallia likes a bright position, but not direct sunlight. Give it 4 good hours of strong light a day. It needs to be in temperatures of around 20°C/68°F in summer (temperatures much over this will reduce the life of the flowers), and cooler in winter.

Water and feeding
In summer water often, always keeping the soil moist, and feed each week. In winter water sparingly, otherwise the roots may rot. Humidity is important so if possible place on a tray of wet pebbles.

Propagation
This plant grows easily from seed; sow in early spring. The seeds will sprout within 14 days. Cover with a dusting of compost and place in a propagator at 18°C/64°F. After the seedlings have germinated, prick off into 7.5cm/3in pots. They will begin to flower 6 months later.

Repotting
Not necessary as most people regard this plant as an annual.

PROBLEMS

When the air is dry, greenfly and whitefly can sometimes be a nuisance. Spray with insecticide.

If the plant becomes leggy, pinch out the growth tips to encourage bushiness.

Brunfelsia (Yesterday, today and tomorrow or morning, noon and night)

QUITE EASY

The common name of this sweet-smelling plant refers to its changing colours: the flowers move from purple through pale violet to white in fast succession.

It is an extremely slow growing but very attractive plant, with glossy green leaves and pretty flowers about 5cm/2in across. In its native habitat of Brazil, where it is found in tropical conditions under semi-shaded canopy, it will grow to 2m/8ft tall, but as an indoor plant it rarely reaches above 60cm/2ft. It can flower almost all year round, and will be particularly encouraged if placed in a sheltered spot on a sunny patio during the summer months.

CARE

Light and temperature
Keep out of direct sun when growing and in flower. During spring and summer keep temperature between 18–24°C/64–75°F. This plant flush flowers so to encourage a second flowering it is important to drop the temperature to 13°C/55°F. After this second flush and with winter approaching, reduce temperatures further to 7°C/45°F to harden off plant.

Water and feeding
Water thoroughly in spring and summer. Stand the pot on a saucer of pebbles almost covered with water since the plant enjoys high humidity. In winter, remove from pebbles and allow to dry out between waterings. During spring and summer feed at monthly intervals with general houseplant fertilizer.

Propagation
Take tip cuttings and place in cutting compost in a propagator at a temperature between 18–21°C/64–70°F.

Repotting
In autumn, when flowering has finished, in no. 2 loam-based compost.

PROBLEMS

Webs on underside of leaves indicate red spider mite. Use systemic insecticide or diluted malathion and raise humidity.

Grey mould may occur in winter if plant is too cold and too wet.

Brunfelsia pauciflora calycina can be found with white or yellow flowers as well as the more common purple variety

Calceolaria herbeohybrida (Pocketbook plant)

EASY

CARE

Light and temperature
Calceolaria likes bright light, but should be protected from the midday sun in a cool and airy position, perhaps a north window. Ideal temperatures are 10–13°C/50–55°F.

Water and feeding
Water well, and spray occasionally, but do not allow the compost to become too wet. Feed weekly during flowering.

Propagation
Generally this is best tackled by professionals.

Repotting
Not necessary as the plant is an annual.

PROBLEMS

Flowers may turn brown if the plant is too hot and dry. Move to a cooler location.

Prone to greenfly. Spray with a systemic insecticide.

This cheerful plant, with unusual pouch-shaped flowers, in blotchy yellow, orange, red or white, rising above large hairy leaves, is bought in flower and has a relatively short life as an indoor plant. None the less it produces an eye-catching splash of colour in the early months of the year. Keep the temperature on the cool side to prolong the flowering season.

The name of the plant derives from the Latin word *calceolus*, meaning small shoe. Originally *Calceolaria* was found on the lower slopes of the Andes mountains of Chile and it reaches about 45cm/18in high. It is best regarded as an annual.

Calceolaria integrifolia (Chilean pouch or slipper flower) looks similar but is grown as an annual, for flowering tubs on patios or in public parks.

Campanula isophylla (Italian bellflower, star of Bethlehem, falling stars)

EASY

Nearly all campanulas are hardy garden plants, but only a few of the 35 genera are suitable as houseplants. By far the most reliable and dazzling of these is *Campanula isophylla*. With its pale green leaves setting off star-shaped blue or white flowers, it is best displayed from a suspended pot or hanging basket. Although blue is the most common colour, a white variety, *Campanula isophylla* 'alba', and a mauve variety, *Campanula isophylla* 'Mayii' (which is difficult to grow), are more readily available these days.

This pretty subtropical plant is a native of Italy and grows to a height of 22cm/9in with a spread of 45cm/18in. It should flower happily throughout the summer. Pinch off flower heads that have faded, and give the bush a sharp trim as the flowering season ends. The plant should be replaced after a couple of years.

C. isophylla 'alba'

C. isophylla

CARE

Light and temperature
Campanula likes bright positions with as much light as possible, but in summer protect it from the hot noon sun. It likes average warmth. Good periods of rest in winter will help the plant to be a successful flowerer the following season. In winter it will tolerate below-freezing temperatures. Adequate ventilation is essential.

Water and feeding
In the flowering season keep the plant moist at all times. Apply liquid fertilizer every fortnight to prolong the blooms. In late winter, cut the plant right back to within 3cm/1in of the soil, leaving 1 pair of leaves. Keep on the dry side, watering only occasionally. Vigorous new growth will appear in spring. Then water the plant regularly. Do not use leaf shine.

Propagation
Start cuttings off in spring from prunings made when cutting the plant back. Tips need to be 10cm/4in long and inserted into a peat and sand compost and placed in a propagating frame with a constant temperature of 18°C/64°F.

Repotting
Repot once in spring, after the first season, using a rich humus potting soil.

PROBLEMS

If leaves turn yellow and fall, red spider mites could be infesting the plant. Spray with a systemic insecticide.

Conditions that are too wet and cold cause flowers to rot and fall before opening. Stand in a warmer atmosphere and allow to dry out before watering again.

Waterlogging can cause the leaves and stems to rot. Allow the plant to dry out.

Should mould appear, apply a fungicide to kill the fungus. Make sure the compost is not left saturated in humid conditions.

C. carpatica 'Karl Foster'

C. carpatica 'Karl Foster' white

C. poscharskyana white

C. poscharskyana blue

Canna hybrida (Canna lily, Indian shot)

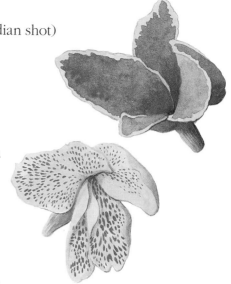

EASY

An indoor bulb which cannot tolerate frost, the canna lily will appreciate a sunny patio after flowering but should never be left outside in winter.

It is a wonderfully colourful plant with large clusters of flowers, on a 60–90cm/2–3ft stalk, which last for 3 weeks or so.

Its native habitat is mostly Brazil, where it grows in tropical conditions in the rainforests.

Dutch and Danish growers have bred a wide variety of colours – reds, pinks, yellows and white. The flowers can be up to 12cm/5in across and many are striped or spotted, though the pure white ones are the most dramatic against the green, dark green or purple leaves. This lily is summer-blooming and should be left in its pot until the foliage has completely died down. The compost should be kept almost dry until growth begins again the next spring.

The canna lily loses its vigour after 4 or 5 years and should be replaced.

Canna indica

CARE

Light and temperature
During the growing period give plenty of light and average room temperatures. Protect from scorching midday sun, particularly when flowering, to make the flowers last longer. Winter rest in a box of peat is recommended.

Water and feeding
Water frequently to keep the soil moist during the flowering season. Ensure good drainage. Feed with a weak solution of liquid fertilizer to encourage growth of the flower stalk. After flowering allow the plant to die down with minimal watering prior to a period of dormancy.

Propagation
Best left to a professional.

Repotting
This bulb likes a rich houseplant compost when repotted easily each spring after the dormant period. Begin watering right away.

PROBLEMS

Mealy bugs can infest this plant. Treat individually and raise the humidity around the plant.

If flowers fail to form, try increasing the dormancy period and ensure the bulb is kept in really cool, though frost-free, conditions for at least 3 months. Thereafter apply fertilizer when watering.

Capsicum annuum (Ornamental chilli pepper, Christmas pepper)

EASY

Capsicum fruits profusely and the peppers last up to 3 months

CARE

Light and temperature
The plant needs to be in a sunny and airy position, but not too hot. Some direct sun is needed. In dim light, it will immediately shed its fruit. It prefers moderate temperatures.

Water and feeding
Keep damp, but not wet, and feed weekly during the growing period with weak solutions of liquid fertilizer.

Propagation
Ornamental chilli peppers can be grown from seed planted in a propagator in winter. If the seedlings are placed outside on a warm patio during summer they will bear more fruit than those continuously indoors.

Repotting
These plants are annuals.

Capsicum annuum is usually available in autumn, when its bright red fruits add festive cheer to windowsills and tables in the period leading up to Christmas.

The plant should be purchased in September, when the starlike white flowers are in bud. From these develop green peppers which ripen into purple, crimson and orangy-yellow edible fruits. It must not be confused with the poisonous *Solanum pseudocapsicum*. The plant grows to a height of 45cm/18in, and lasts only 1 season.

The ornamental pepper is native to Central South America, where it grows as a small tropical shrub.

PROBLEMS

Aphids and spider mites can infest the plant if it is put in a place which is too warm and dry. Move to a cooler position and spray with insecticide.

If the peppers fall the chances are the compost has been allowed to dry out. Increase watering. If this appears not to be the cause, increase humidity by placing the pot over a saucer of damp gravel.

Celosia cristata (Cockscomb)

EASY

This is a weird looking plant, its bright crimson, orange or yellow flowers having a velvet-like texture. The flowers are best described as cockscombs and have a greasy feel to them.

Celosia cristata grows to 45cm/18in and is quite distinct from the other main type, *Celosia plumosa* (the plume flower), which bears red or yellow feathery plumes in summer and grows to about 30cm/12in. Both originate from the cooler areas of tropical Asia, where they grow in semi-shaded areas, often clinging to rocks in the East Indies.

Although they can be raised from seed, nursery-bought plants are generally more successful. They are best regarded as annuals.

C. plumosa will have blooms for 2 months or more

CARE

Light and temperature
This plant is not fond of heat so a cool temperature of 13–15°C/55–60°F suits it best. In higher temperatures it tends to fade quickly. However it likes good light and can even have a little direct sunlight each day.

Water and feeding
Keep the compost moist at all times, but do not overwater as the plant may rot or wilt and never recover. Feed with a general indoor fertilizer each fortnight.

Propagation
Seeds can be sewn in spring at 15–18°C/60–64°F. Prick out the seedlings as soon as they are large enough to handle and pot on using a soil- or peat-based compost.

Repotting
Not necessary, as the plant is an annual. Discard after flowering.

PROBLEMS

Whitefly can be a nuisance. When infested, spray with insecticide.

Celosia cristata

Chrysanthemum

EASY

Potted chrysanthemums are now available all year round in almost every colour except blue. The Danes and the Dutch are developing many new and better varieties, with single or double flowers, in dwarf sizes, bushes or standards.

Chrysanthemum morifolium, or the florists' chrysanthemum, has been cultivated for over 3000 years in China and Japan, where it grows to 1m/3¼ft high and flowers naturally after the summer. The variety sold in stores today is *Chrysanthemum indicum*, which has been adapted to last longer in flower and is raised with the use of both chemicals and light restriction (the first curtailing growth; the second forcing flowering to a specific date). This plant is sold at a height of 24–30cm/9–12in and flowers throughout the year. It should be bought with coloured buds since green buds may fail to open.

Chrysanthemum frutescens (the white marguerite, or the Boston or Paris daisy) is altogether different and grows up to 90cm/36in high and 60cm/24in wide. It is also known as *Argyranthemum frutescens chrysaster*. The bush is covered by masses of small yellow or white daisy-shaped flowers which bloom for weeks on end. It may last for 3–4 years,

given the right conditions. Flowering in early summer, it needs to be firmly chopped back after the flowering season and should be given periods of rest in a greenhouse.

C. morifolium can be planted in the garden when flowering is over; this is a better long-term solution than trying to make these forced specimens last a second flowering period.

The flowering season lasts 6–8 weeks if sited in a bright, cool room; overheated rooms cause the plant to have a short life.

CARE

Light and temperature
Chrysanthemums need to be kept cool, around 13–16°C/55–60°F and in a bright position. Pot chrysanthemums must not be subjected to direct midday sun.

Water and feeding
In summer the plant needs to be kept thoroughly moist, which may mean watering it frequently. In winter, keep the compost just moist. Feed with fertilizer each fortnight while the plant is in flower.

Propagation
C. frutescens and *C. morifolium* can be raised from seed or cuttings in spring and potted into large containers of soil-based compost as necessary. They can then be brought indoors in the autumn, which is the natural flowering time for garden chrysanthemums. Pot-grown dwarf chrysanthemums can be pruned and planted outside in the garden after flowering, or be treated as annuals and discarded. If planted outdoors, they revert to the natural flowering season in autumn and grow taller as the effect of the dwarf hormones given to them by nursery men wears off.

Repotting
In spring, when necessary, using good potting compost.

PROBLEMS

Aphids and spider mites can infest the plants if they are too warm. Move to a cooler spot and spray with insecticide.

Chrysanthemum frutescens

Citrus mitis (Calamondin orange)

QUITE EASY

This miniature orange tree brings threefold pleasure. Its leaves are wonderfully glossy and dark green and carry deliciously fragrant tiny white flowers, borne singly on the branch tips, and decorative edible, if bitter, fruits.

From the Philippines, *Citrus mitis* is a dwarf variety and grows up to 1.2m/4ft high. It may well be a hybrid of the lime and the kumquat. Flowers and fruits develop throughout the year, though the greatest profusion will come in summer. A spell in the garden during this time will benefit the orange tree and may avoid the need to brush-pollinate the flowers. Midday is the best time to artifically aid pollination.

A gentle shake when buying the plant will ensure you do not choose one whose leaves are falling – a sign of an unhealthy specimen. Draughts should be avoided at all times. With good plant management *Citrus mitis* can last for years.

CARE

Light and temperature
Citrus mitis likes a bright, sunny position throughout the year and a spell outdoors in summer. In winter, temperatures of 15–18°C/60–64°F will suit it well. Good ventilation without draughts is important.

Water and feeding
Always use soft water and do not let the soil dry out between spring and autumn. In the growing period, use a weak solution of fertilizer each week.

Propagation
This is difficult to do in the domestic environment, but enthusiasts can try in spring. Dip cuttings in a rooting hormone powder and plant into a rich compost in a base-heated propagator. Plants grown from orange pips are too large for indoor plants in the long run.

Repotting
Lack of new growth indicates soil exhaustion. Repot in spring into a pot one size up when the plant is very potbound.

PROBLEMS

Citrus is prone to scale insect. Remove individually with methylated spirit swabs.

Spider mites, aphids and mealy bug may attack the plant from time to time. Spray with fungicides or insecticides.

If the leaves develop patches of dark grey mould, spray with a systemic fungicide.

Yellow leaves may appear if the plant has been watered using hard water. They may also be a sign of lack of magnesium. Add a plant tonic with magnesium to remedy this.

Brown-tipped leaves indicate the plant may be suffering from draughts. Move to a better site.

Citrus mitis has loose-skinned fruits around 5cm/2in across; they make a good addition to marmalade

Clerodendrum thomsonae

EASY

(Glory bower, bleeding heart vine)

This is a vigorous climbing shrub in the tropical regions of west Africa, where it grows up to 4m/13ft on twining stems, supporting itself on other vegetation. It has attractive dark glossy leaves with startling papery white flowers that have blood-red corollas appearing throughout the summer season.

Here nursery men treat the plant with growth inhibitors and it is sold as a shrub reaching no more that 60cm/2ft high. The plant will live for 4 or 5 years as an indoor plant before becoming too straggly and losing its vigour. Even so, pruning is necessary to encourage further flowering after new growth appears and to keep the plant in check; cut back up to half the previous year's growth. *Clerodendrum* flowers on new growth and the weak stems will need to be supported.

Keep it in a cool place during winter as it cannot cope with heating units or air conditioning.

Clerodendrum thomsonae can look striking in a hanging basket but it is important to pinch out the stem tips to prevent legginess

PROBLEMS

If the air is too dry, flowers and buds can drop off. Keep the air around the plant humid by spraying.

If the plant does not flower, the humidity and temperature must be increased during the growing period.

Spray with a systemic insecticide if the plant is infested with whitefly. White woolly patches on the axils of leaves indicate mealy bug. Spray with diluted malathion.

CARE

Light and temperature
Very bright, but no direct sun. It needs warmth and humidity. Allow it to rest during winter when it loses it leaves.

Water and feeding
Clerodendrum likes warm soft water. Do not let the plant dry out and feed once a week from spring to autumn with a high-nitrogen fertilizer. Make sure there is plenty of humus in the compost at all times, and if possible stand the pot over a tray of moist pebbles.

Propagation
This plant is difficult to propagate and requires a heated propagator if the 10cm/4in cuttings taken in spring are to grow. Dip them in hormone rooting powder and allow 6–8 weeks for new growth to appear.

Repotting
Every spring, cut back and pot on in good peaty compost which has had plenty of leafmould worked into it.

Clivia miniata (Kafir lily)

EASY

From Natal in South Africa, this rhizome develops heads of between 8–10 pretty orange bell-shaped flowers from thick stalks surrounded by glossy leaves. Varieties with red, yellow or cream flowers may occasionally be found as indoor plants.

A subtropical plant originally, it grows amongst rocks and crevices in damp and shaded conditions. It reaches 45cm/1.5ft in height and will flower regularly in early spring, but only when certain rules are obeyed: it needs space, winter rest and does not like to be repotted unless it is absolutely bursting out. Remove the dead flower stalk. The plant will benefit from a spell outdoors during the summer months.

Clivia lives for many years and is a striking plant.

Clivia miniata

CARE

Light and temperature
Bright light, but no direct sun, and cool or average warmth. Keep at a temperature of 8°C/50°F through the dormant period and at room temperature in summer.

Water and feeding
Water moderately in summer but hardly at all in winter. Always ensure good drainage. As soon as the flower stalk emerges from the base of the plant, feed on a weekly basis with general liquid fertilizer until the end of summer. Mist the leaves frequently.

Propagation
In early spring separate young offshoots after flowering with a sharp knife, ensuring the young plant retains its roots. Several growing in the same pot look attractive. The offsets may take 2 or 3 years to flower.

Repotting
Do this only when essential. Established plants only require the top 8cm/3in of soil to be changed using a soil-based compost.

PROBLEMS

White woolly patches on leaves indicate mealy bug. Remove with a swab dipped in methylated spirit.

If leaves become brown and scorched, move the plant out of the sun and do not water in direct sunlight.

Flowers may fall prematurely, in which case move to a cooler position.

If no flower spike appears once the plant has reached maturity, wait a further year and allow a longer winter resting period. Ensure correct watering takes place during the growing phase.

Columnea (Goldfish plant)

DIFFICULT

Columnea gloriosa is one of the
most striking of all hanging
plants, with long green tendrils
producing red, orange and scarlet
tubular-shaped flowers which
appear at various times of the
year. It is, of course, ideal for a
conservatory where its glorious
shape can be shown off to good
effect. Its natural habitat is
Central America, mainly in the
dense jungles of Costa Rica, and
it was named after the sixteenth-
century Italian botanist, Fabius
Columna.

Columnea gloriosa has trailing
stems with hairy leaves and
grows to 90cm/36in or more,
while the hybrid *Columnea
stavanger* has smooth leaves on
stems which grow to the same
length. *Columnea banksii* is one
of the most commonly available
and is also one of the easiest to
make do well.

But be warned – it is a fussy
plant that requires constant
attention, most importantly high
humidity and an enforced period
of rest during winter. It will do
well for 3 or 4 years and should
then be replaced with new
plants.

C. banksii   *C. gloriosa*

Columnea

CARE

Light and temperature
Bright light, but not direct sunshine. It
does not like temperatures to fall below
13°C/55°F and will take up to 24°C/75°F as
long as there is good humidity. The foliage
will scorch if it touches the hot glass of a
window.

Water and feeding
Columnea needs frequent, often daily,
misting, but do not spray in direct sunlight
otherwise the flowers may scorch. Avoid
hard water and alkaline fertilizers. During
summer, keep the soil moist but not wet,
otherwise root rot or botrytis will set in. In
winter keep the soil slightly damp, almost
dry. Feed weekly in summer with a weak

solution of liquid fertilizer. If possible,
stand the plant on a bed of moist pebbles
to provide a humid atmosphere.

Propagation
Use a heated propagator and take cuttings
when the flowering season ends. Dip
them in rooting hormone powder and
plant into a rich compost of sand and
loam. Make sure the cuttings are not
allowed to dry out. They should take in
about 3 weeks.

Repotting
Repot every 2 years after blooming into a
humus-rich compost.

PROBLEMS

If the trailers become straggly, prune them
by about half their length after flowering to
encourage bushiness.

Draughts and central heating will cause
leaves to drop. Spray the foliage daily with
lime-free water.

Red spider mite can attack this plant. Treat
with a systemic insecticide and then
improve the humidity of the plant to
prevent further attacks.

If flowers fail to appear, move the plant to
a brighter spot.

Crossandra infundibuliformis

QUITE DIFFICULT

(Firecracker flower)

As the common name suggests, this is a striking plant with trumpet-shaped flame-coloured flowers in yellow, orange and red, hiding the green triangular bracts on which they form. It was brought from India in the early 1800s, but sank in popularity and was only re-introduced in the 1950s after a Swedish nursery man bred a houseplant variety, 'Mona Wallhead', which is commonly available today. The flowers are salmon-pink.

In its native habitat, *Crossandra* can grow as tall as 90cm/36in, but the indoor plants available only reach 30cm/12in high. It is a pretty, bushy plant which flowers from late spring to early autumn. It starts to flower when only a few months old. With careful plant management *Crossandra* will bloom practically throughout the year and will welcome a spell out on a sunny terrace in summer.

It needs to be sprayed often and flourishes best when it is surrounded by other plants. It will do well for up to 2 years, but should then be replaced.

CARE

Light and temperature
It likes bright light in winter and needs to be warm all year round, with temperatures no lower than 18°C/64°F. In summer place in a bright well-lit position where the plant will get some sunlight.

Water and feeding
In summer water frequently and always use water at room temperature. Do not spray either foliage or flowers. In winter, water only when the soil has dried out. Feed during the growing period.

Propagation
In early spring, top cuttings root well in a heated propagator, taking up to 6 weeks. Pot them on and pinch out the growing tips to achieve an elegantly shaped plant.

Repotting
Each spring into a pot one size larger. Good drainage is essential as overwatering is often fatal.

PROBLEMS

Red spider mite can infest the plant. Spray with insecticide.

If you notice leaves falling and the plant looking droopy, consider draughts and move the plant if necessary.

Lack of growth will be caused by not enough heat. These 'tropical' plants like warmth. Move to a better position.

If flowers do not appear, increase feeding and move to a warmer site. Pinching out leaf growth will stimulate flowering.

The stems of the Firecracker flower grow from the leaf axils; there are yellow and orange flowered varieties available too

Cyclamen persicum (Alpine violet, florist's cyclamen)

QUITE DIFFICULT

This is, deservedly, among the most popular of all flowering plants. In full bloom it is glorious in winter time, with beautiful flowers in a range of colours on long stalks above big heart-shaped leaves in variegated shades of green and silver.

Originally from the Mediterranean region, cyclamen corms grow in poor alkaline soil and in rock crevasses, and like dappled light in semi-shaded conditions. The varieties available commercially have often been forced into flower and can drop dead on you: buy only from a trusted source and never a plant that looks droopy. It likes cool conditions and a north-facing windowsill is ideal. Alpine violets, as the name suggests, can withstand slight frosts and may be planted in window boxes, where they will keep throughout the winter in temperate zones.

There are 3 main varieties, each coming in many different shades of pink, red, white and purple. Some have contrastingly coloured 'eyes'. *Cyclamen persicum* has a height and spread of 30cm/12in. The original species had a delicate scent, but this, sadly, has been bred out of modern plants. New scented varieties are currently being introduced.

The intermediate variety grows to a height and spread of 25cm/9in. It is compact and fast-growing, often bearing more than 30 flowers at a time.

The miniature varieties reach only 15cm/6in or less and bear dainty flowers in a wide range of colours. The 'Puppet' and 'Kaori' series have slightly scented flowers.

Most cyclamens are discarded after a few weeks, but with the right care and attention, they can bloom for up to 2 months in winter, and be kept going for a few years. However it is not worth much effort in trying to recover a plant that has been severely stressed by over- or underwatering.

CARE

Light and temperature
A bright but not sunny spot, airy but not too warm. Optimum winter temperatures are around 15°C/60°F. In summer, when the plant is dormant, place it outside in a semi-shaded position. Good air circulation helps.

Water and feeding
Keep the plant moist but not wet. In summer, reduce water intake. *Cyclamen* is very sensitive to too much water, which is the most common cause of its collapse. Water by standing in a bowl of water at room temperature and then allow to drain thoroughly. Never water the top of the corm where the leaves and flower stalks are clustered. Feed weekly before and during flowering. Pull out old leaves and flowers, as the old stalks rot quickly and

this rot can spread to the rest of the plant. Do not spray flowers as this may cause them to become spotted, but give the plant adequate humidity.

Propagation
Sow from seed in late summer at 18–20°C/ 64–70°F using a heated propagator. Cover the seeds with soil and pot up when germinated. Give young plants a lot of light. Most varieties will take up to 18 months to flower, but the miniature varieties take only half that length of time.

Repotting
In midsummer when the old leaves die back, repot using fresh compost – up to half of the corm should be above soil level – and stand the pot in a cool but bright position.

Cyclamen persicum

PROBLEMS

Too much hot dry air causes the leaves to yellow. Other causes may be too little water or too much sunlight.

If the plant collapses and rots, the cause is likely to be overwatering. Allow it to dry out. Never water the corm.

Shortened blooming periods can be the result of too much warm dry air and insufficient fertilizer.

Minute cyclamen mites may infect the plant, causing curled leaf edges, stunted leaves and withered buds. This pest flourishes in humid conditions and all infected leaves must be destroyed. Insecticide is of no use.

Lack of sunlight and too much heat may cause new leaves to have very long, weedy stems and will discourage new flowers.

Dipladenia sanderi (Rose dipladenia, pink allamande)

QUITE DIFFICULT

This sturdy little climber, also known as *Mandevilla sanderi*, bears pretty purple, dark red or white flowers all summer long. Unchecked, it can reach 3m/10ft or more, but pruned or trained around a frame it is a much smaller bushier plant. It grows fast and is rewarding, the flowers appearing on the current season's growth. It should be pruned back strongly after flowering to encourage new blooms the following year.

From tropical Brazil, where it climbs on neighbouring undergrowth in very humid conditions, *Dipladenia sanderi* is one of the most readily available hybrids and has either pink (*D. s. rosea*) or strong red (*D. s. rubiniana*) flowers. A newer variety is the scented *Dipladenia boliviensis*, which bears white flowers with yellow throats.

This plant is extremely poisonous, both leaves and flowers, and for this reason it has never been very popular.

CARE

Light and temperature
Bright light or semi-shade, but not direct sun. *Dipladenia* likes to be very warm and humid all year round, with temperatures never lower than 15°C/60°F. Fresh air circulation is important.

Water and feeding
Water twice a week with soft tepid water but make sure the soil has dried out first and feed every fortnight during flowering. After blooming, reduce the amount of water and rest the plant from autumn through to spring. Keep humidity at a reasonably high level.

Propagation
In spring, take tip cuttings. These can be successfully rooted with the aid of hormone rooting powder using a heated propagator. Good drainage is important. The plantlets should take in around 3 weeks.

Repotting
Repot only when potbound, or if it fails to produce new growth, using good houseplant compost mixture.

PROBLEMS

Leaves will curl and wither if the air is too dry and the plant will not flourish if its roots are cold and wet.

The leaves will also go yellow if given low humidity in summer. Stand the pot on a tray of moist pebbles.

Whitefly and red spider mite can sometimes attack. Spray with insecticide.

Mealy bug causes white cotton wool patches on the axils of the leaves. Spray with diluted malathion or rub off with cotton wool swabs dipped in alcohol.

Dipladenia sanderi. In Greek *diploos* means 'double' and *aden* 'gland', referring to the glands in the flower's ovary

Echeveria (Firecracker plant, moulded wax, hen and chickens, painted lady)

QUITE EASY

This succulent plant belongs to the cacti family and makes a perfect houseplant as it thrives on the dry hot atmosphere created by central heating. Give it a good rest period during the winter.

Originally from the desert areas of Mexico and the southern states of the US, *Echeveria* forms rosettes of leaves which are fleshy and covered with a 'bloom' that can be easily damaged. The bell-shaped flowers last only a day or so, but the plant itself is extremely long lived.

CARE

Light and temperature
Plenty of direct sunlight will please this plant – a south-facing windowsill, with spells on the sunniest patio during the summer months. For the rest period keep in temperatures as low as 10°C/50°F.

Water and feeding
Water sufficiently to prevent the soil drying out in the rest period; only sparingly during the growth and flowering months. Flat varieties that cover the soil can be watered by standing the pot in 5cm/2in of water for 30–60 minutes; drain well. Feed with cactus fertilizer on a weekly basis when the plant is growing.

Propagation
Remove offsets or take leaf cuttings in spring. Leave them to dry out for a week or so then pot up in sandy compost. Rooting will occur in 2 weeks, provided watering is only just sufficient to keep compost from drying out.

Repotting
Do this in spring into a shallow pot one size larger. Good surface drainage is important so work in some sand.

PROBLEMS

Overwatering will lead to rot and the production of soft leaf growth at the expense of flowers. Cut out rot and water less often.

Scorched leaves – do not allow water to remain on the leaves.

Dry brown spots on the leaf indicate underwatering. Increase watering, particularly in summer.

Mealy bugs find the close-set leaves perfect. Use a brush dipped in denatured alcohol to remove each bug individually.

Echeveria pumila

Echeveria agavoides

Echeveria agavoides

Euphorbia milii (Christ plant, crown of thorns)

EASY

Euphorbia milii 'Selene'

Euphorbia milii 'Rosemarie'

CARE

Light and temperature
Average warmth and as much light as possible. During the flowering period it will do well in temperatures up to 18°C/64°F. Let this temperature drop by only a few degrees in winter.

Water and feeding
As a succulent, water the plant moderately, and scarcely at all in winter. Use cactus fertilizer in the water every 2 weeks while the plant is in flower.

Propagation
Take cuttings and dip them in tepid water to halt the flow of milky sap. Leave them to dry off for 24 hours and then pot in a peat and sand mixture. Keep the cuttings very much on the dry side. Once they have rooted, which takes around 6 weeks, situate in bright light. Make sure there is good drainage.

Repotting
Young plants can be repotted every 2 years. Use cactus soil. Prune or trim before new growth begins in spring.

PROBLEMS

If the leaves drop, check that there is adequate drainage, that the plant is not overwatered and that it is in a warm enough spot. The leaves grow only on new growth and will not be replaced if they fall.

The *Euphorbia* should flower for much of the year. If it fails to, move it to the sunniest spot you have.

This euphorbia, among the 2000 or more known species of the spurge family, is an old trooper. It is not fussy, and can produce cheery bracts of orange to salmon-pink and red all year round.

It comes from Madagascar, where it grows happily in granite crevasses, reaching up to 1m/40in, though as a houseplant it rarely exceeds this height. Its long thorny branches are about as thick as a little finger and are easily trained over a hoop.

Euphorbia lophogona, again from Madagascar, is an evergreen with pink flowers. The two species have been crossed to produce *Euphorbia* hybrids in a range of colours from yellow and pink through to violet.

Euphorbia milii is poisonous, particularly the juice from the woody stems.

Euphorbia pulcherrima (Poinsettia, Christmas star, Mexican flame leaf)

DIFFICULT

In its native Mexico, the tropical *Euphorbia pulcherrima* often climbs to 3m/10ft or more. It flowers when the days are shortest, hence our ability to adapt it to indoors. The Americans were instrumental in developing the plant during the 1960s, from the original which was first recorded in 1834. Today we prepare over 7 acres of poinsettias for sale into the Christmas trade.

The plant grows only to about 45cm/1½ft. The flowers, which are really coloured bracts, make a wonderful show in cream, yellow, pink or red and should last for 2–3 months. There are single-stemmed or standard forms available commercially. 'Pulcherrima' means 'the most beautiful'.

Most people treat this plant as an annual and throw it away after flowering so never buy a specimen whose leaves are falling. It is difficult, but not impossible, to make it flower again. Pinch out the growing tips to help the plant become bushy.

To achieve flowers for a second year, cut off the stems to about 8cm/4in above the pot when the leaves have fallen. Place it in a mild shady spot and let the compost dry off. In early May, water and repot. Keep watering and shoots will soon reappear. Feed regularly and prune the new growth to leave 4 or 5 strong stems.

Lighting then needs to be very carefully controlled from the end of September. The plant must be in complete darkness for 14 hours each day, so you must cover it with a black polythene bag or something similar. Do this for 8 weeks and then bring it into the light and start watering. Nursery men use a growth retardant to limit the size and bushiness of the poinsettia but this is not often on sale at garden centres.

CARE

Light and temperature
Bright light during winter and a minimum temperature of 13–15°C/55–60°F. The plant must be protected from hot summer sun if it is to flower again next Christmas.

Water and feeding
These plants need moist air, so spray frequently. Water well and wait until the compost is thoroughly dry before watering again. Water more liberally in summer or if leaves begin to wilt. Feed weekly from early summer to mid-autumn.

Propagation
Take a stem cutting in early summer. Using a rooting hormone powder, plant the cuttings in small peat pots in a propagator, having been treated in water to stem the milky white juices. They will take in 3 or 4 weeks.

Repotting
Pot on in fresh peat when new growth is evident. Keep the pot the same size to encourage flowering rather than leaf growth.

PROBLEMS

Red spider mite and mealy bug are the main pests and can be sprayed with insecticide.

Overwatering causes the leaves to fall off after wilting. Make sure the compost is dry before you water.

If the temperature is too low, or there is not enough light, leaves will fall without wilting.

Eustoma grandiflorum (Prairie gentian)

DIFFICULT

In the garden or in its native habitat of Central America, this incredibly beautiful plant, with scented violet, pink and cream bell-shaped flowers, grows to 90cm/36in and until recently was sold only as a cut flower known as *Lisianthus russelianus*. It is particularly popular in Europe.

Today nursery men use growth inhibitors to produce plants about a third of the size that are suitable for indoor cultivation. They have lovely blue-green oval leaves and, with the right care and attention, should flower for up to a month. There are usually 2 or 3 plants in a pot. Discard after flowering.

Eustoma grandiflorum

CARE

Light and temperature
No direct sunlight but extremely bright and warm conditions.

Water and feeding
Water moderately and feed each week until the blooms are spent.

Propagation
This is best left to professionals, although the plant can be raised from seed in early summer using a heated propagator. The seedlings should be kept in a bright position, at temperatures of 15–18°C/ 60–64°F. A year after the seed is sown, plants should begin to flower.

Repotting
Not needed if the plant is discarded after flowering.

PROBLEMS

If the plant is in a draught, it will wilt immediately and not recover.

The plant will wilt, too, if overwatered. Never allow the roots to become soggy.

Creamy white

Pink

Double

Exacum affinae (German, Persian, Mexican or Arabian violet)

EASY

The German violet, a member of the gentian family, has tiny, glossy leaves and produces countless white or purple scented flowers in summer through to autumn. It is a small plant, reaching a height of 15–20cm/6–8in, with a spread of about the same. Also available is a pretty double species, *Exacum affinae rokokko*.

It is a biennial from the Socotra Island in the Gulf of Aden, and away from its native habitat is best raised from seed or bought as an indoor plant as it often withers after flowering. Plant in a shallow container about 12cm/4in in diameter. Pick off dead flowers to prolong the flowering season and if attempting to overwinter the *Exacum*, prune it back hard at the end of the flowering period to maintain its bushy character.

Exacum affinae rokokko

Exacum affinae 'Persian Violet'

CARE

Light and temperature
A very bright position, but no full midday sun. Average warmth and good air circulation are important for success.

Water and feeding
Always keep compost moist, never soggy. If the rootball dries out, the flowers will fade and quickly die. Feed once a fortnight and pinch off faded flowers. Keep the pot on a tray of moist pebbles if possible.

Propagation
From seed sown in early winter on the surface of a sphagnum-rich compost, and leave the seed uncovered. The seedlings will flower the following spring and should be potted up in a rich compost with good drainage.

Repotting
Overwintered plants should be repotted in early spring into pots one size larger, using a humus-based compost.

PROBLEMS

The *Exacum* will wilt immediately if placed in a draughty situation.

If flowers fail to form, move to a brighter position and ensure the plant has sufficient humidity.

Fuchsia

QUITE DIFFICULT

Fuchsia is one of the most popular flowering shrubs. Some hybrids can grow as tall as 2m/6ft outdoors, but inside the most suitable are dwarf or hanging varieties. There are certainly many to choose from, with flowers in almost every colour except yellow.

The plant blooms from March through to November, bearing highly ornamental bell-shaped flowers on stems that have small pointed deciduous leaves.

In summer, plants that are normally kept indoors will thrive if given short spells outside in bright light, but not direct sun. Buy small specimens in spring and place the pots in holders filled with wet gravel to increase humidity. In winter, though the leaves will drop, the plant will remain dormant if kept in a cool room.

Fuchsia's original habitat is New Zealand and Central America, where it grows to tree size in full sun.

Fuchsia 'Golden Marinka'

Fuchsia 'Marinka', a red hanging type

Fuchsia 'Lena', one of
the many doubles

Fuchsia 'Winston Churchill', a single hybrid

CARE

Light and temperature
A bright position, but not full sun, with
temperatures of 15°C/60°F in summer
and 8–10°C/46–50°F in winter.

Water and feeding
Fuchsias like humidity, so spray often.
Water plentifully throughout flowering
and feed once a week. When the plants
are not in flower, feed each fortnight. In
winter allow the plant to dry out
between waterings.

Propagation
Cuttings from the tips can be rooted in
spring or autumn and set in a heated
propagator.

Repotting
As necessary, in a potting mixture made
of loam, peat and sand in equal parts.
Hanging varieties need to be pruned by
two-thirds in spring and repotted when
new shoots appear.

PROBLEMS

Aphids and whiteflies can infest the
plant. Spray with insecticide.

Leaves turn yellow and drop if the plant
becomes waterlogged. Allow to dry out
before watering again and ensure good
drainage.

173

Gardenia jasminoides (Common gardenia, Cape jasmine)

DIFFICULT

The scent of a single *Gardenia* bloom can permeate an entire room and it is for this characteristic that the plant is memorable. It is difficult to grow indoors, because it needs high temperatures and high humidity to flower. Therefore it is best regarded as a greenhouse or conservatory plant which is brought indoors when in flower. However the one thing *Gardenia* hates most is a change of environment, which will cause buds to drop and the tips of new growth to blacken – so beware!

Originally from China, there are over 60 known species (named after the American botanist Alexander Garden), but the most generally cultivated here is *Gardenia jasminoides*, which was introduced into England in 1754, and into the US 45 years later.

It is a pretty plant, with attractive glossy dark green leaves and white single or double flowers which bruise easily and fade to creamy yellow before dropping. Nursery men have cultivated double forms of *Gardenia jasminoides*, which have superb scent.

The plant can grow up to 120cm/4ft high and wide, but only at a rate of 15cm/6in a year. It is best discarded after 4–5 years.

CARE

Light and temperature
Bright light, but always away from direct sunlight in summer. To flower, it needs summer temperatures of 15–18°C/60–64°F and, ideally, no fluctuations of temperature between night and day. In winter, it can survive at 12°C/55°F while resting.

Water and feeding
Gardenia needs to be watered frequently in summer. It likes high humidity and should be stood on a tray of moist pebbles at all times. A bright bathroom windowsill is ideal when the plant is indoors. In winter, water less and always use tepid rain water. Feed once a fortnight with half-strength fertilizer and spray regularly, avoiding the flowers, as this causes them to mark and discolour.

Propagation
Young stem cuttings can be taken in early spring and placed in a sand and loam compost in a heated propagator at a temperature of 18–21°C/64–70°F.

Repotting
As necessary when the plant outgrows the pot.

PROBLEMS

Mealy bugs, scale insects and spider mites can attack the plant. Spray with insecticide, and try to find ways of increasing the humidity to deter further attacks.

Yellowing leaves indicate either too little light, or chlorosis from using water with a high lime content. Water with sequestered iron and use only lime-free water or rain water.

If the flower buds drop before opening the plant needs more humidity. Spray daily with soft and tepid water, avoiding the flowers.

Gardenia hates draughts and a change in conditions. Avoid gas fumes at all times.

Gardenia jasminoides is a rewarding plant if kept free from temperature changes

Gerbera jamesonii (African daisy, Transvaal daisy, Barbeton daisy)

EASY

Gerbera jamesonii has lobed leaves which are woolly on the undersides. The long-lasting flowers are most often flame-coloured but may be shades of salmon-pink, yellow or white

CARE

Light and temperature
As bright as possible, with 3–4 hours of sun. The plant needs good air circulation with a summer temperature of up to 21°C/70°F.

Water and feeding
Keep the compost moist and feed once a week during flowering.

Propagation
From seed, sown in early spring and potted on into 14cm/5in pots. Most hybrids flower well in the first year of sowing but the flower stems from home-grown seeds revert to the longer, somewhat ungainly length.

Repotting
Not necessary as *Gerbera* is discarded after flowering.

PROBLEMS

Negligible, as the flower is an annual.

Gerbera is one of the most popular summer pot plants. Its major attraction is its showy, large, daisy-shaped flowers which come in unusual and subtle colours. There are double as well as single forms, although most people agree the latter are more graceful. It is also popular as a cut flower.

Gerbera jamesonii is a perennial from the Transvaal, where it grows in full sun, rooting itself in rocky crevasses. The flowers are long-lasting, which is part of its attraction, and the flower stems are up to 60cm/2ft in length. Nursery men have bred an indoor plant variety, which is generally regarded as an annual, but this has stems around half the length. Buy plants in bud in early summer.

New varieties have now been bred from tissue culture giving up to 6 blooms at a time, with the foliage less vegetative than before.

Gloriosa rothschildiana (Glory lily, climbing lily, Mozambique lily)

EASY

Gloriosa rothschildiana is a tuber which originates from tropical East Africa and is part of the lily family. It is a vigorous climber, reaching over 2m/7ft in height, and in its native habitat it will quite happily clamber over other plants and trees. It has glossy leaves, the uppermost ones formed as tendrils which makes this an interesting plant even when the flowers are not out.

The stunning red flowers, veering towards orange at the base, have 6 petals with wavy edges that curve inwards. There are some entirely yellow varieties.

The plant blooms from June to August each year, but in a greenhouse can be forced to flower from February onwards. Rest periods are important. It should last a good few years – perhaps 6–8 – with the right conditions. The tubers contain poison.

It is a plant that is now becoming much more widely available.

CARE

Light and temperature
Gloriosa needs as much light and direct sunshine as possible. Its favourite temperature is 15–18°C/60–64°F. Protect the flowers from sun and scorching on very hot days.

Water and feeding
Water abundantly during growth and put the pot over a saucer of wet gravel. Feed with a weak solution of liquid fertilizer each fortnight. After flowering, allow the plant to dry out between each watering until it finally withers. Cut back all vegetation to just above soil level and cease watering. Place the pot in a dark spot and keep dry. Do not allow the temperature to drop below 8°C/48°F, then repot tubers into fresh compost in early spring.

Propagation
In early spring, separate the small tubers which have formed among the roots of the parent plant. These can be potted out and left to develop green buds at 15–18°C/60–64°F.

Repotting
Each year. In winter the parts of the plant above ground die off and the tubers should be kept at 10–12°C/50–54°F. In early spring repot these tubers in a mixture of loam, peat and sand mixed in equal parts. Each tuber will produce 3 stems, which need support.

PROBLEMS

Uneven temperatures and a drop in humidity may cause dark spots to appear on the leaves. Keep both constant.

Leaves may wilt if the temperature is too high.

If flowers fail to appear, move to a sunnier position and ensure the right degree of humidity.

Gloriosa rothschildiana is a climber with weak stems needing support. Also found is *Gloriosa superba* that has green and orange flowers fading to red.

Heliotropium arborescens (Heliotrope, cherry pie)

EASY

This flowering herb from Peru gives off a delicious vanilla scent from its tiny flowers which are borne on large heads. Its flowering season is throughout the summer, when the perfume can be easily and deliciously detected in any room. It is a simple plant to grow and can be trained as a standard.

In its native habitat and with sufficient humidity *Heliotropium* will grow into a large shrub. As an indoor plant it can reach up to 1m/3ft high and will live for many years, but it will lose its ability to produce flowers over time. The most commonly available are the purple varieties, but white- or blue-flowering heliotropes may be found.

CARE

Light and temperature
Plenty of light but no direct sun. Average warmth in summer and temperatures of not less than 8–10°C/40–50°F in winter.

Water and feeding
Keep the compost well watered in spring and summer but never allow the plant to become waterlogged. Feed at weekly intervals using a general liquid fertilizer to manufacturer's recommendations. Whilst dormant, allow the plant to dry out between waterings and do not feed.

Propagation
From seed in early spring or from cuttings taken in late spring or summer and rooted in seeding compost in a propagator at 21°C/70°F.

Repotting
Heliotropium thrives best if repotted each spring. Use a humus-rich compost and a pot one size larger.

PROBLEMS

Scale insects on the underside of leaves should be treated by using a swab dipped in methylated spirit.

Aphids can infest the plant. Spray with diluted malathion.

Thrips can cause the leaves to lose their colour and develop flecks. Spray with diluted malathion.

Heliotropum arborescens, sometimes known as *H. peruvianum* has attractively wrinkled leaves

Hibiscus rosa-sinensis (Chinese hibiscus)

EASY

Hibiscus rosa-sinensis

Hibiscus plants look particularly pretty on windowsills where their large flowers with long yellow stamens can bloom almost continuously all summer.

The trumpet-shaped flowers only last a day or two, but given the right care and attention you can achieve a succession of blooms over a few months. The flowers are large and measure up to 15cm/6in across. They can be double or single, in shades of yellow, orange, pink or red.

In its native habitat of tropical Asia and Southern China, the plant grows up to 3m/10ft tall in full sunshine, but indoors generally it reaches a height of around 1m/3ft.

Hibiscus can live for 20 years or more but needs to be pruned to keep it small and bushy. It can also be trained as a standard.

CARE

Light and temperature
Very bright to full sun throughout summer. Warm temperatures during the flowering season. In winter, temperatures of around 15°C/60°F help promote the development of flowers in the next season.

Water and feeding
Water daily throughout summer until autumn, less in winter. From spring to autumn, feed each week; in winter, feed each month. *Hibiscus* must be fed otherwise it will not bloom.

Propagation
From top cuttings in late spring. Pot in fresh compost and keep moist and warm.

Repotting
Young plants need to be repotted each year. Older plants as necessary. Before repotting, cut back long shoots.

PROBLEMS

Dry compost will cause buds to drop.

Leaves will curl if the air is too dry.

Aphids and red spider mite can cause problems. Spray with insecticide.

Hippeastrum hybrids (Amaryllis, Barbados lily)

EASY

Clusters of glorious huge trumpet-shaped flowers in warm colours, from white through to scarlet-red, make *Hippeastrum* a dramatic sight and often there may be 2 flower stalks.

Many large bulbs are sold around Christmas time, specially prepared to come into bloom after around 5–6 weeks, from mid-winter to mid-spring. The bulbs have been forced, and will take up to a year to regain their strength and vigour.

The plant originates from tropical and subtropical America, but only hybridized forms are available today, mostly the result of Dutch breeders crossing *H. leopoldii* from Peru with other species. There are many different varieties: 'Apple Blossom' is sweet-smelling, pink and white; 'Ludwig's Goliath' is fiery red; 'Fantastica' is red-and-white striped and 'Fairyland' is pink. There are also other hybrids with stripes of 2 or 3 different colours.

Occasionally florists sell amaryllis as a cut flower, particularly in Europe; a bunch of pure white trumpets can look totally magical. 'Ludwig's Dazzler' is probably the best of the white varieties; others include 'Maria Goretti' and 'Early White'.

Parts of this plant are poisonous.

CARE

Light and temperature
The bulbs need a very bright and warm position to promote growth.

Water and feeding
Water very little until after growth begins. Once blooming has finished – around 3 weeks – allow the foliage and flower to die back (never cut this off) and keep feeding each week until late summer. This is necessary for the bulb to flower again the next year. In autumn, decrease watering and stop feeding, allowing the bulb a 3-month period of rest. Keep the bulb dry and warm until spring, or until new growth becomes evident.

Propagation
This requires considerable effort from the home gardener, but the truly dedicated can separate side bulbs the size of marbles from the mother bulb, or sow seeds. Generally speaking, it is best to buy fresh bulbs, which will flower for 2 or 3 years and should then be discarded.

Repotting
Plant overwintered bulbs in a roomy pot with good compost every 2 years. Half the bulb must show above the soil. Remove 3cm/1in of topsoil and replace with fresh compost each spring. Always use a mixture of bonemeal and composted leaves with garden soil, rather than peat-based compost, which weakens the bulb.

PROBLEMS

Fire disease can attack the bulb, in which case it should be discarded before the rest of the stock becomes infected.

If the plant fails to produce new leaves or flower stalks it may have been too cold or wet at a critical stage. Move to a warmer site and follow watering instructions.

Leaf tips turning yellow are a sign of overwatering. Cut back on frequency.

Leaf scorch, a fungal disease, can eat at the bulb. Infected areas can be cut out and the bulb dusted with charcoal if the signs are spotted in time. If not, discard immediately.

Hippeastrum 'Red Lion'

Hoya bella (Miniature wax plant, porcelain flower)

EASY

Hoya bella is a delicate tropical plant, originally from India, where it grows in rocky crevasses and in the forks of tree trunks under leaf canopy. The scented flowers are star-shaped and pure white with pink and purple centres. They develop throughout the summer months and the plant flowers more profusely if it is not pruned.

Rather more robust is *Hoya carnosa*, a native of subtropical China and Australia, sometimes known as the honey plant because of its nectar-like smell. It climbs vigorously and has pale creamy pink flowers with crimson centres. It can grow quite easily to a height of 3m/10ft. A variegated form can sometimes be found on sale. It is a shy flowerer.

Hoya bella lives for up to 5 years, though *Hoya carnosa* can be kept going for much longer.

CARE

Light and temperature
Keep the plant out of strong midday sun but give up to 4 hours of direct sun each day. Because of its tropical origins, it needs to be kept warm, around 16–21°C/60–70°F.

Water and feeding
Water often during summer and sparingly when the compost dries out in winter, preferably with rain water. Feed during spring and summer with general houseplant liquid fertilizer, at half strength, on a fortnightly basis.

Propagation
Stem or tip cuttings can be taken from mature shoots, dipped first in hormone rooting powder, and planted in a rich humus-based compost in a propagating frame.

Repotting
Repot in spring when the plant has outgrown its pot into loam-based compost to which a little sand and polystyrene granules have been added. Cut back leggy stems.

PROBLEMS

Mealy bugs and aphids sometimes infest the plant and need to be sprayed with insecticide.

Too much water and cold roots cause the leaves to drop and the stems to die back.

If its position is too dark, the flowers and buds will drop. Move to a brighter spot.

If flowers do not appear, increase fertilizer cautiously. Overfeeding can cause leaf and stem development rather than flowering.

There are up to 12 flowers in a cluster of *Hoya bella*

Hydrangea macrophylla (Hydrangea)

EASY

Hydrangea macrophylla has a short life indoors, of around 6 weeks, but makes a lovely spring or summer outdoor plant, because once its glorious mop heads of blooms are finished it can be planted in the garden, where it will survive for many years. If you want it to flower again the following year as a houseplant, put it into a greenhouse with good light.

The plant comes from Japan and was introduced into Europe in 1790. Its flowers are naturally pink, but will turn blue when watered with aluminium sulphate. There is also a white variety. The recent 'lacecap' varieties are beautifully delicate, with some florets opening on the flower head while the inner ones are still in bud.

Choose plants that are in bud and which have strong healthy foliage with no broken stems. Never allow the roots to dry out.

CARE

Light and temperature
As much light as possible, but not direct sun. When in flower, normal room temperature is quite adequate unless above 18°C/64°F. In winter, the plant prefers a temperature of 7°C/45°F, which should be raised to 13°C/55°F in February for spring flowers.

Water and feeding
Hydrangea loves water and it does not hurt to immerse the pot in a bucket of water every second day. Feed once a week while flowering and in winter water only every 10 days or so. Blue varieties need lime-free water.

Propagation
Prune after flowering and cut the plant back to 2 pairs of new leaves. The tops of the prunings can be rooted in sand mixed with peat at temperatures of 13–16°C/55–61°F.

Repotting
Repot in damp compost at the end of the flowering season and place in the greenhouse.

PROBLEMS

Fungal infections, red spider mite and greenfly can infest these plants. Spray with fungicide for infections and insecticide for mites and greenfly.

Hydrangea macrophylla

Hypocryta glabra (Clog plant, goldfish plant)

EASY

The clog plant, from Southern Mexico and Brazil, is a small shrub with waxy leaves and tiny orange pouched flowers. The German name for this plant means 'little kissing mouths' though some people call it the goldfish plant. At any rate its flowers have an intriguing shape and are around 3cm/1in long.

It is a charming addition to a hanging basket, beginning to trail as it grows larger. It is sold in bloom from late summer until spring but when not in flower it still has the attraction of shiny dark green, almost succulent leaves.

In its native habitat it grows as a creeper in humid undergrowth. As an indoor plant it should last for 2 or 3 years. Prune the stems judiciously in winter to encourage flower buds the following season.

CARE

Light and temperature
Bright but avoid full sun. A windowsill is a good location. A spell outdoors in a semi-shady position will not go amiss, but take care that the plant does not get too cold. Average warmth in summer. In winter, temperatures of 12–15°C/54–60°F will encourage the development of flower buds.

Water and feeding
Keep the soil just damp throughout the flowering season. Fertilize fortnightly with a weak-strength fertilizer. In winter, do not feed and water sparingly.

Propagation
Cut 5cm/2in cuttings from young growth in spring or summer and pot up in good houseplant compost. They should take in 6–8 weeks.

Repotting
Repot in spring every 2 years in fresh compost.

PROBLEMS

If the plant has few flowers, prune more vigorously in the 'rest' period.

Buds that rot before opening usually indicate overwatering. Reduce frequency and ensure good drainage.

The name of *Hypocryta glabra* has been changed 2 or 3 times recently. Sometimes it is known as *H. nummularia*. The stems are red and somewhat hairy on this semi-epiphyte

Impatiens hawkeri hybrida

EASY

(Bizzie lizzie, patient Lucy)

The New Guinea *Impatiens*

Impatiens 'Blitz', the flowers of which are 5cm/2in across

Impatiens 'Sultani' variegata

CARE

Light and temperature
Bright to sunny position; the more sun the heavier the flowering. Good air circulation helps a lot. Room temperature throughout the year is fine. Never below 13°C/55°F.

Water and feeding
Water freely in summer, keeping the soil damp, but not wet; in winter, watering to prevent stem rot. *I. hawkeri* hybrids need humidity so stand over a tray of damp pebbles. Feed weekly throughout summer with a very weak dose of liquid fertilizer.

Propagation
Take tip cuttings of 5cm/2in long and root them in water. When the roots develop transfer to a rich potting compost. Seed can be sown in springtime.

Repotting
Clip back now and then to prevent plants from becoming straggly and leggy. You can repot in spring using potting mix, but unless the plant has retained its shape well it is better to start again.

Until just after World War II, the bizzie lizzie was hardly known. Now it is one of the most common indoor plants, and is also used extensively for bedding outdoors during summer months. It is easy to propagate and children are often taught about plant life through taking cuttings of this colourful, fast-growing 'annual'. 'Tango', 'Red Magic' and 'Fanfare' are common examples.

A native of the tropical highlands of New Guinea, it was hybridized with several cultivars to produce the elliptically-leaved plants which will bloom throughout the year in the right conditions. The flowers range from reds and pinks to white. New breeding seeks to produce varieties with larger flowers.

The old-fashioned bizzie lizzie is *Impatiens walleriana*, coming originally from the spice island of Zanzibar, where it covers rocky surfaces and even roots itself in sandy beaches. 'Blitz' is probably the most pure of the reds. There is also a charming variegated form.

The name means impatient, and that it is. With regular attention success comes easily. After a year or two start again with fresh cuttings – the plant can go on much longer but will lose vigour.

PROBLEMS

Leaves may drop or wilt. The most common cause is underwatering. Immerse the pot for a good drink and allow it to drain thoroughly. Keep the compost moist, even if this means daily watering.

Flowers failing to form is usually a sign of lack of light – move to a sunnier position. Only repot when essential.

Red spider mite, aphids and whitefly can attack this plant. Treat appropriately.

Leggy growth often comes from warmth without sufficient light. Sunlight has increasingly become recognized as very important for success.

Ixora stricta (Dwarf lemon)

QUITE DIFFICULT

Ixora, a member of the madder family, has never been hugely popular as an indoor plant. It is a tropical evergreen shrub, originally from Eastern Asia, where it thrives in humid and warm conditions as undergrowth in semi-shaded glades.

Ixora stricta, or *Ixora chinensis* as it is sometimes known, is a rounded plant with pretty pale yellow flowers which fade into shades of warm orange. Hybrids of *Ixora coccinea* (flame of the woods) and *Ixora javanica* (jungle geranium) are also commonly available and come in a range of colours, such as reds, oranges and pinks. The flower heads, which have flat tops and comprise many individual tubular flowers, appear from spring onwards, and over 4–5 years the plant will reach a height of 1.3m/4ft.

The leaves are quite glossy and thick, and are arranged in pairs. It is a bushy plant and the new foliage often has a bronze tinge, which matures to dark green.

Ixora is hungry for light and will do well if given the growing conditions it craves; otherwise there will be poor flowering and a lacklustre plant. It should not be subjected to cold water or cold draughts.

CARE

Light and temperature
This plant likes full sun on the windowsill. Direct sunlight is important for at least 5 hours a day, in temperatures which must not fall below 16°C/60°F.

Water and feeding
During the summer months, when *Ixora* is growing, feed every 2 weeks with a liquid fertilizer. Watering should be regular, though less frequent in dormant months. Use soft rain water at room temperature. The potting medium should be allowed to dry out before rewatering in winter.

Propagation
Cuttings are the best method, particularly if you have a propagating frame or can use artificial methods. Cut just below a leaf, with 8cm/3in of stem. Dip into a hormone rooting powder before potting into a mixture of peat, moss and sand. Place in the propagating frame at a constant temperature of at least 21°C/70°F. When the cutting has taken, acclimatize it slowly.

Repotting
Every spring for the first 4 years. Then just dig out the top 3cm/1in of soil and replace, using a mixture of peat, leafmould and sand.

PROBLEMS

Ixora is a tetchy plant; flower drop is caused by changes in temperature, as is leaf drop. Keep away from draughts and give the right amount of sun.

If the rootball is kept too moist or cold chlorosis may set it. Allow to dry out immediately and then water less frequently.

Scale insect can infest this plant. Treat with swabs of cotton wool dipped in methylated spirit.

Ixora stricta does not like changes in its conditions

Jasminum polyanthum (Pink jasmine)

QUITE EASY

Jasminum is a member of the olive family and needs a cool winter season followed by warmer temperatures to bring it into flower. It is a plant well worth keeping, for the flowers have a magnificent perfume, even if they are short lived. This is a vigorous grower, and can be trained on a hoop or allowed to romp in a conservatory.

Jasminum polyanthum comes from the Far East, where it grows in subtropical conditions, often to vast heights, scrabbling up other trees in wooded areas in semi-shady conditions. It was brought to Europe in the 1890s. The garden form of jasmine is *Jasminum officinal.*

The flowers have between 4 and 9 white petals which open from pinky buds in large clusters. There is always an odd number of leaves on the branches of this woody stemmed plant. Buy ones in bud and bring them on indoors in spring.

The plant will appreciate spending the summer months after flowering on a warm patio. Cut the plant back to half its size and pinch out growing tips to encourage side shoots to grow in order to produce a good compact plant for the following year.

Jasminum polyanthum

CARE

Light and temperature
The temperature is best kept at 13°C/55°F. In summer, when the plant is not flowering, it can rise to 21°C/70°F, but do not place it in direct sunshine. Good light is important.

Water and feeding
Water once every 4 or 5 days when flowering, using soft, tepid water. Feed fortnightly. When out of flower in summer water every second day. Resting the pot on a tray of moist pebbles helps humidity.

Propagation
Root stem-tip cuttings with at least 2 pairs of leaves taken in spring or autumn and set them at a temperature of 16°C/61°F, using a rooting hormone powder. They should take within 21 days.

Repotting
In spring after flowering, when potbound. But more usually these plants are regarded as annuals and if you do not have a conservatory or greenhouse, discard them. Older plants become straggly and woody after 4 or 5 years, at which time young cuttings can be brought on.

PROBLEMS

Red spider mite or greenfly can infest this plant. Spray with insecticide.

Dried up leaves indicate too little water. Follow the instructions in 'Water and feeding' carefully.

If the buds brown, the plant is too hot or too dry. Move to a cooler position, and increase the humidity by placing on a tray of moist pebbles.

If the buds fail to open the plant needs more light.

Kalanchoe blossfeldiana (Flaming Katie, Palm Beach belle)

EASY

Kalanchoe blossfeldiana is the most commonly found variety of this succulent, and indeed perhaps the most commonly sold houseplant. In its native Madagascar its bright red flowers appear during the winter, though Dutch breeders have manipulated hybrids which flower throughout the year, in colours from yellow and orange to pink and purple. It will appreciate a spell out of doors in a sunny sheltered spot in summer months, and can reach a height of 30cm/12in, though dwarf varieties are sometimes seen for sale.

Kalanchoe manginii is a spring-flowering type, demanding higher humidity, so stand on a tray of moist gravel and mist the leaves frequently. The flowers hang downwards, making good display of this plant important. 'Wendy' and 'Tessa' are just two of the many hybrids available.

CARE

Light and temperature
An east- or west-facing windowsill from spring to autumn and a south-facing windowsill in winter. It needs average warmth, with a minimum 10°C/50°F in winter. Remember these plants only develop flowers when they receive 8–10 hours of light each day for 4–6 weeks.

Water and feeding
Use high-potash fertilizer every 4 weeks during spring and summer. Water very sparingly during winter.

Propagation
Mostly done from seed sown in March or April. Leaf cuttings or whole shoots can be taken in spring and summer. Use a sharp knife and dust with hormone rooting powder. Either lay leaves or insert stems into a sand and peat compost.

Repotting
Best to do this straight after flowering if retaining the plant for a further season's flowering.

PROBLEMS

White woolly patches on leaves are caused by mealy bug. Remove with a methylated spirit swab.

Black patches on leaves can be removed by dusting the flowers with sulphur.

Wet and cold conditions cause leaves to drop and stems to become black. Dry the plant out.

Right: *Kalanchoe manginii* 'Tessa'

The fleshy leaves of *Kalanchoe* look a rich reddy-green in sunlight

Lantana (Yellow sage, shrub verbena)

QUITE EASY

Originating in the West Indies, this plant grows up to 2m/6ft and is a vigorous and fast-growing shrub, flowering throughout the year if it has sufficient light. Only dwarf hybrids are cultivated for indoor use. If left untrimmed, *Lantana* will reach 1.2m/4ft, but it is best pruned into a smaller, bushier shape. It can look good in a hanging basket.

It has pretty white, pink or yellow tubular flowers, which darken with age, on prickly stems that have rough leaves. It will bloom between May and October, but the only reliable indoor cultivar is *Lantana hybrida* 'Nana'. It should be discarded after 3–4 years.

Lantana hybrida 'Nana'

CARE

Light and temperature
Lots of sunlight – it will not flower unless it gets 3–4 hours of direct sun each day throughout the year. It likes good air circulation and copes well with summer room temperatures. Rest in winter at about 10°C/50°F.

Water and feeding
Water freely while in flower and feed with liquid fertilizer each fortnight. In winter, allow the compost almost to dry out between waterings.

Propagation
From 10cm/4in cuttings taken from a non-flowering branch in August. Strip off the leaves, dip in rooting powder and plant in a mixture of peat and sand. Place in a greenhouse at 18°C/64°F, in bright but filtered light. Leave the cuttings over winter. In early spring, pinch the tips to encourage a bushy shape. In March, pot into standard growing soil.

Repotting
When potbound in compost made up of organic soil, sand and peat.

PROBLEMS

Lantana is very prone to whitefly. Spray with insecticide.

Leptospermum scoparium (Tea tree, Manuka)

EASY

Leptospermum grow to form small upright bushes

CARE

Light and temperature
Requires full sun all year round and likes at least 6–8 hours of daylight. You may need artificial light during the winter months.
Winter temperatures can be those of an unheated greenhouse but never subject the plant to frost.

Water and feeding
Use soft rain water, preferably at room temperature. Lime is abhorrent to the plant. Keep the compost moist throughout the flowering season and in winter water sparingly, allowing the compost to dry out between waterings. Feed on a fortnightly basis during the flowering season.

Propagation
New growth can be potted on in spring, or after flowering more mature cuttings can be dipped in hormone rooting powder. Use a mixture of humus-rich compost and sand. Plants should take root in 6 weeks.

Repotting
Each spring the tea tree should be moved into a pot one size larger. Use a rich houseplant compost.

PROBLEMS

If the flower buds fail to form, increase the dose of liquid fertilizer and ensure that the compost does not dry out.

Occasionally aphids will attack this plant. Make sure that it has sufficient air circulation.

The tea tree is a subtropical plant native to Australia and New Zealand where it climbs to 6m/20ft, using other vegetation as a means of support. The extraordinary thing about this plant is the fragrant oil glands in the leaves. There are masses of flowers, which in many ways resemble roses, on the upright foliage. In some species these may be white and in others pinkish. The plant will flower from late spring until the beginning of autumn.

L. s. 'Album' has bigger flowers, with equally silky foliage, and *L. s.* 'Ruby Glow' has crimson flowers in considerable profusion. There are both single- and double-flowered varieties and some forms have deep bronze leaves. The leaves of all varieties have very sharp tips.

It is possible to keep *Leptospermum* going for a number of years, but judicious pruning at the onset of spring is helpful.

Lilium (Lily)

Lilium

EASY

These types of lilies come mostly from China or other parts of South East Asia, where they grow in a warm and temperate climate. The glorious blooms and scent can last for up to 3 weeks indoors.

Lilies are bulbs and it is important to buy plump firm bulbs with no signs of wrinkling or softness. The autumn is the best time to plant them. Until growth begins, they need to be kept cool, dark and moist, then, when growth starts, they can be moved to a brighter position. All lilies need to be staked otherwise their tall stems can easily topple.

There are 3 main types of lily:

Turk's Cap-shaped lilies – swept back petals with small flowers. Popular varieties include *L. citronella*, which produces yellow flowers with black dots in summer and reaches 90cm/3ft high, with 10cm/3in flowers. *L. fiesta* hybrids are taller, reaching 1m/3ft.

Trumpet-shaped lilies – also flower in summer. *L. longiflorum eximium* (Easter or Madonna lily) has fragrant white flowers 12cm/5in across. There is a 'Mt Everest' variety.

L. regale (regal lily) bears white flowers with yellow throats and has a powerful scent. The yellow variety is 'Royal Gold'. There is a group all reaching the 1.1m/4ft mark, called the 'Mid-century' hybrids, dramatically coloured with medium-sized flowers appearing in early summer. Varieties included 'Brandywine', 'Cinnabar', 'Destiny', 'Enchantment' and 'Prosperity'.

Bowl-shaped lilies – flared petals opening to produce a wide bowl. These include *L. auratum* (goldband lily) and *L. speciosum* (Japanese Lily).

Consider lilies as annuals when grown indoors. The bulbs have been specially treated to force them into flower. Plant them in the garden after the blooms have faded and the foliage has shrivelled.

L. speciosum rubrum

L. auratum

CARE

Light and temperature
In winter, prepare the pot with charcoal at the bottom for good drainage, overlaid with sphagnum moss and bulb fibre or a sandy soil. Bury the bulbs with at least 3cm/1in compost above their heads. Set the pot in a dark frost-free place with the temperature at around 4°C/40°F. Move to a warmer, better lit spot when growth begins in spring. Gradually give more light and warmth, eventually providing bright light, but no direct sun.

When the flower fades and the stalks yellow, allow the plant to die down completely before planting outside in the garden in a sandy, humus-rich soil.

Water and feeding
During the growing season water well but never let the bulb become waterlogged. Reduce watering to allow bulb to dry off after flowering.

Propagation
Difficult. Best left to a professional.

Repotting
Plant on into a garden.

PROBLEMS

Overwatering and bad drainage can lead to rot. Yellowing flower tips are a sign of this. Allow the plant to dry out as fast as possible.

If grey mould appears on new growth as the plant develops, the ventilation is insufficient and should be improved. A dusting with sulphur will help.

Medinilla magnifica (Rose grape)

DIFFICULT

As the common name suggests, from March to June this bushy plant bears arching stems of drooping rose-pink flowers shaped like bunches of grapes and set in sensationally pretty pink bracts. The pairs of leaves have no stalks and measure up to 30cm/12in long and 12cm/5in wide. The stem of the plant is woody and has many branches.

Its native habitat is the tropical jungles of the Philippines, where it was discovered in 1888. There it grows to 2.5m/8ft, but as an indoor plant it reaches no more than 1m/3ft. It is difficult to make a success of indoors because it needs controlled temperature and humidity levels. Thus it is expensive. It is also best suited to a conservatory where it should last for a good number of years.

Medinilla magnifica

CARE

Light and temperature
In summer, it needs bright light but no direct sun. In winter it can take direct sunlight. It needs high temperatures of 18–27°C/64–80°F in summer. In winter it can tolerate 15–18°C/60–64°F when the plant is at rest, which is essential for further flowering.

Water and feeding
Water moderately, letting the soil almost dry out between waterings. In winter, water less. Humidity needs to be high and the foliage sprayed each day. The plant should be placed in a saucer of wet gravel. Feed with liquid fertilizer each fortnight from when buds form until September.

Propagation
Leave to the professionals.

Repotting
Every other spring in a compost made up of leaf mould, sphagnum moss, peat and sand. Pinch out tips of stems to encourage branching.

PROBLEMS

Prone to red spider mite. Spray with diluted malathion.

If flowers do not form, increase the difference in seasonal treatments, giving higher, more humid conditions in spring and cooler temperatures in the rest period.

Mimosa pudica (Sensitive plant, humbleplant)

QUITE EASY

This small shrub from the tropical areas of Brazil grows like a weed in the wild and is a different genus from the yellow-flowered mimosa sold by florists. *Mimosa pudica* has pom-pom flowers which bloom from July through to September, and feathery leaves like an ash tree. The leaf axils are also hairy.

The plant loses its beauty as it ages and because of this it is usually cultivated as an annual and discarded after flowering.

It is an extremely reactive plant, hence its common name. The small leaves will fold up tightly if they are touched or if the plant is shaken, and similarly if subjected to heat from a lighted candle or cigarette. The stalks may also droop. If left alone for about 30 minutes, the leaves will gradually unfold and the stems straighten. This behaviour only occurs during the daytime and it is thought that heat is the trigger.

The plant needs high humidity, having been adapted for the house from a plant found on the constantly moist forest floor. It grows from seed to a height of about 60cm/2ft.

Mimosa pudica

CARE

Light and temperature
It needs bright light and direct sun (though not midday sun) for 3–4 hours each day. It does best at normal room temperatures of 18–22°C/64–71°F.

Water and feeding
Mimosa pudica needs high humidity, so place the plant over a saucer of wet gravel. Allow the soil to dry out before watering and feed with liquid fertilizer each fortnight while the plant is in bloom.

Propagation
Sow seed in February or March, 2–3 seeds to each 8cm/3in pot. Keep in bright filtered light at 18–20°C/64–68°F. Water sparingly and keep only the strongest seedling when it reaches 4–5cm/2in.

Repotting
Discard after flowering.

PROBLEMS

Failure to flower is caused by not enough humidity. Place in a position that has better light and ensure the tray of pebbles is sufficiently moist at all times.

Musa cavendishii (Dwarf banana plant, dwarf ladyfinger banana)

EASY

This plant, also known as *Musa nana*, was named after Antonium Musa, doctor to Octavius Augustus, the first Emperor of Rome, as it was first brought back from the tropical areas of southern China by Roman troops. It was introduced into England in 1849. Smaller varieties were very popular with Victorian gardeners, who favoured the plant for their conservatories. It is cultivated commercially in the Canary Islands and Florida and can be grown successfully indoors in a well-lit position.

In its native, tropical habitat, the plant bears fruit and grows to a height of 12m/40ft or more. Indoors, it will still produce edible fruit but will reach only 1.8m/6ft, with dramatic leaves up to 1m/3ft long.

As the fruit is seedless, the banana must be propagated from suckers. These grow quickly, often as much as 60cm/2ft a year. Take great care with the leaves as they are delicate and can be easily torn.

Plants only last 4–5 years.

Musa cavendishii

CARE

Light and temperature
Place in strong light and normal room temperature, with a minimum winter temperature of 15°C/60°F.

Water and feeding
Water liberally in summer, every 10 days in winter. Feed in summer each fortnight with liquid food and provide rich compost. Place the pot on wet pebbles and spray often, but make sure that there is no surplus water on the leaves as this will cause scorching if the plant is in direct sunlight.

Propagation
This plant is seedless and can only be propagated by splitting suckers from the adult plant in spring and potting on in high temperatures (21–27°C/70–80°F) and humidity.

Repotting
Every spring, using fresh compost.

PROBLEMS

White woolly patches in the axils of leaves indicate mealy bug. Remove with a swab dipped in methylated spirit.

If the trunk appears to rot the plant is breaking down due to overwatering and low temperature. Raise the temperature and dust the flowers with sulphur.

Nerium oleander (Oleander, rose bay)

DIFFICULT

The oleander is native to the whole Mediterranean region, where in summer it blooms almost continuously. It grows on sunny slopes and rocky hillsides to a height of 3m/20ft as a dense bushy shrub covered with white, pink, peach, red and yellow flowers. The leaves are a lovely silvery green and the flowers can have a delightful fragrance.

When this plant is cultivated for indoors, it generally reaches about 60cm/2ft and flowers only during July and August. It needs full sun. A variegated variety is to be found occasionally.

The whole plant is extremely poisonous – men have died from drinking liquid stirred with an oleander twig – so keep well away from children. It needs pruning once flowering is over; be sure to wash your hands thoroughly after touching it.

PROBLEMS

Prone to attacks by scale insects. Spray with insecticide.

If no flower buds develop, increase the light and hours of sunshine if possible. Make sure there is good ventilation too.

CARE

Light and temperature
It needs direct sun and is best placed outdoors during summer, where strong light will help promote flowering. Indoors it lives at summer room temperature, provided it has strong direct light each day. In winter temperatures can drop to 12–14°C/53–57°F. It can stand temperatures as low as 8°C/46°F, but will not tolerate frosts. The oleander is not a lover of heating systems.

Water and feeding
In summer, water moderately, letting the soil surface dry out between waterings. Given the sun it craves this could mean watering daily. Do not allow the roots to dry out or the flower buds will fall before opening. In winter, reduce watering. Feed with a weak liquid fertilizer each fortnight between May and September or one that has a high nitrogen content.

Propagation
From 15cm/6in cuttings taken from non-flowering shoots in June. Root these in water and transfer into good compost when they begin to show growth. The cuttings can also be rooted into a mixture of peat and sand.

Repotting
Every spring, with fresh soil.

Nerium oleander

Nertera granadensis (Bead plant, coral bead plant, baby tears)

QUITE EASY

This member of the madder family is a curious-looking but attractive low-growing creeping plant. Its fleshy green leaves intertwine to form a thick mat, with the whole plant growing no more than 7–8cm/3in high. Small white flowers are produced in June, followed by orangy-red berries covering the entire plant. These berries fall after a few months, and there are often so many of them that the foliage is hidden.

The native habitat of the bead plant stretches from the Andes to Cape Horn, New Zealand and Tasmania. It grows in high mountain zones at least 2000m/6500ft above sea level and so requires a lot of direct sunlight.

The plant is low, and should be grown in a container where the decorative berries can be displayed well.

CARE

Light and temperature
Needs 3–4 hours of direct sun a day, so a south-facing windowsill is ideal. However it requires cool temperatures of between 14–17°C/57–62°F. The plant will become straggly and refuse to bear fruit if it is placed in rooms which lack light or are too warm.

Water and feeding
Water thoroughly as needed, but let the surface soil dry out before repeating. Place the plant in a saucer of wet gravel. In winter reduce watering, but do not allow the plant to become completely dry. Feed only once a month, when the berries begin forming.

Propagation
In spring, divide clumps of old plants into 5 or 6 small portions and repot individually into fresh soil made up of peat, sand and organic mulch.

Repotting
Repot each year in spring when dividing.

PROBLEMS

Do not over-fertilize, or you will promote leaf growth rather than flowering.

If the flowers open but berries fail to form move to a better ventilated position.

Nertera granadensis is also sometimes sold as *Nertera depressa*.

Orchids: Cymbidium hybrids

EASY

(Cymbidium orchids)

Orchids are probably the largest flowering plant family, with about 750 groups of *genera* and more than 30,000 species. The most spectacular of those cultivated as indoor plants are cymbidiums.

These orchids are native to tropical Asia and Australia, where they grow either in the forks of rainforest trees, on rocks (epiphytes) or on the ground (terrestrial).

As cut flowers they are long-lasting – up to 6 weeks – and can be found in a dazzling range of colours, from red and yellow, to pink, brown, green and white.

The leaves are tough and ribbon-shaped and when the plant produces long racemes of heavy waxy flowers, up to 30 per stalk, it makes a truly exotic display. Because most orchids available are grown in hothouses, they are usually available all year round. If you buy a plant with good healthy-looking buds, the flowers should bloom for up to 8 weeks, given the right care. The rhizomes like to be potbound.

The Victorian idea that orchids were hideously difficult to grow is no longer the case, particularly with cymbidiums, the easiest orchids to cultivate indoors. Two types are commercially available, the hybrids which grow to more than 1m/3ft tall and the miniature indoor cymbidiums which reach a height of around 60–90cm/2–3ft. The smaller varieties tolerate heated rooms best, and have flowers around 4–7cm/1½–3in across.

green hybrid with spotted lip

'Lemforde Surprise'

'Miniature Delight'

CARE

Light and temperature
Cymbidiums need a very airy, bright and sunny location and can be placed out of doors from early summer to early winter in a sheltered spot, but not full sun. Ensure plenty of contrast between warm daytime temperatures and cool night air when the buds are setting. A spell in a greenhouse where the orchid receives multi-directional light is helpful.

Water and feeding
Water from early spring to early autumn, but not too enthusiastically. It is best to let the compost dry out between waterings. Cymbidiums love humidity, so spray with water often and keep on trays of damp pebbles. Over 50 per cent humidity is needed for success. Feed with special orchid fertilizer every 4 weeks. Do not overdo feeding, as you will only produce more leaves at the expense of flowers.

Propagation
The easiest way is to divide the rhizome directly after flowering. Remove the plant from the pot, wash the roots thoroughly and cut through the rhizome with a sharp knife so you have 2 or 3 pseudobulbs (the bulbous fibrous growths at the bottom of the plant) and a fair clump of leaves on each new plant. Discard the dead growth. Water newly separated orchids sparingly, but spray well.

Repotting
Orchids, like most plants, like to be left alone and only need repotting every 2 or 3 years. The potting mixture should be one part sphagnum moss, one part organic soil, two parts of osmunda fibre and a pinch of bonemeal and charcoal. This mixture can be bought readily.

PROBLEMS

Scale insects and mealy bug can cause problems, so spray with an appropriate insecticide. It is advisable to wipe the leaves down each week.

Mildew on the leaves may be caused by over-misting in cool temperatures. Treat with fungicide and move to a warmer position.

Lighter leaves and those with yellow spotting indicate a viral disease for which there is no cure. Destroy the plant immediately.

Lack of flowers but vigorous growth of leaves indicates too little light.

Orchid cymbidium

Orchid phalaenopsis (Moth orchid)

DIFFICULT

These demanding plants are quite stunning during their long flowering period, which can last almost throughout the year. Several flower spikes can follow on after each other and the arching stalks carry many blooms. It is a pseudobulb, with fleshy light green leaves.

Many people fail with the moth orchid because it is very difficult to emulate the conditions in which the plant grows in its native habitat of Malaya.

A constant temperature is required – in summer 25°C/70°F and 16°C/60°F in winter. A cool night temperature helps. The difficulty of keeping the moth orchid at home is providing 10–15 hours light each day, so artificial light in winter is essential. The plants need no rest period. They can last for 4–5 years with the right care.

PROBLEMS

If the leaves shrivel and rot at the stem this may be caused by overwatering. Allow compost to dry out and reduce future waterings.

If the plant fails to produce new flower stalks, the most likely cause is insufficient light and humidity. Use artificial light if necessary and increase humidity.

Greenfly may attack this plant. Use insecticide before infestation becomes too serious.

CARE

Light and temperature
High temperatures by day and cooler at night is the secret of success with this plant. Place in a warm spot with as much daylight, but no direct sun, as you can manage.

Water and feeding
Humid conditions help enormously; stand the plant over a tray of damp pebbles if at all possible and spray the leaves often. Water weekly during flowering, ensuring the plant has good drainage.

Propagation
The moth orchid produces side bulbs, which may be separated from the parent plant. Remove the plant from the pot and delicately sort out the roots, washing thoroughly. Cut the bulb away if necessary with a sharp knife and pot up into specially prepared orchid compost which has been pre-moistened. The growth should start in 3–4 weeks. Water sparingly during that time.

Repotting
Only when absolutely essential if the plant is potbound, every 2 years or so. Use a special orchid compost, rich in sphagnum moss and osmunda fibre.

Osteospermum (Trailing African daisy, Burgundy mound)

EASY

In its native habitat of the Cape and Natal province of South Africa, *Osteospermum* grows as ground cover and spreads easily. In the last year or so Danish nursery men have hybridized an indoor variety which is now marketed successfully throughout the summer months.

Its leaves have several points and are smallish. The cheerful flowers are a delicate purple fading to white on the upper side, with a deeper purple colour on the underside of the petals, the centres are dark purple. A most attractive and unusual plant, the flowering season lasts for 2 to 3 months. A white variety, *Osteospermum fruticosum* 'Album' is occasionally found on sale.

Osteospermum throws out long trailing branches which root easily, and can be cut and planted to increase stock. The plant will last for a couple of years but then loses vigour and is best replaced.

Osteospermum fruticosum

CARE

Light and temperature
Normal room temperature is fine; keep plant on a sunny, south-facing windowsill if possible, and give plenty of light during the winter months. Artificial light is not necessary.

Water and feeding
Keep the compost moist, but provide good drainage. Weekly watering in the winter rest period should be sufficient. Feed with a weak solution of houseplant fertilizer on a 7-day basis when in bud and flowering.

Propagation
Use the plantlets from the trailers and pot up into moist compost in spring. Water sparingly until new growth is obvious, then treat as a mature plant. Three or four months later flowering should commence.

Repotting
In early spring, into ordinary houseplant compost. Use a pot 1 size larger. This should only be necessary if trying to keep plant for a second season. Otherwise discard.

PROBLEMS

Whitefly needs to be treated with insecticide.

If plant becomes leggy, pinch out growing tips to encourage flowering and bushiness.

Pachystachys lutea (Lollipop plant)

QUITE DIFFICULT

The lollipop plant is often confused with *Beloperone* and was recently introduced into Europe as a variety of this plant. It does look similar, with its bright yellow bracts and long oval dark green leaves. The stems are erect and become woody with age. The bracts last for 3 months or more and from them emerge the 5cm/2in-long white flowers with green tops – these are very fresh but live for only a few days.

It comes from Peru, where it grows as a perennial. It can be kept going for a fairly long time but, in practice, 2–3 years will see it past its best.

Pruning is important to keep the plant from becoming straggly. In spring it will shoot again if cut back all over to 9cm/3in. Buy plants with well-leafed stems, particularly at the base – a lack of these leaves indicates it has been subjected to the wrong conditions.

CARE

Light and temperature
Full sun in summer; away from direct light in winter. The maximum summer temperature is 21°C/70°F. When resting keep in cooler condition but not less than 16°C/60°F or the lower leaves will fall.

Water and feeding
Keep well watered in summer. Do not allow the plant to become waterlogged. In winter, keep the soil just moist, allowing the topsoil to dry out before rewatering. Feed only in summer, every 14 days.

Propagation
In spring take young stem-tip cuttings from prunings. The cuttings should be about 8–10cm/3–4in long. Root them in sharp sand and peat, ensuring very good drainage, and place in a propagator at 18°C/64°F.

Repotting
Every spring, using new soil. The bigger the pot, the taller the plant will grow, and this may cause the lower stems to become deleafed and unattractive, so use a pot just one size up.

PROBLEMS

If the plant is allowed to dry out, the leaves will droop, then fall. Soak the pot, allow to drain thoroughly and water more regularly.

Lack of ventilation and humidity will cause the flowers to rot and drop off. Keep humidity constant by placing the plant in a saucer of wet gravel. Keep well ventilated.

If flowers fail to form apply a high-potash fertilizer for one season.

Pachystachys lutea

Passiflora caerulea (Blue passion flower)

QUITE EASY

The blue passion flower has a colourful background. It was named by Jesuit missionaries who discovered it growing in Brazil in the 1720s and likened its petals to the Ten Apostles who witnessed Christ's crucifixion. The anthers were the five wounds in Christ's side, the rays of the corona His crown of thorns, and the 3 stigmas represented the nails that pinned Him to the Cross.

The plant grows in tropical conditions, clinging by its tendrils to the trunks of other jungle trees. It will reach a height of 5m/16ft but is commonly sold as an indoor plant trained on a hoop.

The flowers of *Passiflora caerulea* are greeny-blue and purple. You may occasionally find *Passiflora violacea*, with its more pinkish flowers; this variety requires higher temperatures. It is a vigorous grower, which will go on for years. In a conservatory or greenhouse it should be grown in a close-fitting container as this will encourage flowering.

The passion flower needs heat, sun and ventilation to do well. It can be trained against an outdoor wall in a sheltered position or used with great effect in a hanging basket.

The intriguing flowers of *Passiflora caerulea* live for only for a day or so

CARE

Light and temperature
It needs bright light and 3 or 4 hours of sunshine each day. Bring it indoors for only a short time. It enjoys good ventilation and temperatures of around 21°C/70°F. Give the plant a good rest in winter at cooler temperatures.

Water and feeding
Water freely in summer and once a week or once a fortnight in winter. Feed every 2 weeks in summer during the growing season with liquid fertilizer at half strength.

Propagation
Cuttings of stem tips about 18cm/7in long can be rooted into pots of half sand and half peat moss at 21°C/70°F. Keep well sprayed until they begin to grow, which will be in 3 weeks time. Prune plants down to around 25cm/9in of the soil's surface each spring, despite the age of the plant.

Repotting
Passion flowers bloom best if their roots are restricted. Repot annually for the first year or two, then every spring add a fresh layer of compost to the surface. They will live for many years given the right conditions.

PROBLEMS

A lack of flowers means there is insufficient light. Move to a sunnier spot. If the leaf growth is strong yet no flower buds appear, reduce feeding.

Greenfly can infest the plant. Spray with insecticide.

Pelargonium (Geranium)

EASY

Originally from the warmer areas of South Africa, *Pelargonium* was widely bred and hybridized by nursery men in the last century, since when nothing has diminished the plant's extraordinary international popularity.

It flourishes almost everywhere, happily tolerates dry atmospheres and is easy to grow from seed or from cuttings. It has no dormant period and modern hybrids will flower almost continuously for up to 10 months of the year, given ample light and sufficient water.

There are thousands of named varieties ranging from dwarf plants to standards of considerable height. The flowers come in shades of pink and red. Some have scented or variegated leaves and vary widely in shape and size. When buying, it is best to consult a specialist nursery catalogue.

Four of the biggest groups are zonal, ivy-leaf, regal and scented-leaf varieties. Many of the zonal geraniums (*P. x hortorum* or *P. zonale*) can be grown in pots for indoor use. The term 'zonal' comes from the leaf markings of most varieties, which are shaped like a horseshoe, giving the popular alternative name of 'horseshoe geraniums'.

Ivy-leaf varieties are classified as *P. peltatum* and have trailing stems with fleshy leaves. They can be trained along a trellis, or left to cascade from hanging pots or baskets. Indoors, they will flower most of the year if given good sunshine. There are over 200 varieties, including single, double and semi-double flowers. They are sometimes known as trailing pelargoniums.

Regal pelargoniums (*P. domesticum hybridus*) are often called just that and not geraniums. These have larger flower petals than other types and a plain green papery leaf. Indoors they will bloom for up to 9 months of the year, although older strains only flower for 2 months, so choose carefully. There are more than 1000 varieties of regal pelargonium, sometimes known as the Martha Washington pelargonium.

The main attraction of the scented-leaf varieties is the foliage, the flowers being rather insignificant. Leaves may be patterned in reds, browns, greens and yellows or have simple white or cream edgings. Their common names describe the different fragrances produced as the leaves are gently rubbed, ranging from nutmeg and ginger to apricot and lemon. The varieties are endless and breeders are working to make their flowers more dramatic.

Zonal pelargoniums

'Gazelle Ravenskeck'

'Frank Headley'

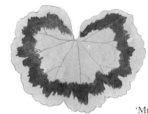

'Mrs Quilter'

'Mrs Henry Cox'

'Distinction'

Scented-leaf varieties

p. tomentosum
mint geranium

p. crispum
lemon geranium

p. x Fragrans variegatum

CARE

Light and temperature
Full light. It is a plant that is greedy for sun. Ordinary room temperature in summer, but no hotter than 24°C/75°F. In winter keep cooler at around 13–16°C/55–60°F.

Water and feeding
Water generously in summer, but keep almost dry in winter. Feed with liquid fertilizer each fortnight in summer. They like a dry atmosphere, so do not spray.

Propagation
By seed, or stem-tip cuttings taken in spring – both are easy. Seeds should be sown in spring at 16–18°C/60–64°F in sandy compost. Also in spring cut back by as much as a third; *P. x domesticum* can stand up to half. Always deadhead the plants.

Repotting
Pelargoniums like to be potbound, so only repot as they grow on from young cuttings.

regal

zonal

ivy leaf

cascade

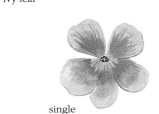

single

regal

'Stellar'

PROBLEMS

A lack of flowers is caused by overfeeding, which encourages leaf growth at the expense of flowers. It may also be caused by too much winter heat.

Lack of light causes thin growth, and too little water causes the lower leaves to go yellow and develop brown patches. Ideally leaves should occur regularly and close together up the stems. Do not allow the plant to get leggy.

If pale yellow circles appear on the leaves, a virus has attacked the plant. Destroy the plant as there is no cure. Also fatal is black leg disease, where the stems blacken and rot near the soil's surface. This is caused by overwatering.

If a mass of distorted leaves begin to sprout, leafy gall disease is usually the problem. Again, there is no cure. Destroy the plant.

Geraniums are often infested with whitefly. Spray with malathion.

Plumbago auriculata (Cape leadwort)

EASY

This South African perennial has light blue flower clusters or racemes which provide real joy in summer. In warmer climates, *Plumbago* is used as a particularly attractive hedge, or a cascading plant over walls and rockeries, where it grows with great vigour.

Indoors, it is best planted in a conservatory, where it can remain in a constant position, or in a narrow border, where roots have a freer spread than in a pot. It grows as much as allowed and needs its stems to be guided on some kind of support. It can live for many years. Cuttings take easily, so if the plant becomes straggly you should replace it. A white-flowered variety, *P. a. alba*, can be found.

Plumbago indica (scarlet leadwort) comes from South East Asia and is again a perennial in its native habitat. The zigzag stems are fascinating and the flowers a stunning shade of red. This plant is rarer to find for sale but is none the less rewarding and unusual.

Both varieties can do with pinching out the growing tips to encourage bushiness.

PROBLEMS

Young shoots can be attacked by aphids. Spray with fertilizer.

CARE

Light and temperature
Plumbago needs at least 3 hours of sunshine every day. It survives happily at room temperatures, but requires a rest in winter, preferably at around 10°C/50°F.

Water and feeding
Water regularly from spring to autumn, and feed every fortnight. In winter, reduce watering and let the soil dry out, though not completely. The plant appreciates a fertilizer high in potash during the growth period.

Propagation
In June or July, take 10cm/4in cuttings and plant in pots filled with a peat and sand compost. Cover with plastic bags and expose to filtered light. Uncover when rotting occurs.

Repotting
In early spring, move into a pot one size larger. Older plants can just have the top 5cm/2in of compost replaced with rich soil.

Plumbago auriculata used to be known as *Plumbago capensis*. It flowers on new growth

Portulaca grandiflora (Rose moss)

EASY

Portulaca is a delightful low-growing plant (up to 15cm/6in in height), covered with masses of brilliant coloured flowers which range from reds and purples to whites and yellows. These open only in strong sunlight. It has fleshy leaves on low-spreading branches and is ideal for hot dry spots or south-facing window boxes. It can also thrive in a hanging basket, liking the well-drained soil. Very popular in the southern states of America.

Its original habitat is in the drier areas of Brazil where it grows in open terrain, clinging to rocks and burying its roots in the sandy arid soil. Occasionally a double-flowered variety of rose moss may be found, *P.g. flore pleno* 'Jewel'.

CARE

Light and temperature.
Full direct sun in a hot dry position.

Water and feeding
Water to keep the top of the soil moist, but do not overwater. Feed each fortnight with liquid fertilizer, throughout summer.

Propagation
Through seed sown in spring. A propagator is not necessary. Keep warm and prick out seedlings into pots. They will develop 2 or 3 weeks after sowing.

Repotting
Not necessary as the plant is an annual.

PROBLEMS

If no flower buds appear, move plant to a sunnier position. Full sunlight is essential.

Portulaca grandiflora

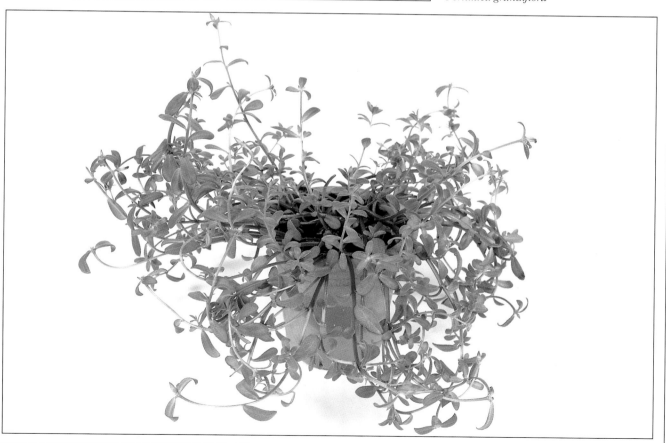

Primula (Primrose)

EASY

Primroses are perky little plants, useful for the colour and cheer they bring to the house. They come from the cooler regions of the Yunnan province of China and flower for up to 6 weeks, given the right conditions.

There are 4 varieties of *Primula*, which are perennial in their native habitat, growing under leaf canopy in wooded areas. However, when kept indoors they are usually treated as annuals.

Primula acaulis (or *P. vulgaris*) is a hybrid of the modern primrose, which comes from southern Europe, and is available in a wide range of colours.

Primula malacoides (the fairy or baby primrose) is naturally purple but also comes in bright pinks and whites as an indoor plant. It is very free-flowering in early spring, with large clusters of flowers on stems up to 15cm/6in high, sometimes producing additional tiers of flowers.

Primula obconica (the poison primrose) has round heart-shaped leaves, again with large flower clusters of up to 25cm/10in high. It comes in blue, white, apricot, red and crimson varieties. Some people are skin-sensitive to the leaves of this plant.

Finally comes *Primula sinensis* (the Chinese primrose), which is smaller, with compact flower heads, and altogether more delicate.

CARE

Light and temperature
Plenty of light and sunshine in the morning and evening. Cool temperatures (10–15°C/50–60°F) will help to make the flowering season longer.

Water and feeding
Always keep the soil moist and feed with a half-strength dose of liquid fertlizer every 2 weeks or so while in flower.

Propagation
Seed can be sown up to the end of the summer in a propagator with the temperature set at 16°C/61°F. Once germination has taken place and the seedlings are established, pot up individually for flowering plants the following spring. Pick off dying flowers of the plant to encourage it to continue in flower in the hopes of producing seed.

Repotting
P. acaulis will move happily into the garden. *P. malacoides* may be repotted into a humus-rich compost to last for a second season and should then be discarded. Other primulas are best treated as annuals.

PROBLEMS

Primulas are prone to grey mould and red spider mite. Spray with fungicide and insecticide.

As soon as the leaves start to brown, cut them off with a sharp knife at the base of the plant.

Never allow the plant to droop as it will not recover fully. Keep the compost moist at all times, and ensure good drainage.

Primula obconica come in a multitude of colours

P. obconica

P. malacoides

P. acaulis

Rhipsalidopsis (Easter cactus)

DIFFICULT

This is an attractive hanging plant with stunningly bright red flowers. It is not an easy plant to cultivate and tends to shrink and shrivel away for no reason at all.

In its natural forest habitat in Brazil, it is a subtropical epiphyte, and grows on forest trees. It belongs to the group of cacti called leaf cacti, because the plant bodies are flattened and the leaves are actually stems. The flowers are either produced from notches in these stems or from their tips. They can grow up to 30cm/1ft if kept going for several years. There are records of *Rhipsalidopsis* living for a century or more. Two kinds commonly sold as indoor plants are *R. gaertneri*, with crimson flowers, and the slightly smaller *R. rosea*, with pink flowers.

The plant should be placed outdoors and needs some shade in summer. It should not be allowed to dry out in winter. A resting period in the early part of the year is essential if the plant is ever to flower again.

CARE

Light and temperature
Medium light, but no direct sun, as it is a forest cacti. Winter temperatures should be cool but not below 10°C/50°F. In the flowering period this should be increased to around 15°C/60°F at least.

Water and feeding
Keep the soil moist but not wet, and spray with lime-free water. Feed with liquid fertilizer each fortnight once the flower buds start to form, thereafter only on a monthly basis. Use rain water at room temperature if possible.

Propagation
In spring, break off leaf segments and plant them upright in compost. Rooting takes place in several weeks.

Repotting
After flowering, only when the roots have filled the container. Use a bromeliad type compost.

PROBLEMS

Scale insects and mealy bug may infest this plant. Spray with insecticide.

If the Easter cactus fails to flower, make sure the correct winter treatment is given. Flowering occurs as the result of good growth being ripened. When the plant is resting thereafter, it should have less light and water for the flower buds to set.

Rhipsalidopsis gaertneri

Rosa chinensis (Pygmy rose, China rose)

QUITE EASY

Rosa 'Judy Fisher', double flowered

Rosa 'Baby Darling'

Rosa chinensis

Although roses in all their beautiful and infinite varieties are undoubtedly the most popular of all garden plants, it is only over the last ten years that they have proved popular as indoor plants. This has been due to the introduction of new miniature varieties in Holland and Denmark where, with the use of artificial lighting, roses are available all year round, in a wide range of colours.

Roses are among the most ancient of cultivated plants and there are many varieties which will thrive in a conservatory, porch or garden room as long as there is adequate light, water and food. Of the new varieties, 'Parade' is one of the best plants for staying in flower longer. There are many variations of this plant – 'Royal Parade' (a beautiful pink), 'Fashion Parade' (a lighter shade), 'Victory Parade' (a red) and 'Dreaming Parade' (a soft salmon colour).

Rosa chinensis grows to around 30cm/1ft and, as its name suggests, originated in China.

CARE

Light and temperature
For summer blooms, bushes should be left outside and pruned severely in midwinter, then brought indoors to a well-lit position, with temperatures slowly increasing from 5°C/41°F to about 13°C/55°F over the next few months until spring. Roses need gradual acclimatization.

Water and feeding
The soil should always be moist, and once buds start to form liquid fertilizer should be added every 10 days. Spray the foliage. Stand over a tray of damp pebbles as high humidity promotes good health. After flowering, move them outdoors again.

Propagation
Through cuttings taken in spring, dipped in hormone rooting powder and potted in good rich potting mixture.

Repotting
Repot with fresh soil in autumn, but do not expect to do this more than 2 or 3 times. After that, move the plant permanently outdoors.

PROBLEMS

Roses are very suceptible to red spider mite and aphid infestation, and fungal diseases such as black spot. Watch carefully and spray with insecticide and fungicide when necessary. It is important to ensure good air circulation.

If the plant becomes leggy, encourage bushiness by pruning shoots back to just above growth buds that point away from the centre of the plant.

If the leaves curl up and look dry, underwatering is the cause.

Ruellia (Monkey plant, trailing velvet plant)

Ruellia makoyana

DIFFICULT

Ruellia makoyana, a pretty native of Brazil, has glorious carmine trumpet-shaped flowers and velvety leaves with silver veins and purple edges. The oval leaves are particularly subtle and beautiful, with the plant flowering in late autumn and early winter.

The species was named after Jean de la Ruells, who was both botanist and physician to Francis I of France in the sixteenth century, and grows in its native habitat in high humidity under a semi-shade canopy.

Ruellia macrantha (Christmas pride) again has carmine flowers and is somewhat larger; however the leaves do not have the attractive veining of *Ruellia makoyana*.

In the home you should be able to keep these plants going for 2 or 3 years. Pinch out growing tips to encourage bushiness. Both can be used in hanging baskets.

Ruellia makoyana
flower and leaf

CARE

Light and temperature
Bright indirect sunlight with an average summer household temperature. Do not let it go above 21°C/70°F and, at this temperature, you should provide plenty of humidity by placing the plant on pebbles in a saucer of water. This is not really a plant for heated rooms. During winter do not let the temperature drop below 13°C/55°F.

Water and feeding
During spring and summer water well, but wait until the surface of the soil has dried out between waterings. Feed fortnightly with general liquid fertilizer to the manufacturer's recommendations. In winter water weekly but do not fertilize.

Repotting
Repot in early autumn in a loam-based compost and add granules.

Propagation
Take stem-tip cuttings with 4 pairs of leaves in summer and root into potting mixture. Place in a propagator but ventilate once a day.

PROBLEMS

Greenfly insects can cover the leaves and growing points. Spray with diluted malathion. Also spray with diluted malathion if whiteflies jump around the plant.

Whitish mould on the leaves and stems can be caused by botrytis, or stem rot. The plant is too wet and cold. Spray with fungicide and move to a warmer position.

Webs under the leaves are caused by red spider mite. Spray with a systemic insecticide. Water the plant thoroughly and spray over the leaves frequently to increase humidity.

If leaves turn black, the location is too cold. Move the plant to a warmer position.

If the leaves shrivel up, the plant is too dry or too hot. Check the compost and water if dry. If the compost is moist enough, move the plant to a cooler spot.

Schizanthus retusus (Butterfly flower, poor man's orchid)

EASY

Only hybrids of the butterfly flower from Chile are available; there it grows as an annual in subtropical conditions in full sunshine to a height of 1m/3ft. Cultivated as an indoor plant, it remains an annual and should be bought in bud, to be discarded after flowering, which can last 4 or 5 months until late autumn.

The foliage is gracefully fernlike, the stems of the plant being somewhat sticky. The flowers look similar to those of the orchid and are around 5cm/2in wide, coming most commonly in a salmon-pink colour with a yellow centre on which there are purple markings. Other colour bands include bright red, purple and pink varieties, *S. x wisetonensis* hybrids, again with yellow centres marked with purple.

Both dwarf and larger varieties can easily be grown from seed. If sown in spring it produces autumn-flowering plants, and if in autumn spring blossoms.

A good plant for hanging baskets, the tips of the growing specimen should be pinched out to encourage bushiness.

Schizanthus needs good air circulation and bright light to do well

PROBLEMS

If foliage begins to look dry and flower buds fail to open, increase watering. Make sure you protect the plant from potential sun scorch.

CARE

Light and temperature
Full light. South-facing window boxes and hanging baskets are ideal. Keep at cool or average warmth – 13–18°C/55–64°F is best.

Water and feeding
Keep the soil moist, but not wet. Feed each fortnight with liquid fertilizer until flowering has finished.

Propagation
Sow seed either in spring or autumn. Pinch out tips of young plants to encourage bushy growth.

Repotting
Not necessary as the plant is an annual.

Saintpaulia (African violet)

QUITE DIFFICULT

These delicate plants, with their attractive, fleshy leaves and stems bearing small daisy-shaped flowers in mauves, pinks and white shades, have many admirers – and deservedly so. But be warned: they can be temperamental. When given the right (and difficult to achieve) balance of warmth, shade and moisture, they can bloom happily all year round.

The species was discovered in the Usambara mountains in South Africa by Baron St Paul St Claire in the late 1800s and was first grown commercially in America. It came originally from Tanzania, in a delicate deep-blue colour, and grew on steep and wind-swept rocks and in crevasses, its flowers up to 3cm/1in wide.

Saintpaulia has round, slightly hairy, heart-shaped leaves and there are variegated varieties, ones with serrated edges, crinkled edges or rolled edges. The flowers may be single, double, frilled, multi-coloured or star-shaped – the choice is endless . . . White African violets will revert to purple quite quickly.

In its native habitat *Saintpaulia* will last for a number of years – as it can as an indoor plant, though it is better kept a couple of years and then replaced with fresh flowering stock.

S. hybrida

'Fancy Pants'

S. Rhapsodie

CARE

Light and temperature
Warm conditions (16°C/60°F) help the plant to flourish. It likes adequate light, but no direct sun, as the leaves and flowers scorch easily.

Water and feeding
Always water from the bottom since water over the leaves and flowers will mark them. Stand in a saucer and fill twice weekly. After 30 minutes drain off the excess water. Use lukewarm water. Feed fortnightly during spring and summer with liquid houseplant fertilizer diluted to half strength.

Propagation
Can be grown from seed but the seedlings vary in quality. Much simpler are leaf cuttings. These root easily in a peat and sand mixture at about 20°C/68°F and will be in flower 6 months later. Rest the plant for 6–8 weeks at a lowish temperature, keeping it on the dry side every now and then. This helps to form flower buds and, when brought back into warmer temperatures with more water, will produce a flush of flowers.

Repotting
Only every second year and make sure the new container is only just bigger than the old one.

PROBLEMS

When leaves turn pale, the plant needs feeding or is receiving too much direct sun. Feed or move to a darker spot.

The plant needs repotting if there is more than a single crown or the leaves are small and too close together. You may limit flowering unless you separate out the crowns so that only 1 grows in the pot.

If the plant does not flower, but looks healthy, add a little superphosphate to the water. A lack of light is the most common cause of no flowers.

Mouldy leaves and flowers are caused by botrytis. Destroy affected leaves and spray with a systemic fungicide.

Whitefly and mealy bug should be treated with insecticide.

Rotting leaves and flowers are caused by too much water. Always water from below, and never overwater.

Some of the many Saintpaulia leaf types

| Variegated | Serrated | Spoon-shaped | Lance-shaped |

The most commonly-seen African violet

Schlumbergera (Thanksgiving cactus, Christmas cactus, claw cactus)

QUITE EASY

In its natural habitat of tropical Brazil, this member of the cactus family is epiphytic, attaching itself on to trees that grow on mountains up to 1500m/4800ft.

Forced by hybridizing and the treatment meted out by nursery men, it is a strikingly attractive plant growing to about 30cm/1ft, and has stems formed of flat joints with a few well-marked 'teeth'. The flowers appear in winter and, for a cactus, are long-lasting – maybe 3 or 4 days. They are usually pink, but modern hybrids include white, red, yellow and purple varieties.

S. bridgesii is the Christmas cactus and *S. truncata* (sometimes known as *Zygocactus truncatus*) the Thanksgiving cactus, also called the claw cactus. They both come into flower in early November and can last for 50 years or more.

Schlumbergera bridgesii looks extremely handsome in a hanging basket or against plain terracotta pots.

CARE

Light and temperature
Some direct sun all year round. It does fine at room temperature. An abundance of flowers can be encouraged by keeping the plant out of artificial light for long periods during early autumn when buds are setting. An outdoor spell is recommended – a shady protected position in summer.

Water and feeding
Keep the soil moist but not wet, using rain water if possible. When flowering finishes, reduce the amount of water. Use high-potassium fertilizer every fortnight all year round except in the 2 months after flowering.

Propagation
In spring take cuttings of 2 to 3 joints, let the surface dry out and pot into a humus-rich compost. Rooting occurs in about 3 or 4 weeks.

Repotting
In spring, but only when roots fill the container. Use a mixture of leaf compost, soil, peat and sand, and keep dryish for the first 2 weeks.

PROBLEMS

Scale insects and mealy bug may infest the plant. Spray with insecticide.

If the plant shrivels up, it has probably been kept too dry. Increase watering and keep the compost moist.

If flowers fail to appear, the plant has been kept too warm during the rest period. Increase contrast in temperature and ensure 2 months' rest for the plant.

Senecio cruentis hybridus (Florists' cineraria)

QUITE EASY

This plant comes in almost every colour imaginable except yellow. It grows to 60cm/2ft and is covered with masses of small daisy-shaped flowers in early spring. There are dwarf, single and double varieties available, but the doubles are limited in their range of colours and will flower less freely. Buy plants with a few open flowers and plenty of buds; the flowering season lasts up to 2 months.

Senecio cruentis is very popular with parks departments for display purposes and is a good conservatory plant, preferring cool temperatures and little direct sun.

Its original habitat is the Canary Islands, where it grows as a half-hardy perennial, high up on the damp mountainsides in cool conditions. As a houseplant, it should be discarded after flowering.

Cineraria likes to have plenty of air circulation and humidity

Two of the many colour variations of singles   Double   Stellata

PROBLEMS

Yellow leaves are caused by draughty conditions. Move the plant to a more protected position.

Wilting leaves and drooping flowers are caused by the plant being either too dry and hot or overwatered. Resite the plant and reduce watering.

Flowers die prematurely if the plant is underwatered or receives too much sunlight.

CARE

Light and temperature.
Cinerarias like cool temperatures between 13°C/55°F. A north-facing windowsill is ideal. Keep out of direct sun, which will cause the plants to wilt and they will never recover completely.

Water and feeding
Water, then allow to dry out. Take care not to overwater and ensure good drainage. Feeding is not necessary as this only produces coarse plants with excessively sized leaves.

Propagation
From seed in summer, but earlier sowings will produce plants that bloom in midwinter. Do not bury the fine seed, but cover with glass or polythene. When the seedlings appear, spray them often, pot up in September and keep in an unheated greenhouse. When buds appear, raise the temperature to 13°C/55°F.

Repotting
Not necessary; plants are discarded after flowering.

Sinningia hybridus (Florist's gloxinia)

QUITE DIFFICULT

With its large bell-like flowers and luxuriant velvety leaves, *Gloxinia* is among the prettiest and most striking of flowering plants. The majority of varieties available now are hybrids, developed by nursery men from *Sinningia speciosa* crossed with *S. regina* way back in the early 1900s. Much of the work was done by a German botanist, Wilhelm Sinning, hence the genus name. From this, numerous other hybrids have been developed in almost every imaginable colour.

In its native habitat of southern Brazil it grows on damp, rocky slopes and has violet-blue flowers which face outwards rather than up. Modern hybrids have much larger flowers, which come into bloom from early spring to late summer. With proper care, they will remain in flower for up to 2 months. Gloxinias are tubers – they should only be purchased if plenty of flower buds are obvious and the leaves look glossy. They will do well as indoor plants for 2 or more years.

Never wet the leaves of the gloxinia

CARE

Light and temperature
Bright light, away from direct sunlight. Average warmth, with a minimum of 16°C/60°F throughout the flowering season. During winter months, keep at lower temperatures and move the plant back to the warmth in order to 'force' it into flowering.

Water and feeding
Keep the soil moist at all times while the plant is blooming. Water with soft, warm water and feed every fortnight with a weak solution of liquid fertilizer during the flowering season. Never allow the leaves to get wet. After flowering, reduce water and stop feeding. Allow to dry out when the leaves turn yellow and store the pot at 10°C/50°F.

Propagation
Take leaf cuttings in summer and pot in fresh compost at a constant temperature of 22°C/71°F or more. Artificial light is essential from late autumn to late winter for seeds sown in spring; not an easy task for the enthusiastic amateur.

Repotting
Wait for tubers to produce shoots in spring before repotting them. Then only repot firm tubers; those that feel at all soggy will not do well. Plant hollow side up with the top of the tuber level with the surface of the soil. Keep warm and on the dry side until leaves emerge, then grow on in a warm, bright and humid position.

Gloxinia has one of the richest and most varied type of flower

PROBLEMS

If the plant collapses, it has been overwatered, or has poor drainage, or has been watered with cold instead of room-temperature water.

Hot dry air causes curled leaves with brown tips. Place the plant in a saucer of wet gravel to increase humidity and ensure that the plant does not get too much sun.

If the leaves become pale, place in a brighter position, but keep away from direct sunlight. Feed the plant more than usual.

The plant hates draughts and will droop if placed in an over-exposed position. Move to a warmer, more sympathetic place.

Solanum (Winter cherry, false Jerusalem cherry)

EASY

Solanum capsicastrum has bright red berries for up to 6 months during wintertime

CARE

Light and temperature
Plenty of light, but not too warm – 13°C/ 55°F is ideal, with the maximum temperature 18°C/64°F. In summer place outdoors, as *Solanum* appreciates a good bake.

Water and feeding
Water very frequently while flowering and never let it dry out. Feed with weak solutions of liquid fertilizer every fortnight. Humidity is important; mist often and stand the plant on a tray of damp pebbles if possible.

Propagation
Sow seed in spring in a propagator at about 16°C/61°F. Stem-tip cuttings can also be attempted at this time.

Repotting
Repot when the plant outgrows its container, which could be several times in its first season. If kept for a second year, repot after pruning quite stringently in spring.

The winter cherry, introduced from Brazil and Uruguay at the end of the seventeenth century, belongs to the potato family.

Solanum capsicastrum (the false Jerusalem cherry) produces fruit berries which ripen from green to red, yellow and orange. These berries are poisonous so keep well away from children. It is a popular plant usually bought in fruit around Christmas and lasts well indoors. Delicate but cheerful white flowers, similar to those of the potato, appear in June and July, but the berries are the more attractive feature. It can reach 30–38cm/12–15in high and will grow to that height from seed in one season.

Solanum pseudocapsicum is the true Jerusalem cherry. There is a pretty variegated form of *S. capsicastrum* available on occasions.

The plant can be kept for 2 Christmas seasons; thereafter it fruits less freely and should be discarded.

PROBLEMS

Grey mould can attack the plant. Spray with systemic fungicide.

If yellow rings appear on the leaves, destroy the plant. It is infected with tomato spotted wilt virus for which there is no cure. Spray with fertilizer containing magnesium if the lower leaves turn yellow with brown spots.

If the berries fall this is usually due to insufficient light. Move the plant to a south-facing windowsill.

Spathiphyllum (Sail plant, peace lily)

QUITE EASY

Spathiphyllum wallisii, which originates in Colombia, is one of the best plants for indoor gardening as it is undemanding of light and care. It comes as no surprise to find that it is a member of the lily family and has exceptionally attractive leaves as well as flowers.

Its glossy bright green leaves lean out like sails from the centre, 30cm/12in high and 90cm/36in across. *Spathiphyllum* 'Mauna Loa' is bigger, growing to 1m/40in high and wide. This is probably a hybrid, bred from *Spathiphyllum floribunda* crossed with a Hawaiian hybrid developed in America. The flower head comprises a white spathe encompassing a 9cm/3in long spadix which is usually coloured white or pale green. For the first few days the flower has scent; thereafter this will fade but the flower should last for around 6 weeks. The plant itself should live for 10 years or more if not maltreated.

Spathiphyllum is a rhizome. It can grow enormously in a single season, doubling in size given the correct conditions. A most rewarding plant to grow.

CARE

Light and temperature
In summer, keep away from direct sun and maintain the temperature at 18–21°C/64–70°F. Research in Holland has shown that less light, rather than more, makes for more flowering. In winter, as much light as possible and keep at 16–18°C/60–64°F.

Water and feeding
This plant grows naturally in high humidity and warmth. With temperatures over 16°C/60°F, the leaves should be misted daily. Place the plant in a saucer filled with wet pebbles. Always keep the soil moist. Feed each fortnight while in flower.

Propagation
Offsets can be separated and planted into humus-rich compost. Seed can be grown but this is a demanding method for the amateur indoor gardener.

Repotting
When repotting divide large plants, in late spring, using humus-rich houseplant compost. New growth will be encouraged.

Remove the old flower stalks of *Spathiphyllum*, as they brown quickly

PROBLEMS

Red spider mite and greenfly can infest the plant. Spray with insecticide.

Floppy leaves indicate too little water. Immerse the pot in a bucket or sink and soak thoroughly, then drain well. Never allow the rootball to get soggy.

If the plant does not bloom, consider feeding and repot if potbound. Large plants can be divided.

If the leaves begin to yellow, the plant could be suffering from too much sunlight. Remove yellow leaves and place in a more shaded position.

Stephanotis floribunda

(Brides's flower, wax flower, Foradora jasmine, Madagascar jasmine)

DIFFICULT

This is a glorious climber when in flower during early summer, with its waxy white flowers much prized by florists for bridal bouquets.

Stephanotis is similar to the gardenia in that it hates changes of environment and temperature. It is ideal for a conservatory, where the white flowers hang down in bunches from the trailing stalks that can be left to climb or weave along a roof beam. However, it is often sold trained around hoops.

It comes from tropical Madagascar and was introduced into Europe in 1839. It can reach 6m/20ft or more, but if grown in a pot it should be kept compact by regular pruning. Plants may rest for several years and then suddenly burst into flower when there is sufficient light stimulus. A period of baking in sunlight helps this light-hungry plant enormously.

The *Stephanotis* has intoxicatingly scented flowers, usually in summertime

CARE

Light and temperature
It must be placed on a windowsill for light, but shielded from the midday sun. The ideal summer temperature is 15–21°C/60–70°F, with somewhat lower winter levels of 10°C/50°F

Water and feeding
Water frequently in summer but in winter just keep the compost from drying out. Use lime-free, warm water. Feed once a fortnight in summer and place the pot on wet gravel in a saucer, keeping the water level just below that of the pot. To induce humidity spray the leathery leaves, but never the flowers, at least once a week.

Propagation
For young plants growing at a great rate repot in good houseplant compost, perhaps as often as twice a year.

Repotting
Repot each spring. Cut back any straggly growth. After 5 years, replace the topsoil.

PROBLEMS

If the pot is moved or turned, the flower buds may drop so try to avoid handling the plant as much as possible.

Leaves will turn yellow if limey water is used. Make sure it is tepid and lime-free.

Red spider mite, scale insect and mealy bug often attack this plant. Spray each month with diluted malathion. Remove scale insect with methylated spirit swabs.

Streptocarpus (Cape primrose)

EASY

The delicate *Streptocarpus* or Cape primrose, which as its name suggests comes from subtropical Southern Africa, was brought to Europe in the 1820s. It grows naturally in humid, leafy shaded soil, often clinging to rocky surfaces, and can cope with semi-shaded conditions within the home.

Recently plant breeders have produced a range of hybrids. Purple or mauve is still the predominant colour, and 'Constant Nymph' the old favourite, but there are many different shades within this spectrum, from the deep purple of 'Amanda' to the soft mauve petals and darker throat stripes of 'Heidi'. White, pink and red varieties are also found.

Other varieties include the pretty mauve *Streptocarpus saxorum*, which can be trained into an attractive hanging plant, and the extraordinary *Streptocarpus wenlandii* with only one enormous leaf, that is red underneath.

The plant flowers twice a year and will live for 2 to 3 years before it needs replacing. After flowering cut the stems at the base to encourage new flower shoots. Mature plants grow to a height of 30cm/12in.

PROBLEMS

Streptocarpus is vulnerable to remarkably few pests and diseases. Give it the conditions outlined and it will thrive.

Shrivelled leaves suggest the plant is too dry. Increase watering.

Droopy leaves again indicate it is too dry. Increase watering.

Leaf stems may rot if the plant is too wet and too cold. Water less and move to a warmer place. Dusting with sulphur may help.

Prone to greenfly. These tend to attack the flower stems rather than the leaves or flowers themselves. Spray with insecticide. The stems may also be attacked by thrips; treat in the same way.

'Falling Stars'   'Stella'

'Heidi'   'Amanda'

CARE

Light and temperature
Streptocarpus is a remarkably tolerant plant in most respects, but it does need plenty of light. Protect it from direct sunlight in summer. The ideal temperature is 16–18°C/63–67°F.

Water and feeding
Water 2–3 times a week in summer, but do not let the plant stand in water. In centrally heated rooms, increase the humidity by placing the pot in damp pebbles. Good drainage is vital. It does not require much feeding – a half-strength dose once every two weeks is plenty.

Repotting
Repot every spring in peat-based compost into a pot one size up. *Streptocarpus* likes fresh soil even if it doesn't need more space, so replace the top 2.5cm/1in of soil.

Propagation
They are easy to propagate. Leaf cuttings should be taken in summer. Cut a leaf along the central vein, cover the cut with rooting hormone and plant the cut surface in sharp sand.

Thunbergia alata (Black-eyed Susan)

EASY

This is one of the most effective flowering climbers, suitable for covering a trellis or being trained in a hanging basket for a conservatory or garden room. It has orange, yellow or white flowers with dark purple centres, and pale green serrated leaves.

Its native habitat is subtropical East Africa, where it grows to 4m/10ft. As an indoor plant it is unlikely to exceed 2.5m/6ft.

It can cover a large area very quickly but must have support. It is often treated as an annual but is actually a perennial which can be kept going for 2 or 3 years. After flowering, cut back the growth to 15cm/6in above soil level, fertilize regularly and repot in early springtime.

Thunbergia alata

CARE

Light and temperature
The plant needs some direct sun to flower successfully and should ideally be placed on a sunny terrace after flowering finishes, at the end of summer, until the frost arrives. Room temperature is adequate. Good air circulation is important.

Water and feeding
Regular watering throughout the flowering period should be cut back through the winter with the compost kept just moist. Mist from time to time and feed with liquid fertilizer each fortnight during flowering.

Propagation
Sow seeds in spring to flower through summer.

Repotting
In early spring into a humus-rich compost.

PROBLEMS

The leaves will shrivel easily if the plant is underwatered.

If flowerbuds fail to appear in the second season, increase fertilizing and move to a sunnier spot.

Torenia fournieri (Wishbone plant)

QUITE EASY

The flowers of this charming and delicate plant are very distinctive; the pale violet blooms have a lower lip with 3 lobes of velvety deep purple and then a yellow lobe in the middle of the lower lobe. A white version, *T. fournieri alba*, can be found occasionally, as well as the larger *T. fournieri grandiflora*.

The leaves are lightish green in colour and have an attractive serrated shape.

Torenia comes from tropical Vietnam, where it grows as an annual in moist conditions under semi-shade. It should never be subjected to direct sunlight or to draughts. It will grow to a height of 30cm/1ft and, in the right conditions, will flower almost continuously throughout the summer months. At the end of the flowering season the plant is best discarded. As and when *Torenia* starts to become straggly, pinch out the tips to encourage bushiness. It may be necessary to provide some kind of support system for this plant, or you can use it to good effect in a hanging basket.

CARE

Light and temperature
Torenia needs good light but not direct sun. In prefers to be at a constant temperature, and will be happy at 15°C/60°F throughout the summer.

Water and feeding
The plant needs regular watering and the compost should not be allowed to dry out. Feed with weak liquid fertilizer every 2 weeks.

Propagation
It is possible to grow from seed, planted into good seeding compost and raised at a constant temperature of 18–21°C/64–70°F. The young plants should be potted up into a humus-rich compost and treated with extreme care.

Repotting
The plant is an annual so repotting is not necessary.

PROBLEMS

If the plant fails to flower, move to a sunnier and warmer position. Ensure at least 3 or 4 hours sunshine each day.

Red spider mite can infest the plant. Treat with melathion.

Torenia fournieri

Zantedeschia (Calla lily, trumpet lily, arum lily)

QUITE EASY

This is an elegant plant from the Cape area of South Africa where it is known as the pig lily. There it grows from its tuber almost like a clump of weed in an area that is marshy through winter and dry in summer. It is a subtropical plant, able to tolerate quite differing day and night temperatures. *Zantedeschia* has broad arrow-shaped leaves up to 50cm/20in long and 20–25cm/10–12in wide on stems of up to 1m/3ft. Its flowers, which bloom in winter or early spring, are spectacular having a golden spadix circled by a velvety white spathe.

Z. aethiopica (arum lily), the most commonly seen, has the white spathe; *Z. rehmannii* (pink calla), from Natal, has leaves spotted with silvery white and in summer produces a delicate pink spathe; *Z. elliottiana* (golden calla) from the Transkei region has a rich deep yellow spathe in late spring to summer.

Provided callas are given a 2-month period of dormancy, when the leaves will die down, the plants can go on for many years.

Z. rehmannii

CARE

Light and temperature
In summer, the rhizome should be kept outside in the sun until late autumn. In October, bring it inside and keep in bright light at reasonably low temperatures. When growth starts, keep at 10–14°C/50–57°F for 3 months, then increase the temperature to over 16°C/61°F.

Water and feeding
Keep the rhizome dry in the summer dormancy period. In winter, water little at first, increasing as growth begins. During full growth keep the soil moist and place the pot in a bowl of water. Feed with liquid fertilizer each fortnight before flowering and weekly when in flower; thereafter cease feeding. Humidity is a natural demand of the calla during the flowering season so place over a tray of moist pebbles.

Propagation
Divide the rhizomes in autumn, keeping at least 1 shoot on each portion. Offsets can be removed and potted on.

Repotting
Each autumn, in humus-rich compost. There are often up to 3 or more rhizomes in a pot for effect.

PROBLEMS

Spray scale insects with insecticide, if infested.

Aphids and red spider mite will attack if conditions are too hot and dry. Treat and increase humidity.

Zantedeschia aethiopica, the arum lily

Glossary

aerial root A root used for climbing that grows above the soil from nodes on the stem. It absorbs moisture from the air. For houseplants aerial roots can be fed back into the soil or trained around a support. Commonly found in the Aracea family, e.g. the *Philodendron*

annual A plant which grows from seed, produces flowers and seeds in one year and then dies.

anther The male part of the flower from where the pollen is produced

aphid A tiny insect, also known as greenfly, that sucks sap from the plant. It is especially fond of flowering plants. (See page 244.)

assimilation The absorption of light by the leaves. (See *photosynthesis*.)

axil Where leaf or leaf stalk joins the stem. Buds sometimes grow here, called auxillary buds

biennial A plant which grows from seed, produces leaves in its first year, flowers in its second, and then dies

bipinnate A compound leaf shape which is double pinnate (see *pinnate*), i.e. each pinnate segment is itself divided into segments

bleeding When sap seeps from a wound on a leaf or stalk that has been cut or broken, e.g. on the rubber plant

bloom Synonym for 'flower'. Can also be used to describe a waxy coating on leaves

botrytis A fungus also known as grey mould because it covers the leaves, stem and flowers with a grey fluffy coating. It is often caused by too much humidity. (See page 245.)

bract A modified leaf which is very close to, or is even part of, the flower. It protects the flower and, as it is often brightly coloured (e.g. poinsettia), also attracts insects for pollination

bud The embryo of stem, leaf or flower, usually protected by outer scales. It can form either on the end of a stem or side shoot (terminal bud) or in the leaf axil (auxillary bud)

bulb An onion-like underground storage organ containing a central bud surrounded by fleshy scales. The bud will produce a single flowering stem

capillary action The upward movement of water – for example, when the potting compost absorbs and draws up water from a saucer under the plant

chlorophyll The green colouring in leaves and stems and a vital ingredient of photosynthesis. (See *photosynthesis*.)

chlorosis A condition caused by a lack of iron or magnesium which inhibits production of chlorophyll, thus causing pale or yellowing leaves

cordate Heart-shaped

corm Swollen storage organ, usually underground. Its bud forms the roots and shoots of the plant

corolla A ring of petals, either separate or fused

cultivar A variety of plant which is adapted from its natural (usually tropical or subtropical) environment and developed or bred in artificial conditions

cutting A section of stem or leaf which can be used to propagate a new plant. (See page 239.)

deadhead The removal of dead or faded flower heads to improve the plant's appearance and prolong the flowering season

deciduous Plants which lose their leaves after the growing period, which is most commonly autumn to winter. Rarely kept as houseplants because of this. (See also *evergreen*.)

division Propagation by separating a plant into sections, each with its own roots and leaves, then repotting each section as individual new plants

dormant period (also known as the rest period) The period, usually winter, when the plant stops (or slows down) growing. During this time, the plant may shed its leaves and lose its top growth

double flower A flower that has a greater number of petals than those found on the single flower. (See also *single flower*.)

epiphyte Plants which grow on other plants, trees or rocks for support or to receive a better position in terms of light and moisture. They are non-parasitic, i.e. they do not receive nourishment from the host plant. Most bromeliads are epiphytic, also known as air plants

evergreen Plants that retain their leaves through the whole year. Most houseplants are of this type

exotic Plants native to tropical and subtropical regions of the world

family Group of plants linked by botanically common characteristics. The family will include different genera, for example *Aechmea*, *Guzmania* and *Tillandsia* are all members of the bromeliad family, Bromeliaceae. (See also *genus*, *species*, *variety*.)

filament Thin stalk of an anther. (See *anther, stamen.*)

F1 hybrid A first-generation cross of two non-hybrid parents. (See *hybrid.*)

forcing The process by which nursery men force a plant to grow, flower or fruit (by controlling temperature and light) at unnatural times of the year. (See page 26.)

frond Leaf of a fern or palm

fungicide A chemical treatment for fungal diseases, such as powdery mildew or botrytis. (See page 245.)

genus (plural genera). A subdivision of a family of plants (e.g. *Hedera*). Each genus can be sub-divided again into species, e.g. *Hedera canariensis, Hedera helix.* (See *family, species, variety.*)

germination The first stage of growth, when the seed sprouts a seedling

greenfly see *aphid*

ground cover A low plant which covers the floor of its native habitat, spreading between other plants

growing tip The tip of a shoot, from where growth occurs. Also known as the growing point

half hardy A plant that requires temperatures no lower than 10°C/50°F for healthy growth. (See *hardy.*)

hardening off The period during which plants become acclimatized to colder temperatures

hardy A strong plant that can withstand temperatures below 5°C/45°F. (See *half hardy.*)

herbaceous A plant with fleshy (as opposed to woody) stems

honeydew Sticky substance excreted on leaves by pests such as mealy bug, scale insect and aphids. Can cause black mould to form. (See pages 244–5.)

humidifier An instrument that increases the humidity of a room. Can be bought from garden centres. Often comes with an air circulation fan. (See page 235.)

humus see *leafmould*

hybrid A plant formed from the cross-fertilization either of two species from the same family (e.g. *Fatshedera* was formed from *Fatsia* and *Hedera*) or, most commonly, from the same genera (e.g. *Gynura x. sarmentosa*)

hydroculture The method of raising plants in nutrient-enriched water

insecticide A chemical treatment for removing insect pests

inflorescence The term used to describe the various arrangements of flowers on a stem

leafmould Also known as humus. Partially decayed leaves which can be added to a potting mixture to provide additional nutrients

leggy Growth that has become long and spindly

loam Potting mixture made from good quality soil mixed with sand, peat and additional nutrients. (See page 243.)

mealy bug White, sap-sucking pest that excretes honeydew on leaves. Can form colonies which appear as woolly patches. (See page 244.)

misting Covering the leaves with a very fine spray of water in order to raise the humidity level around the plant and clean the foliage. Misters can be bought from garden centres. (See page 235.)

node Swollen part of the stem or a joint on the stem from where a leaf or bud sprouts

offset A plantlet, identical to the parent plant, which forms at the base or on a secondary stem. Can be cut away carefully and planted into its own pot as a form of propagation. (See page 238.)

osmunda fibre Added to orchid compost as it has good air-filled porosity. It is derived from the roots of the *Osmunda regalis* fern

overwinter To give a plant its required conditions during the winter months, usually in a greenhouse, to rest throughout the dormant period

palmate A leaf consisting of sections which originate from the same point and fan out like fingers on an open hand

panicle A type of inflorescence – a cluster of flowers on a short stalk

parasite A living organism that lives on and feeds off another living organism. Examples of parasites which affect houseplants are sap-sucking insects such as aphids or spider mites. (See page 244.)

peat Partially decomposed vegetable matter, added to potting mixes. (See page 243.)

pendant Hanging downwards

perennial A plant which lives for more than three years, and possible indefinitely if given the right conditions (see *annual, biennial*)

pH Hydrogen ion concentration – the measurement of acidity/alkalinity. Most houseplants prefer acidic soil. (See page 239.)

photosynthesis The action of light on the chlorophyll in the leaves, which converts the carbon dioxide that has been absorbed by the plant from the atmosphere into carbohydrate (food)

pinch out The removal of the growing tip, either by cutting or pinching off with the fingers, to encourage bushiness and/or flowering. (See page 240.)

pinnae Leaflets, or sub-sections, of a pinnate leaf

pinnate A compound leaf structure, with pairs of leaflets (pinnae) arranged opposite each other along the stalk

pistil The collective name for the ovary, style and stigma – the female reproductive parts of the plant

plantlet see *offset*

potbound A plant whose roots have filled the pot, therefore having no room for further growth

potting on Moving a plant into a larger size pot

powdery mildew A fungal disease which coats leaves with a white, powdery deposit. (See page 245.)

pricking out Transplanting seedlings into larger containers or individual pots

propagation Multiplying plants to increase supply or to replenish old stock. Can be achieved in a number of ways, e.g. by seed, by division, from leaf cutting, from stem cutting or from offsets. (See page 238.)

propagator Piece of equipment that provides the right conditions for propagating seeds and cuttings, i.e. warmth and a moist atmosphere. Can range from just a plastic dome over a seed tray to the electrical kind which provides and controls heat

pseudobulb The swollen base of the stem of an orchid with leaves and flowers. Used to store water, and often found growing from a rhizome

raceme A type of inflorescence – a central stem along which are spaced flowers on short stalks. Flowers usually bloom from the bottom upwards

red spider mite Sap-sucking, 8-legged insect noticible from black dots of excreta on leaves. (See page 245.)

repotting Removing a plant from its container, discarding topsoil and pruning roots, then replacing in same pot with fresh topsoil. (See page 242.)

rest period see *dormancy period*

rhizome A thick-stemmed storage organ, found either underground or lying on the surface. May have roots, leaves and flowering stems. (See also *bulb, tuber.*)

rootball The clump of roots and compost in the pot

rosette Arrangement of leaves spreading out from the central base of the plant

scale insect Sap-sucking pest usually attacking underside of leaf. Ferns and citrus plants are particularly vulnerable. (See page 245.)

scorching The burning of leaves or petals by the rays of the sun through a window

seed Fertilized ovule of a flowering plant, from which germinates a new plant

seedling The young plant sprouting from the seed

shrub Woody-stemmed plant which is smaller than a tree and has no trunk

single flower Flower which has only one row of petals. Many species have single and double varieties. (See also *double flower.*)

spadix A tongue-like flower spike, protruding from or surrounded by a spathe, for example as found on *Anthurium*

spathe A large, prominent bract bearing or surrounding a spadix

species Sub-division of a plant genus, written after genus name, e.g. *Celosia cristata, Celosia plumosa*. (See also *family, genus, variety.*)

sphagnum A young moss, with a very high air-filled porosity, used in potting mixes

spike A type of inflorescence – stalkless flowers growing alternately up a central stem

spore Minute seed of the fern family

stalk Arm of plant which bears the leaves and flower or flowers

stamen Pollen-bearing lobes or anthers – the male reproductive parts of the flower

stigma The point on the flower where fertilization occurs. Coated with a slippery substance, it is the upper part of the pistil and vital in the reproductive system

style The stalk of the female reproductive system, it supports the stigma and connects it to the ovary

succulent Used to describe indoor plants with thick and fleshy leaves. Often found growing natively in dry desert-like conditions where rainfall is short. Some have the ability to store moisture in their leaves; others can tolerate a little rain

systemic Usually refers to a pesticide taken from the leaves into the plant via the sap flow (or vascular system)

tendril A spiralling growth which some climbing plants use to attach themselves as a means of support. Tendrils are usually far finer than the stems from which they grow; some are grown from the leaves and others from the stems of the plants

terrarium Glass growing units for small plants which need high humidity. Also called Wardian cases after the botanist who invented them. Today's versions come with all services such as heat, humidity and ventilation

thrip Minute black insect which either flies or jumps to spread its influence, distorting flowers and leaves as it goes. (See page 245.)

throat The inner areas of a flower from which protrude the anther, filament and eye. Usually a different colour from the petals

transpiration Although it varies with the prevailing conditions, transpiration measures the loss of water vapour through the pores in the leaf structure. Transpiration (evaporation) increases with higher temperatures

tuber Storage root, usually underground. It is fleshy, and may seem thickened. From it grow leaf structures from which buds are borne. Important in the propagation of certain plants

umbel A type of inflorescence – a cluster of flowers, either flat or rounded, which arise from the same point, such as found on *Hoya bella*

variegated Two- (or more) coloured leaves. The white or yellow markings are patches that contain no green chlorophyll, be they in the form of stripes, leaf edges or flecks. Therefore the plants should be placed in good light to increase assimilation wherever possible. Chlorophyll is stored in this way and essential to healthy development

variety A sub-division of a plant species, written in inverted commas, e.g. *Leptospermum scoparium* 'Album', *Leptospermum scoparium* 'Ruby Glow'. May sometimes be called a cultivar. Usually indicates differences in size, colour or other features (See also *family, genus, variety.*)

white fly A sap-sucking, small white winged pest that clusters on the underside of plant leaves. (See page 244.)

whorl Three flowers or leaves which grow from the same node (or point) and radiate like the spokes of a wheel

Light

Light comes from two main sources: the natural (the sun) and the artificial (the electric light bulb).

All the plants we have in the home need varying degrees of light. The nearer this is to the conditions in their native habitat the happier the plants will be. For growth to be *sustained* it is important that the plant receives between 12 and 16 hours of light a day. For nursery men with enormous glasshouses this is easy to achieve and the plants you purchase have been treated in this way before they arrive at the store. How do you then adapt them to the home?

Basics:

1 Only cacti and succulents can be happy with high temperatures and full sunlight. Such conditions are common on windowsills in the Sun Belt states of the US or in the northern states of Australia. Even in the UK in summer such conditions can cause scorching.

2 Plants with variegated leaves require more light than those with plain green leaves. If a variegated plant has little or no variegation move it to a more light-intensive position.

3 There are foliage plants that can survive in little light for *short* periods, such as the aspidistra (see page 40). Plants classified as flowering in this book are *not* able to survive in shade.

4 Many foliage plants, though still requiring light, prefer diffused sunlight. They burn if subjected to bright sunshine and high temperatures.

5 Blue/violet and red are the most important colours of the spectrum for the successful growth of plants; they are obtained in differing quantities from artificial light.

Why plants need light

To grow is the simple answer. The growth of the plant and the development of adequate flowers depends on sufficient light, of the right intensity, being received by the plant. This occurs when the days are long. When nights draw in the plant receives less light and so ceases growing. This is called the rest or dormancy period. It allows the plants to take stock of their situation and prepare for the oncoming growing season.

Measuring light

The intensity of light is measured in lumens. Photographic stores or garden centres sell luxmeters for assessing light.

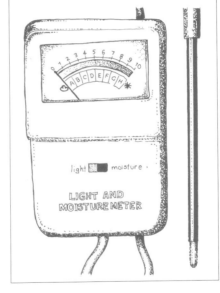

Lack of light

Signs of lack of light:
New leaves may be less intensely coloured and smaller. The older leaves seem pale. The leaf tips or edges are sometimes browned and variegated leaves may become plain green. Little growth, or all growth in one direction and a lack of flowers are also indicators.

Remedies for lack of light:
Rarely the *whole* cause, light starvation problems can be overcome. Consider other possible causes, such as watering, humidity and temperature, in conjunction with light.
1 Move the plant according to its individual light requirements given throughout this book.
2 Look to the basics given above.

Too much light

Signs of too much light:
Despite other suspected causes – such as lack of water – plants still do not thrive and have grey-brown scorch patches or leaves that are similarly coloured. Plants may wilt during the middle period of the day.

Remedies for too much light:
1 Scorching: move the plant to a place with less direct sunshine, e.g. from a windowsill to further back into the room. Direct sunlight through glass is extremely powerful and can burn leaves very fast.
2 Wilting: this may be caused by over- or underwatering, and partly by lack of light. If you suspect your plant has a problem, move it in any case to a position with less direct sunlight.

Artificial light

Ordinary light bulbs (incandescent light) can be used to increase light, though the greater part of their energy is emitted as heat so plants must not be placed too close to a naked bulb in case of scorching. Light from this source is not satisfactory for the long term.

Fluorescent tubes provide a better quality of light for houseplants. Specially manufactured, they can be obtained as straight or circular tubes in a variety of colours. Either 20- or 40- watt, they are fixed in reflector housing which can be sited above a bookshelf or hung from the ceiling. The number of hours of light can be controlled and burning is less likely to occur.

Artificial light has an advantage: tropical plants which in their native habitat are close to the equator receive relatively regular hours of light throughout the year, whereas on windowsills hours of daylight vary considerably between summer and winter. Artificial light compensates for this.

In an average room setting it is important to consider light sources so that the different light requirements of the various plants can be met.

Full sun

Brightly lit

Sunless, but good light

Moderate light, 1.5–2.5m (5–8 ft) from window

Temperature

Plants survive a remarkably wide range of temperatures but what can be fatal is fluctuation of heat. Plants will withstand short periods in temperatures either too high or too low, but in the long term will die.

The right room temperature
The first stage is to consider the temperatures in which *you* want to live, and to select plants that will tolerate those temperatures. The vast range of plants do well with normal heat, given of course that other conditions such as light and humidity are also well suited to their needs. Most plants will tolerate a maximum temperature of 24°C/75°F and minimum of 10°C/50°F. During rest periods for certain groups lower temperatures are preferred, usually during the winter months – down to conditions in which one would not wish to live, such as 10°C/50°F.

Temperature and humidity
For each plant I give the ideal temperature. The second important factor is the ratio between heat and humidity: the higher the temperature the greater the humidity must be. Plants will tolerate summer heat rising to 26–32°C/80–90°F only if there is commensurately an increase in humidity levels. At this time for many of the plants that were used to steamy conditions in their native tropical habitat, trays of damp pebbles become doubly essential. Conservatory rooms should be kept as humid as possible, because the greater area of glass causes temperatures to rise quickly. Good air circulation is important too.

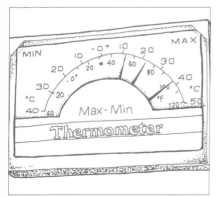

Winter also brings problems for plants. There are draught-hating species and those that wilt with temperature fluctuations – such as when heating systems are turned off during the middle of the day. Whilst temperatures can acceptably be 2–4°C/5–10°F lower during the night than the day, there are danger spots where plants will suffer more.

Measuring temperature
To know precisely what is going on you need a maximum/minimum thermometer which will accurately give you the fluctuation in heat. These are widely available and record differentials over a given period. They are useful for plants that are particularly sensitive to temperature fluctuation, such as *Gardenia* or *Stephanotis*, and for delicate plants in judging, for example, the differences between being in a position at ground level or higher up on a shelf. Temperatures do vary more than you imagine in a relatively small growing area.

The effect of temperature extremes
* Flowering may not occur in species used to different conditions in their native habitat, and that is why in this book I have tried to give as much idea of native circumstances as room permits. If certain plants are used to low or high temperatures for a season and you are unable to give similar conditions then growth will be stunted.
* The plant may wilt despite the compost feeling moist; always try to control temperature changes over a number of *days* rather than hours if the plants are to survive in a healthy condition.
* Growth may die back in extremes of temperature, and a great many of the plants in this book will not survive frost.

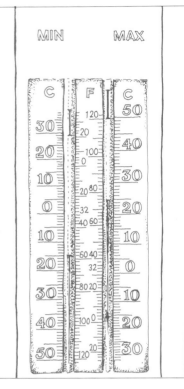

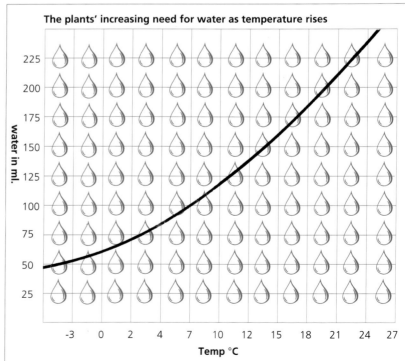
The plants' increasing need for water as temperature rises

Most rooms have different climate areas. It is important to consider these when siting your plants

Doors can be a source of draughts

Windows: if open, draughts may be a problem, but if the window area faces the sun for any length of time it may become very hot

Air-conditioning units may be a source of cold draughts which will harm sensitive leaves

Televisions, fridges, cookers can be sources of intermittent hot air which may or may not suit different house plants. In order to avoid hot draughts many plants would be better sited on a shelf above in order to deflect the full blast

Radiators: hot, dry air can be harmful to many plants

Watering and humidity

Watering

'Not too much', 'not too little', 'just a cupful' – the instructions are endless, both on the care cards of the plants you buy and in the books. But watering is all about common sense and yes, at times, a feel for plants.

I liken watering plants to watering humans. Would you want to stand in a bowl of cold water all day long, or keep drinking and drinking and drinking? Of course not; on the one hand you would get a cold and on the other you would be fit to burst. The same can be said for indoor plants for they are living things just like us, and their roots need both air and water to survive.

Indoor plants come in many sizes, and almost all will benefit from being stood in a bowl or bucket of water for 30 minutes, with the pot totally immersed. Then take them out and allow them to drain thoroughly before putting them back into a room setting. This will give them a really good drink at field capacity, as the professionals say. Wait for the compost to dry out and repeat the dunking process.

If pot plants are already in containers, water them thoroughly, leaving some water in the container to be taken up by the plant. But remember to empty any excess after approximately 30 minutes or the plant will become waterlogged. I have often wished manufacturers would put a lip on the inside, 3cm/1in from the bottom of the container, so that waterlogging would be impossible. **Remember that more plants die from overwatering than from anything else.**

Type of water

Plants do best with water at room temperature. Much tap water has heavy lime content, obviously to be avoided for lime-hating plants such as azaleas. If the water is left in the can or jug to reach room temperature, the chemicals added to the water have a chance to dissipate. Use rain water if possible.

When to water

if the soil feels dry or if the pot feels too light
if the leaves droop and the compost feels dry

Water more frequently

if the plants are grown in unglazed containers as they will require more water than those in ceramic or plastic pots
if heating units are working overtime to cope with drastic temperature drops
if the temperature is higher, i.e. in summer, and if the plant is growing
if plants have not been repotted for a while

Watering whilst on holiday

If you are away for only a few days the plants should be able to cope, if properly watered just before you leave. Beyond that, the best way, if a neighbour cannot help, is to use a capillary mat (available from garden centres). The mat is placed with one end in a sink that is filled half-full of water (make sure the plug doesn't leak!), with the other end over the draining board. Place the plants on the part of the mat which is on the draining board. The mat absorbs the water which is then absorbed by the plants through drainage holes. This method works for plastic pots.

For clay pots, use an oil-lamp wick. One end is planted into the potting medium and the other into a basin of water. Capillary action transfers the water from one to the other.

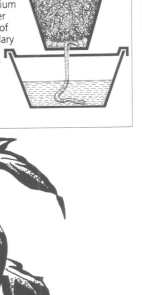

How to water

by immersion – dunk the plant thoroughly in water and wait for the air bubbles to rise to the surface. When they stop, remove the plant and allow it to drain completely before placing in a container.

This is a particularly good method for any plant which does not like water to be in contact with its leaves or crown, such as cyclamen and gloxinias. Orchids and epiphytes thrive on this method of watering, as do azaleas and hydrangeas.

by top surface watering – this method should only be used where there is a good drainage system at the base of the pot. When fertilizer is added to the water, it will be distributed evenly to the potting medium. You will find a watering can with a long narrow spout particularly useful.

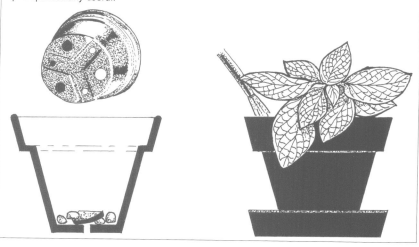

left standing in water – a few of the semi-aquatic plants, such as *Scirpus* and *Cyperus,* all appreciate continually standing in a dish of shallow water. The unglazed clay pots allow air to reach the roots more effectively than the glazed ceramic or plastic pots.

by watering from the bottom – the advantage of this is that you can control the amount of water absorbed by the potting compost, particularly useful for plants that have leaves prone to spotting (due to cold water on the leaves) or to rot (caused by a soggy potting medium). *Episcia* and *Saintpaulia* are often affected. It may be that plants require less fertilizer when watered by this method than when water is allowed to run through the potting medium, carrying the nutrients out through the drainage holes at the bottom.

Bromeliad watering – never allow the central cup of overlapping leaves to dry out. Pour water directly into this cup, for it is in this unique way that the bromeliad quenches its thirst.

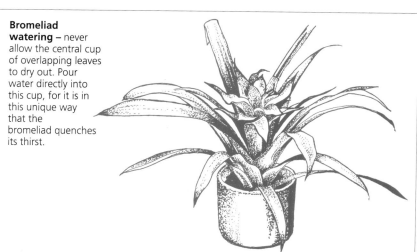

233

Problems of watering

Overwatering
Signs of overwatering:
Green moss on the surface of plants; leaves and flowers falling prematurely; poor growth of the plant generally; new leaves becoming yellow in colour and developing curly edges or soft patches of mould. If the potting medium is waterlogged the roots will rot from lack of oxygen.

Remedies for the overwatered plant:
Remove the plant from its pot and repot into fresh compost into which you have introduced some sand and grit in equal proportions. Loosen the roots gently if possible. Allow the plant to dry out before commencing watering again, and then water less often until the plant's demands appear to change.

Underwatering
Signs of underwatering:
Few flowers develop; flowerbuds and leaves fall prematurely; overall growth is stunted and there may be few or no new flowers developing. When buds come into flower they may fade fast and fall.

Remedies for the underwatered plant:
1 When the compost shrinks back from the sides of the pot, or becomes compacted so that water is not absorbed, the plant should be cut back, properly watered and the following year's growth allowed to develop.
2 An alternative is to remove the plant gently from its pot and to break up the root system including the potting medium – a fork will help. Then dunk the plant up to its neck in water and allow all the air bubbles to escape. Place into a pot with good drainage. Spray the leaves with fine mist and stand the plant in a cool place.

Moisture meters
If you are worried about over- or underwatering your plants you can buy moisture meters or gauges from garden centres or nurseries which will show you the moisture content of the potting compost.

The meter usually comprises a gauge – with either a numbered scale or reading 'Wet', 'Moist' and 'Dry' – attached to a thin probe which is pushed, carefully, into the compost.

Also available are the less elaborate moisture indicator sticks. When these are inserted into the potting mixture they change colour according to the amount of moisture present.

These meters and sticks can be helpful in caring for large delicate plants but they are not an essential piece of equipment for the houseplant gardener.

Confusions between over- and underwatering
It is often difficult to decide what to do if a plant has wilted but the compost is moist: should you water or not? If there is any doubt, don't. The following two conditions are difficult to judge.

Condition
Water runs straight through the potting medium

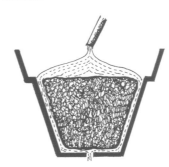

Treatment
The compost is compacted and has shrunk from the sides of the pot. Total immersion treatment is recommended

Condition
The surface of the potting medium becomes clogged and blocks the water from reaching the rooting system

Treatment
The surface should be picked over to allow air in

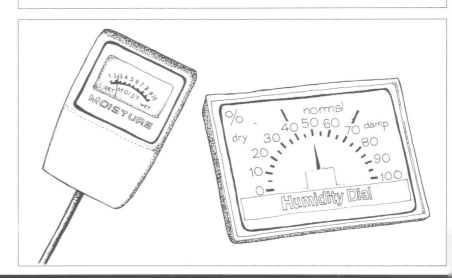

Humidity

As a general rule, plants that grow among dense jungle canopy and in rainforests require high humidity; succulents and cacti, coming from desert regions, require low humidity. Plants with transparently thin leaves need higher levels of humidity than those with thicker, rubbery leaves. The vast majority of plants live happily in moderately humid conditions – that is to say, humidity of around 50–60 per cent in room temperatures of 18–20°C/64–70°F.

Plants absorb moisture from the atmosphere. In summer, when windows are open and plenty of air is circulating, lack of humidity is less of a problem, but in winter dry atmospheres prevail, and heating and air conditioning units make matters worse. Remember, the higher the temperature the greater percentage of humidity is required to keep the plants healthy.

Humidity, after all, is only the measurement of the amount of water in the air. The higher the temperature in a heated room, the more moisture is evaporated from the atmosphere and the drier it becomes. You can purchase hydrometers from garden centres that can measure relative humidity. A humidifier with an air circulation fan can be used in cases of low humidity during winter months and will also prevent furniture from being cracked by heating units doing overtime.

Too much humidity
Signs of too much humidity:
Both leaves and blossoms become covered in patches of grey mould and the plant looks weedy. The leaves near the base of the plant may rot and fall.

Remedies for too much humidity:
Give individual plants more space and open windows a little to allow air to circulate more efficiently. Parts of plants affected with mould should be removed immediately.

Too little humidity
Signs of too little humidity:
Leaf tips become brown and curl under, or the edges may turn yellow; this is particularly true of thin-leaved plants. Newly developing leaves may not reach their right size. Flower buds may die without opening properly.

Remedies for too little humidity:
See 'How to increase humidity' above. A plant must not be allowed to suffer a lack of humidity for too long.

How to increase humidity
The best way to increase moisture in the atmosphere around a plant is to stand it on a tray of pebbles filled with water to just below the top of the pebbles.

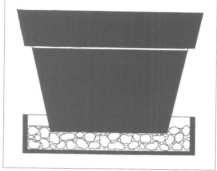

Another method is to sink the plant into a larger pot filled with granules, pebbles or peat.

Misting or spraying the foliage is not a long-term solution to the problem of low humidity. The leaves will be dampened with a fine spray – which is both refreshing and removes dust – but the humidity is improved only for a few moments.

Grouping plants together may help marginally in that an eco-system is produced: each plant will aid the others. Unglazed clay pots are best for this.

Feeding

Like humans, plants need food in order to grow healthily. Photosynthesis (the action of light on chlorophyll in the leaves) produces light energy which combines with gases absorbed from the air (through the leaf's pores) to form carbohydrate – or food. In the plants' natural habitat they absorb essential minerals such as nitrogen, phosphorus and potassium (potash) from the soil. For the home, they are sold in compost that has often been sterilized and had sufficient minerals added to it to last a couple of months. The minerals will gradually drain out through the base of the pot as the plant is watered so thereafter feeding will be necessary. This is particularly important for foliage and flowering plants, though the succulents and cacti can survive a fair amount of starvation.

Look at the label on a bag of compost and you will see what it contains. Some manufacturers add nutrients, others don't. Where peat-based mixes are used begin feeding 6 weeks after purchasing the plant; for repotting, 8 weeks. Loam- or soil-based mixes release nutrients from the soil for a longer period and so can last longer, but again it is important to look at the label on the compost if not mixing with your own soil.

Feeding a plant with foliar food

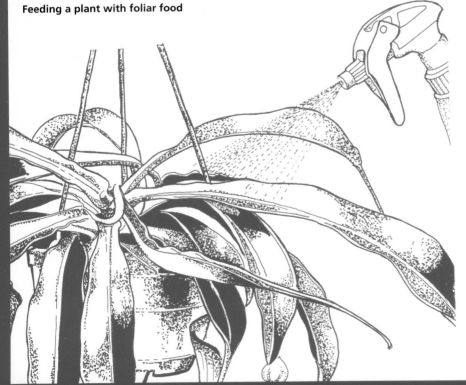

What food does what

Potassium (potash) leads to flowers, and is as essential for indoor plants as it is to those in the garden. A lack of flowers, or fruits, on the ornamental cherry, for example, may be due in greater part to a lack of this mineral. Potassium is also responsible for strong growth. Weak stems on the peace lily could well be due to lack of potash. The sign on the label of your compost may be abbreviated to **K**.

Nitrogen (nitrates) is also responsible for strong stems and for the production of chlorophyll. Yellowing leaves, or indeed yellow spots, are signs of a lack of nitrates. Weak leaf growth in summer can be caused by over-fertilization. The sign on the label of your compost may be abbreviated to **N**.

Phosphorus (phosphates) aids both the development and the growth of new roots and the strength and disease-resistance of the plant. It is also fundamental to the production of flower buds. It is abbreviated to **P** on the compost bag labels.

Trace elements include, amongst others, copper, iron, magnesium, manganese and zinc. These aid processes such as respiration and photosynthesis. They are sometimes shown on the label too.

How fertilizers are sold

General houseplant fertilizers are available from many manufacturers. Garden centres also carry high-nitrate, high-potash (tomato) and high-phosphate fertilizers.

Plant food is sold in different forms – pills, plant sticks, granular, soluble powders, crystals, or in concentrated form to be diluted with water. Foliar food is sprayed on to the leaves where plants have trouble absorbing minerals through the roots system.

Effectiveness
* Foliar foods have an immediate effect, boosting a starved plant.
* Flower spikes release concentrated fertilizer into a small area of the plant, so the roots can develop unevenly if you are not careful. Over-feeding is possible.
* Powders and granules take time to work down from the surface to the roots system where they are required, but they are long lasting.
* Liquid feeding is probably the easiest and most effective method for the majority of plants. It is combined with the watering exercise.
* 'Every time feeding' can be practised by feeding a very weakened dose of liquid fertilizer at each watering, thus keeping up a constant supply of food. This is effective for peat-based composts and annuals.
* There are times when a plant does not need feeding – the resting period. If you do feed it the plant is encouraged to grow rather than rest, a self-defeating exercise.

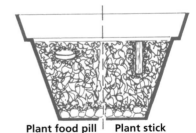

Plant food pill | Plant stick

When to feed

Plants need added nutrition, particularly when emerging from the rest period into a season of growth, budding and flowering. Many plants *prepare* for budding before the rest period: then the buds should be allowed to form before feeding commences, and liquid fertilizer only applied when the plant has a healthy display of buds. Feed at regular intervals during the growing and flowering season and then reduce gradually as the flowers die off and the dormant season approaches.

Grooming

This chiefly concerns leaves. Just as a table surface becomes dusty, so do the leaves of any plant and there are several disadvantages of dusty plants:

* they look unsightly;
* the plant will not be able to 'breathe' efficiently as the leaf pores will be blocked by the dirt. Carbon dioxide, oxygen and water need to be absorbed or emitted from the leaves;
* light will not reach the parts of the plant where photosynthesis occurs in the correct amounts; the plant can literally be 'starved' of light, with devastating consequences;
* industrial dirt is more dangerous to indoor plants than practically anything else; in particular, fumes from oil or gas heating systems or from stoves can damage the future growth of the indoor plant.

How to groom plants

Dust and dirt should be gently sponged from the leaves of houseplants. This can be done with a sponge or damp cloth – do not use a duster which deposits fluff all over the place. Dip the cloth or sponge in tepid water and only use a little household soap if water is apparently not strong enough (then rinse thoroughly). Take care with the stems of plants; they should be supported as they are easily broken when the leaves are dusted.

Leaves which have deep indentations because of veining may need more severe treatment than just a damp cloth wiped over the surface. A soft, dryish brush (even an old toothbrush) can do wonders to remove dust from quilted leaves.

Leaves should only be cleaned (or wetted) when there is time for them to dry out during daylight hours. If the plants have moist leaves through the hours of darkness disease may attack the plants.

Many plants welcome dusting by total immersion in tepid water.

Leaf shine

Many proprietary potions are marketed in liquid form and have been successful because they give leaves a 'rejuvenating' shine. At the same time, however, long-term use of leaf shine lotion may well block the pores on the leaf's surface, causing damage. Leaf shine is therefore only recommended for the very short term.

Deadheading indoor plants

Indoor plants need to look good – compact and flourishing, with plenty of new growth and flower buds in prospect. Seed heads should not be allowed to develop and, as flowers begin to die back, the flower heads should be removed. Many a healthy plant can be drained of energy if seed is allowed to set. *Primula* and *Hippeastrum* are two good examples where the flower head should be discarded immediately following flowering. *Cyclamen* requires both the flower and flower stalk to be removed.

Shaping plants

A well-shaped plant attracts praise; one that is allowed to become straggly will need a great deal of work if it is ever to recover its shape. Summer-flowering plants do best if they are trimmed in winter before the spring growing period which sees the plant into bud. 'Pruning' (page 237) deals with this.

Cosmetic improvements

* Leaf tips that have browned can be trimmed up.
* Pruning should be done to just above a leaf axil.
* Support weak growth with good sturdy poles. The more natural such supports are, the better the overall appearance of the plant.

Propagation

Propagation is undertaken for two reasons:
1 to increase supply
2 to replenish stock too old to go on sensibly

Many of the plants chosen for this book can be multiplied easily and simply, without the use of a heated propagator. There are two main methods of propagation:
1 Planting the seeds ripened on flower heads through the sexual act of pollination
2 Vegetative propagation (asexual) which can be as basic as removing an offset (e.g. *Clivia*) or dividing a clump (e.g. *Zantedeschia*), or by leaf cutting (e.g. *Streptocarpus*) or by stem cutting (e.g. *Fuchsia*) or by replication (e.g. *Tolmiea*).

Here we will outline the various methods, many of which become totally engrossing – there is nothing more rewarding than watching the first flowers on a seedling you have grown yourself, or the stem-tip cutting that has been painstakingly rooted over 2 or 3 months.

Division
Characteristics: Plants that usually grow in clumps. Species that produce rosettes are particularly suitable. Best done in spring or autumn.
Propagation: Remove plant from pot, gently ease away compost to separate as much root system as possible from 'division'. Use a sharp knife if necessary. Replant parent carefully and pot on divided segment into fresh cutting compost. Fill pot to avoid any air pockets.

Offsets and plantlets
Characteristics: Identical to parent plant. Appear at plant base or on secondary stems. May have roots already. Usually seen to develop after parent plant has flowered.
Propagation: Cut away carefully as near the main stem as possible once suitable size is reached. Use a sharp knife. Push offset down into fairly moist compost. Support if necessary and keep warm, with just sufficient water until new growth appears.

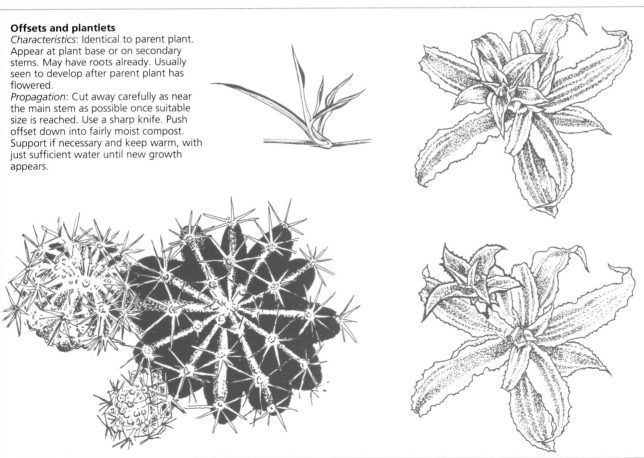

Leaf cuttings

Characteristics: New plants develop from leaf stalk or base of leaf or segment.
Propagation: Use mature leaf and stalk, cut from parent and insert into pre-made hold in pre-moistened compost. Use rooting bag or propagator if possible.

 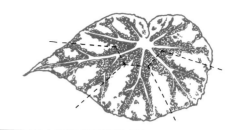

Stem-tip or slip cuttings

Characteristics: Soft-stemmed plants root easily. More commonly practised on woody-stemmed plants. Tip cuttings are taken from new growth. Good for the many plants that do not grow true to species from seed. Usually dipped in hormone rooting powder. Most successful in spring or autumn.

Propagation: Essential is a sharp knife to cut cleanly without damage to the cutting. Make incision below node. Try to have 3 nodes, as close together as possible. Dip in rooting powder and insert cutting into pre-made hole, in centre of pot filled with pre-moistened compost. Firm up soil to cutting. Cause as little damage as possible or decay will set in. Rooting bags or propagators are useful for bringing stem cuttings on.

Seed

Characteristics: Few indoor plants can be raised easily in this way. Mainly annuals. Large numbers can be grown. Demanding and difficult except where specifically recommended.
Propagation: Use mixture of sand and peat. Keep at temperatures of 21–28°C/70–75°F. Heating cables are available – both for small trays and greenhouse use. Seed should be sown as evenly and sparingly as possible. The more the seed is like dust the less soil it should be covered with. The general rule is to cover seed with the equivalent of its diameter. Cover seed tray or put in polythene bad until seedlings appear. Water delicately if compost dries out.

Air layering

Characteristics: Used for plants that will not root easily from cuttings. Suitable for thick-stemmed plants. Parent plant not harmed; stem will usually shoot again when layering has been removed.
Propagation: Take accessible stem and strip bark from 1–2cm/Hin section below node (point where stem and leaf join, usually obvious but occasionally only marked by thickening in stem). Paint with rooting hormone powder. Wrap damp spaghnum moss round the wound. Seal into a polythene bag at both ends. Dampen moss only when absolutely essential. Allow nature to take its course: roots will develop in 6–8 weeks and fill the moss. Remove plastic, cut below the moss rootball, which is now firmly fixed, and pot up new plant. Now treat as mature plant.

Important factors

Compost: the right kind of soil, though even that may be poor in composition. 'Fine' is the most important word to stress; if the soil is too coarse, dense or impenetrable the propagation will not work. Half sand, half peat is as ideal as you'll get home-made.

Position: Light makes most plants grow and is important in generating new growth or germination. Warm, sunny (but not scorching) and constantly high temperatures around 21°C/70°F help a great deal.

Watering: The tendency is to overwater. On the other hand compost should not be allowed to dry out ever (or the growth that has been made, albeit undetectable, will fail).

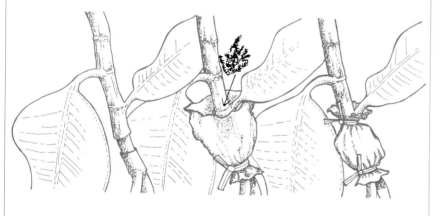

Pruning

Why prune?
Plants bred for cultivation indoors have, on the whole, been hybridized and hybridized again, to give specimens that do not require much pruning, as opposed to outdoor garden plants which need to be kept in check. But there are reasons to prune:

to keep the plant under control
to keep it well shaped
to encourage further flowering
to achieve a goal, such as training on to hoop

When to prune
The onset of the growing season is the optimum time for major cutting back; if this is done at other times of the year the growth of dormant buds may well become stunted.

When *not* to prune
Always consider with flowering plants whether the blooms develop on new or mature growth. Then prune as and when the 'Care' sections of this book specify.

How to prune
Pinching out: this is the most obvious form of pruning and is usually done by hand, though it may be done with secateurs or a razor blade. Pinch out above a node on the stem. This minor pruning encourages bushiness and is therefore particularly good for many recently established plants. It is also useful in preventing more mature plants from becoming straggly.

Cutting back
This is done to encourage certain plants to flower more profusely and to keep the plant vigorous. Sharp secateurs or scissors should be used to cut cleanly. Do not break stems or crush them, otherwise there is a danger of rot setting in. Cut straight across the stem first, above a node, or cut from above the node sloping down to the other side of the plant.

What to prune
1 Start with any obviously dead or diseased parts of the plant. Then remove weak stems and those that have grown straggly.

2 Tackle over-long and often leafless stalks next. Always deadhead the plant or it will put energy into producing seed rather than growth.

3 Remove any all-green growth which develops on a variegated specimen to prevent plant reverting.

Advantages of pruning
1 Plants are encouraged to become bushy.

2 Air circulation is increased once unwanted stems are removed.

3 More light reaches the plant.

Training

Supports and climbing

Many tropical plants use other vegetation in their native habitat to support their growth. As indoor plants they need a structure on which to climb and lean. These can be provided using a variety of resources – wire or plastic, cane and rattan structures, moss-covered poles or twine. Below I give a few ideas for methods of training on various supports.

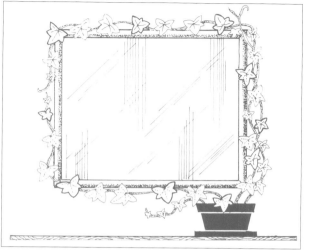

Training around household objects

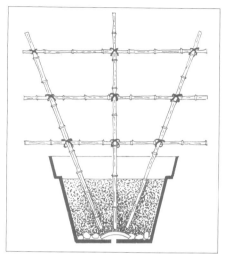

Cane trellis

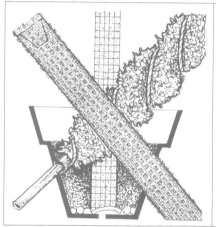

Training around a moss pole (behind) or a wire netting pole (front)

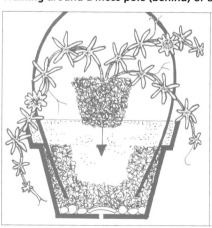

Training around a hoop

Repotting and potting on

What is repotting?

There is a great deal of confusion between *repotting* – literally removing a plant from its pot and repotting it in the same container, perhaps with fresh soil – and *potting on* – moving a plant into a larger sized pot. The most important reason to repot or pot on is when a plant shows signs of distress: repotting rejuvenates, potting on allows further development.

The time to repot/pot on

* When plants are potbound and have no room to grow larger root systems.
* When the leaves discolour from lack of nutrients taken from the soil, which has become exhausted.
* When the plant outgrows the pot – this happens frequently in certain plants during the early part of the growing period.

The optimum time to pot on is when the growth season is commencing – for most plants in early spring – so that the new growth has room to develop properly. Never repot unless you have to during the dormant period.

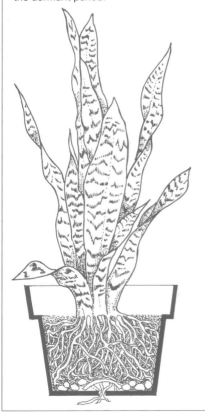

Repotting

Remove the pot. Gently discard about 4cm/1½in soil from the surface of the compost, taking care not to expose the roots. Prune the roots if the plant is really potbound. This should only be done in drastic cases or to encourage new growth where roots are blackened and decaying, but plants need very special care to survive the experience. Ensure good drainage and repot the plant using fresh compost to top dress it to its original level. Indoor plant fertilizer can be incorporated into the dressing.

Pots

Clay, terracotta and plastic ones are commonly available. Each has advantages and disadvantages. Terracotta and clay look more natural than plastic, and hence suit some plants better than others. Plastic ones are 'unbreakable', although they do split on occasion: they come in a range of different colours – browny red, green, black and cream are commonly seen.

Pots are normally round and as wide as they are deep (i.e. the diameter = the depth). There are square pots too, and half-pots, useful for shallow-rooted plants.

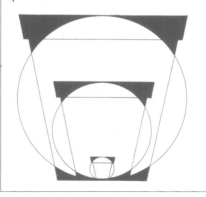

The potting on process

1 Begin by immersing the plant in a bucket of tepid rain water for an hour to give it a thorough soaking. Remove any moss that has grown on the surface of the soil.

2 Choose an appropriately sized new pot, ideally just a little bigger than the previous one. (New, unglazed clay ones should be soaked in water until air bubbles cease to rise to the water's surface; this prevents them from absorbing the moisture intended for the plant.) Why shouldn't you choose a much bigger plant to avoid the messy repotting business and provide for years of future growth? Because the compost becomes sour with age, and, with the extra amount of compost not occupied by the roots, the plant stands a much higher chance of becoming waterlogged.

3 Set up the new pot with good drainage: a concave crock from an old broken pot to cover the hole in clay pots, and a shallow layer of pebbles over the many holes in plastic pots will suffice. Top this with a layer of appropriate compost, then place the plant on top. Fill the sides with more of the new compost. Pack it in firmly but gently. Air pockets should be forced out but the compost should not be so compact that water cannot penetrate it. Water the new compost thoroughly around the edges of the pot from the top, ensuring it drains well.

Removing the old pot

This can be difficult and exasperating. Turn the plant over and tap the base firmly. A sharp knife can be used to loosen the sides. In extreme cases you may have to push a blunt piece of wood up through the drainage holes or even break the pot.

Compost and potting mix

Compost is the source from which indoor plants can thrive and flourish. It comes in two different types – soil-based (loam) and soil-less (peat). Loam is good-quality soil which has been mixed with coarse sand and peat, together with additional plant foods.

Indoor plants do well in both but due to the variability of good loam most commercial nurseries use more peat-based composts.

Advantages of loam-based compost
* The weight of the potting mixture is able to support larger plants.
* It dries out more slowly than a peat-based compost.

Disadvantages of loam-based compost
* Not easy to gauge quality as the composition of the soil is uncertain. Always buy from a reputable supplier.

Advantages of peat-based compost
* Quality does not vary.
* It is lighter and easier to handle.

Disadvantages of peat-based compost
* It can be difficult to water once it has dried out.
* Due to its lightness there is little anchorage when potting on a large plant.

Exceptions
Orchids and cacti all need specially mixed composts, which are widely available at superstores and garden centres.

There are a range of composts readily available to meet your every need, but first read the instructions carefully to ensure that you have the right product.

Acidity/Alkalinity
Indoor (and indeed many garden) plants prefer a slightly acidic soil to an alkaline soil. The tell-tale sign of unsuitable soil is the leaves turning yellow (chlorosis, see glossary).

The term Hydrogen ion concentration (pH) is used to measure acidity/alkalinity in soil. The scale is from 0–14 with 7 being neutral. Soil-testing kits are readily available at garden centres. The band that indoor plants will tolerate on the pH scale is between 4.5 and 8, i.e. on the acidic side.

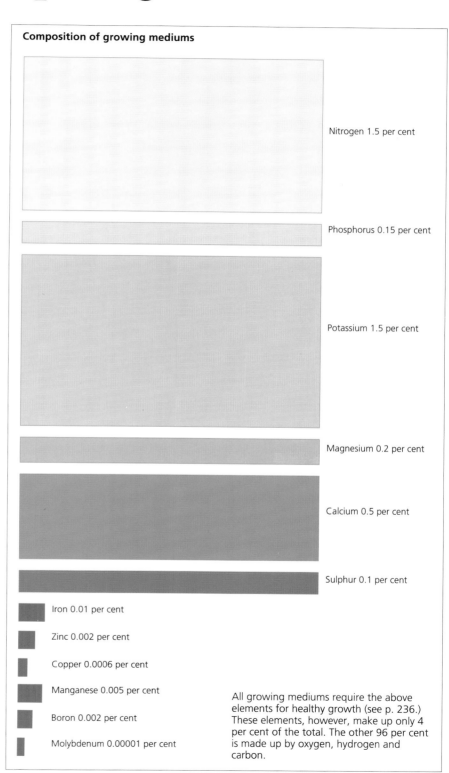

Composition of growing mediums

Nitrogen 1.5 per cent

Phosphorus 0.15 per cent

Potassium 1.5 per cent

Magnesium 0.2 per cent

Calcium 0.5 per cent

Sulphur 0.1 per cent

Iron 0.01 per cent

Zinc 0.002 per cent

Copper 0.0006 per cent

Manganese 0.005 per cent

Boron 0.002 per cent

Molybdenum 0.00001 per cent

All growing mediums require the above elements for healthy growth (see p. 236.) These elements, however, make up only 4 per cent of the total. The other 96 per cent is made up by oxygen, hydrogen and carbon.

243

Pests and diseases

Pests

Small pests do a great deal of harm to indoor plants, and their size often allows them to go undetected until the infestation is serious. Watch for the following and treat as detailed below, making sure the pest is properly eradicted and will not reappear.

Mealy bug
The creature: named for the white, mealy wax that coats it, below which is the pinkish body. Excretes 'honeydew' which in turn draws ants. Sap sucker.
Signs: visible with human eye in leaf axils, or on leaves. Forms colonies (woolly patches). Leaves yellow, wilt fast then fall.
Treatment: wipe off with methylated spirit swabs or spray with diluted malathion. Can be picked off individually. Granular pesticide can be added to the potting mix.

Vine weevils
The creature: grub is cream-coloured, up to 2.5cm/1in long, living in potting compost and eating roots of plant. Develops into similarly sized dark brown/black beetle which chews leaves. Rosette-shaped succulents (e.g. *sansevieria*) often attacked.
Signs: badly stunted new growth, often wilted. Grubs fall from compost. Leaves have chewed patches.
Treatment: once badly infected, discarding plant is probably the best solution. Remove and destroy beetles. Immediately spray both plant leaves and compost with pesticide, repeating once a week for 2 weeks

Root mealy bug
The creature: similar to mealy bug, sucks the sap from roots. Cacti, succulents and African violets are prone.
Signs: wilted leaves, stunted growth. When plant roots are exposed white woolly bugs can be seen.
Treatment: where roots are badly affected cut away, soak remainder in solution of pesticide before repotting in new compost. The entire compost should be drenched 3 times over 6 weeks with systemic insecticide where plants are too big to have roots exposed.

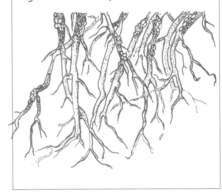

Leaf miners
The creature: grub of a small fly; long, thin caterpillar-like. Sap sucking, it tunnels through the surface layers of leaves. Chrysanthemums and cinerarias particularly prone.
Signs: can be seen occasionally, more often long, white, irregular pattern develops quickly on leaf.
Treatment: discard all affected leaves. Spray plant with pesticide or use systemic insecticide on plant compost.

Whitefly
The creature: Young larva is greenish, mature insect up to 4mm/⅛in long, mothlike and white. Attacks underside of leaves, depositing sticky 'honeydew'; infestation multiplies quickly. Sap sucking. Usually found on flowering plants, particularly pelargoniums. Excreta encourages black mould (see page 245).
Signs: small white blobs apparent when plant gently tapped. Leaf growth distorted.
Treatment: spray with malathion, pyrethrum or dust with derris. Change pesticide used as whitefly quickly becomes resilient to a constantly applied formula.

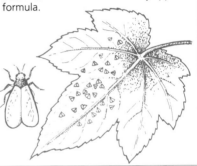

Aphids/greenfly/plant lice
The creature: six-legged insect up to 4mm/⅛in long when mature, usually green but can be brown or grey. Attacks all parts of plant, especially soft tissue – growth tips and flower buds – sucking sap, depositing sticky 'honeydew' from which black mould (see page 245) easily develops. Carries incurable viral disease. All plants bar bromeliads may be infested.
Signs: distorted leaf growth, sticky patches, leading to black mould.
Treatment: spray with malathion or dust with derris powder according to instructions on packet.

Red spider mite
The creature: small, red or pinky, 8-legged insect that deposits black dots (excreta) on leaves. Sap sucker.
Signs: yellowing leaves, black spots; confirm with magnifying glass.
Treatment: remove badly affected leaves; spray remainder with malathion or a systemic insecticide or use derris dust. Treat until all signs of infestation have gone.

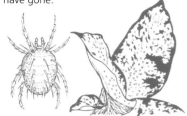

Cyclamen mite
The creature: Minute 8-legged insect, but eggs appearing as dust coating on underside of leaves. Sap sucking. Attacks cyclamen and other plants.
Signs: leaves curl eventually becoming covered with scabs, buds wither, stems become twisted.
Treatment: spray over a period of months with pesticide until no signs of egg dust. If plant doesn't respond, discard.

Thrips/thunderfly
The creature: tiny winged insect, usually blackish, jumps rather than flies from plant to plant. Sap sucker. Attacks soft-tissued plants.
Signs: Excreta on leaves or flowers turns black. Patches of silvery streaking or mottling appear on any part of plant.
Treatment: remove seriously infected growth and spray remainder with malathion or dust with derris powder.

Scale insect
The creature: up to 4mm/⅛in long. When young it moves around plant but when mature stays in one place, usually the underside of a leaf near central vein, covering itself with waxlike brown oval disc. Sucks sap, excretes 'honeydew', possibly causing black mould. All plants can get scale, particularly ferns and citrus families.
Signs: leaves wither and may become infested with ants; sticky patches of mould appear.
Treatment: remove by hand if possible, using cotton wool swabs dipped in methylated spirit. Treat over a period to ensure infestation is completely dealt with. Spray whole plant with pesticide afterwards – however, spraying is not wholly effective against protective wax coating of mature scale insect.

Diseases

Overwatering and poor air circulation allow disease to become established. Pests can transmit diseases, and a plant is more prone to a disease if it is damaged. On the whole, however, there are not many diseases that you have to deal with. The main ones are:

Black or sooty mould
Signs: a fungus that grows on the sticky 'honeydew' secreted by sap-sucking insects. Quite a thick layer of 'soot' appears on the upper side of the leaf. It feels sticky, clogs up the pores and reduces photosynthesis in the leaf by blocking light. Damages plant in long term and its appearance in short term. Members of the citrus family are particularly prone.
Treatment: Eradicate the insects causing this disease and use soapy water to wash off mould.

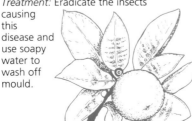

Botrytis/grey mould
Signs: A fungus affecting soft-stemmed plants, which can be introduced from water lodging in leaf axils. Cool, dampish still air is perfect for development of botrytis. Both leaves and stems can become covered with fluffy grey mould, occasionally buds and flowers too.
Treatment: Discard affected and fading parts of the plant. Use a fungicide/benomyl. Increase air circulation and move to a warmer, drier position.

Blackleg/black stem rot
Signs: affects plants where stem and compost meet, and spreads both up and down the stem. Rot sets in and the plant dies. The plant should be burnt. Pelargoniums are susceptible.
Avoidance treatment: the cause is a potting mix that has been too wet over a period. Avoid this mistake by using good draining compost. Cuttings should always be taken with a sharp knife to avoid damage, which can allow blackleg to set in. Dip cuttings in hormone rooting powder containing fungicide.

Powdery mildew
Signs: grows on surface of the leaves, marking them with a white powdery deposit.
Treatment: remove badly marked leaves and spray with systemic fungicide or dust with sulphur.

Useful addresses

Below I give a list of addresses which I hope will be of use to you, wherever you live. For the United Kingdom I have listed garden centres that are members of the Garden Centre Association and who sell plants for the home. For Canada and Australia I give the main horticultural societies, from which you can receive much information about plants and suppliers in your area.

UNITED KINGDOM

All-in-One Garden Centre
Rochdale Road
Slattocks
Middleton
Manchester M24 2RB
Tel: 0706 32793

Alton Garden Centre
Arterial Road
Wickford
Essex SS12 9JG
Tel: 0268 726421

Armitage Pennine Garden Centre
Shelley
Huddersfield
Yorkshire HD8 8LG
Tel: 0484 607248

Astbury Meadow Garden Centre
Newcastle Road
Astbury
Congleton
Cheshire CW12 4RL
Tel: 0260 276466

Auldene Garden Centre
Southport Road
Ulnes Walton
Leyland
Lancashire PR5 3LQ
Tel: 0772 600271

Aylett Nurseries
North Orbital Road
London Colney
St Albans
Hertfordshire AL2 1DH
Tel: 0727 822255

Badshot Lea Garden Centre
(Caffyn Parsons Ltd)
Nr Farnham
Surrey GU9 9JK
Tel: 0252 333666

Peter Barratt's Garden Centre
Head office
Gosforth Park
Newcastle-upon-Tyne
Tyne & Wear NE3 5EN
Tel: 091 236 7111

Barton Grange Garden Centre
Barton
Preston
Lancashire PR3 5AA
Tel: 0772 864242

Baytree Nurseries Garden Centre
High Road
Weston
Spalding
Lincolnshire PE12 6JU
Tel: 0406 370242

Bayley's Garden Centre
Bayston Hill Nurseries
Shrewsbury
Shropshire SY3 0DA
Tel: 0743 874261

Bents Nurseries & Garden Centre
Warrington Road
Glazebury
Lancashire WA3 5NT
Tel: 0942 671028/262066

Bernhard's Rugby Garden & Leisure Centre
Bilton Road
Rugby
Warwickshire CV22 7DT
Tel: 0788 811500

Bickerdike's Garden Centre
London Road
Sandy
Bedfordshire SG19 1DW
Tel: 0767 680559

Birds Garden Centre
Cowbridge
South Glamorgan
South Wales CF7 7YP
Tel: 0446 772001

Bloomingdales Garden Centre
150 Staines Road
Laleham
Staines
Middlesex TW18 2SF
Tel: 0784 460832

Booker Garden & Leisure Centre
Clay Lane
Booker
Marlow
Buckinghamshire SL7 3DH
Tel: 0494 533945

Bourne End Garden Centre
Hedsor Road
Bourne End
Buckinghamshire SL8 5EE
Tel: 06285 23926/29411

Bournville Garden Centre
Maple Road Bournville
Birmingham
West Midlands B30 1AE
Tel: 021 472 0303/8812

Brambridge Park Garden Centre
Kiln Lane
Brambridge
Eastleigh
Hampshire SO5 7HT
Tel: 0962 713707

Brampton Garden Centre
Buckden Road
Brampton
Huntingdon
Cambridgeshire
Tel: 0480 453048

Bridgemere Garden World
Bridgemere
Cheshire CW5 7QB
Tel: 09365 381/239

Burford Garden Centre
Shilton Road
Burford
Oxfordshire
Tel: 0993 823117

Burleydam Garden Centre
E. H. Williams (Nurseries) Ltd
Chester Road
Little Sutton
South Wirral
Cheshire L66 1QW
Tel: 051 339 3195

Bybrook Barn Produce & Garden Centre
Canterbury Road
Ashford
Kent TN24 9JZ
Tel: 0233 631959

Byrkley Park Centre
Rangemore
Burton-on Trent
Staffordshire DE13 9RN
Tel: 0283 716467

Cadbury Garden Centre
Smallway
Congresbury
Avon BS19 5AA
Tel: 0934 876464

Cantilever Garden Centre
(R Tilling & Company Ltd)
Station Road
Latchford
Warrington
Cheshire WA4 2AB
Tel: 0925 35799

Carnon Downs Garden Centre
Quenchwell Road
Carnon Downs
Truro
Cornwall TR3 4LN
Tel: 0782 863058

Chatsworth Garden Centre
Calton Lees
Beeley
Matlock
Derbyshire DE4 2NX
Tel: 0629 734004

Cheal's Garden Centre
Horsham Road
Crawley
Sussex RH11 8PL
Tel: 0293 522101

Chenies Garden Centre
Chenies
Hertfordshire WD3 6EN
Tel: 0494 763545

Clacton Garden Centre
St John's Road
Clacton-on-Sea
Essex CO16 8DY
Tel: 0225 425711

Clay's Garden Centre
Silksworth Lane
Sunderland
Tyne & Wear SR3 1PD
Tel: 091 522 0911

Country Garden Centres plc
Head office
Turnpike Road
Thatcham
Berkshire RG13 3AN
Tel: 0635 873700

Cowells Garden Centre
Ponteland Road
Woolsington
Newcastle-upon-Tyne
Tyne & Wear NE13 8BW
Tel: 091 286 3403

Crowders Garden Centre
Lincoln Road
Horncastle
Lincolnshire LN9 5LZ
Tel: 0507 525252

Daisy Nook Garden Centre
Medlock Hall
Daisy Nook
Failsworth
Lancashire M35 9WJ
Tel: 061 681 4245

Donaghadee Garden Centre
34 Stockbridge Road
Donaghadee
Co. Down
Northern Ireland BT21 0PN
Tel: 0247 883603/883237

Duncans of Milngavie
Flower & Garden Centre
101 Main Street
Milngavie
Glasgow
Strathclyde G62 6JJ
Tel: 041 956 2377

Edem Park Garden Centre
Grove End
Tunstall
Sittingbourne
Kent ME9 8DY
Tel: 0795 478108/471583

Endsleigh Garden Centre
Ivybridge
Devon PL21 9JL
Tel: 0752 892254

Ferndale Nursery & Garden Centre
Dyche Lane
Coal Aston
Sheffield
Derbyshire S18 6AB
Tel: 0246 412763

Findlay Clark Garden Centre (Aberdeen)
Hazlehead Garden Centre
Hazledene Road
Aberdeen
Grampian AB9 2QU
Tel: 0224 318658

Turfhills
Head office
Boclair Road
Milngavie
Glasgow G62 6EP
Tel: 0360 20721

Forest Lodge Garden Centre
Holt Pound
Surrey GU10 4LD
Tel: 0420 23275

Forth Valley Garden Centre
18 Cauldcoats
Linlithgow EH49 7LY
Tel: 0506 834346

Frinton Road Nurseries
Kirby Cross
Frinton-on-Sea
Essex CO13 0PD
Tel: 0225 674838

Frosts Garden Centre
Newport Road
Woburn Sands
Milton Keynes
Buckinghamshire MK17 8UE
Tel: 0908 583511

Fruit Export Garden Centre
Les Banques
St Peter Port
Guernsey
Channel Islands
Tel: 0481 723881

Garden Paradise
Avis Road
Newhaven
East Sussex BN9 0DH
Tel: 0273 512123

Garson Farm Garden Centre
Winterdown Road
Esher
Surrey KT10 8LS
Tel: 0372 462261

Gateacre Garden Centre
E. H. Williams (Nurseries) Ltd
Acrefield Road
Liverpool
Merseyside L25 5JW
Tel: 051 428 6556

Gordale Nurseries
Chester High Road
Burton
South Wirral
Cheshire L64 8TF
Tel: 051 336 2116

Roger Harvey Garden World
The Farm House
Bragbury Lane
Stevenage
Hertfordshire SG2 8TJ
Tel: 0438 811777

Haskins Garden Centre
Head office
Tricketts Cross
Ferndown
Dorset BH22 9AL
Tel: 0202 872282

Hayes Gardenworld
Lake District Nurseries
Ambleside
Cumbria LA22 0DW
Tel: 0539 433434/5

Heighley Gate Nursery Garden Centre
Morpeth
Northumberland NE61 3DA
Tel: 0670 513416

High Legh Garden Centre
High Legh
Nr Knutsford
Cheshire WA16 0QW
Tel: 0925 756991

Hillier Garden Centres
Head office
The Stables
Ampfield House
Hampshire SO51 9BQ
Tel: 0794 68944/68733

Holland Arms Garden Centre
Gaerwen
Anglesey
Gwynedd
North Wales LL60 6LA
Tel: 0248 421655

Hurrans Garden Centre
Head office
Unit B Staverton Technology Park
Gloucester Road
Staverton
Gloucester GL5 6TQ
Tel: 0452 714111

Jackmans The Garden Centre
Egley Road
Mayford
Woking
Surrey GU22 0NH
Tel: 0483 714861

Jack's Patch Garden Centre
Bishopsteignton
Teignmouth
Devon TQ14 9PN
Tel: 0626 776996

Jardinerie
Bath Road
Haresfield
Gloucestershire GL10 3DP
Tel: 0452 721081/723823

Kennedys Garden Centre
Head office
Kennedy House
11 Crown Row
Bracknell
Berkshire RG12 3TH

Kiln Nurseries
Common Road
Stanmore
Middlesex HA7 3JF
Tel: 081 954 8029

Knights Garden Centre
Head office
Rosedene Nursery
Woldingham Road
Woldingham
Surrey CR3 7LA
Tel: 0883 653142

The Landscape Centre
J. K. Nurseries
24 Donegore Hill
Dunadry
Antrim
Northern Ireland BT41 2QU
Tel: 08494 32175

Marlows DIY & Garden Centre
Hollow Road
Bury St Edmunds
Suffolk IP32 7AP
Tel: 0284 763155

Mayfield Garden Centre (Sinclair Horticulture
& Leisure)
Kelso
Borders TD5 7AU
Tel: 0573 224124

Mid Ulster Garden Centre
Station Road
Mahera
County Londonderry
Northern Ireland BT46 5BS
Tel: 0648 42324

Millbrook Garden Centre
Tubwell Lane
Jarvis Brook
Crowborough
East Sussex TN6 3RJ
Tel: 0892 663822

Millets Farm Garden Centre
Kingston Road
Frilford
Abingdon
Oxfordshire OX13 5HB
Tel: 0865 391923

Monkton Elm Nurseries & Garden Centre
West Monkton
Taunton
Somerset TA2 8QN
Tel: 0823 412381/413123

Narey's Garden Centre
Bury Road
Stowmarket
Suffolk IP14 3DQ
Tel: 0449 612559

North Devon Garden Centre
Ashford
Devon EX31 4BW

Notcutts Garden Centre
Head office
Woodbridge
Suffolk IP12 4AF
Tel: 0394 383344

Otter Nurseries Garden Centre
Head office
Gosford Road
Ottery-St-Mary
Devon EX11 1LZ
Tel: 0404 815815

Pennell & Sons Ltd
Head office
Neward Road
South Hykeham
Lincoln
Lincolnshire LN6 9NS
Tel: 0552 682088/500091

Pilkington Garden Centre
Bold Heath
Nr Widnes
Cheshire WA8 0UU
Tel: 051 424 6264

Planters Garden Centre
Woodlands Farm
Freasley
Tamworth
Staffordshire
Tel: 0827 251511

Plymouth Garden Centre
Bowden Battery
Fort Austin Avenue
Crownhill
Plymouth
Devon PL6 5NU
Tel: 0752 771820

Podington Garden Centre
High Street Podington
Wellinborough
Northamptonshire NN9 7HS
Tel: 0933 53656

Polhill Garden Centre
London Road
Badgers Mount
Sevenoaks
Kent TN14 7BD
Tel: 0959 534212

Ransoms Garden Centre
St Martin
Jersey
Channel Islands JE3 6EB
Tel: 0534 56699

Redfields Nursery & Garden Centre
Ewshot Lane
Church Crookham
Fleet
Hampshire GU13 0UB

Roots & Shoots Garden Centre
Nags Head Lane
Upminster
Essex RM14 1TS
Tel: 0708 342469

Roots Garden Centre
1 Caskieberran Road
Glanrothes
Fife KY6 2NR
Tel: 0592 756407/756236

Rouken Glen Garden Centre
Rouken Glen Road
Giffnock
Glasgow G46 7JL
Tel: 041 620 0566

Roundstone Garden Centre
Angmering
West Sussex BN16 4BD
Tel: 0903 776481/2/3

Ruxley Manor Garden Centre
Maidstone Road
Sidcup
Kent DA14 5BQ
Tel: 081 300 0084

Scotsdale Nursery & Garden Centre
120 Cambridge Road
Great Shelford
Cambridgeshire CB2 5JT
Tel: 0223 842777

Secretts Garden Centre (F. A. Secrett Ltd)
Old Portsmouth Road
Milford
Nr Godalming
Surrey GU8 5HL
Tel: 0483 426633

Stephen H. Smith Garden & Leisure Centre
Head office
Wharfe Valley
Pool Road
Otley
West Yorkshire LS21 1DY
Tel: 0943 462195

Snowhill Plant & Garden Centre
Snowhill Lane
Copthorne
Crawley
Sussex
Tel: 0342 712 545

South Ockendon Garden Centre
South Road
South Ockendon
Essex RM15 6DU
Tel: 0708 851991

Squires Garden Centre
Head office
Sixth Cross Road
Twickenham
Middlesex TW2 5PA
Tel: 081 977 9241/2/3

St Bridget Nurseries & Garden Centre
Head office
Old Rydon Lane
Exeter
Devon EX2 7JY
Tel: 0392 873672/3/4

St Peters Garden Centre
St Peter
Jersey
Channel Islands JE3 7BP
Tel: 0534 45903

Stewarts Country Garden Centre
God's Blessing Lane
Broomhill
Holt
Nr Winborne
Dorset BH21 7DF
Tel: 0202 882462

Stewarts Garden-Lands
Lyndhurst Road
Somerford
Christchurch
Dorset BH23 4SA
Tel: 0425 272244

William Strike Ltd
Elton
Stockton-on-Tees
Cleveland TS21 1AQ
Tel: 0642 583838

Strikes Garden Centre
Urley Nook Road
Eaglescliffe
Cleveland
TS16 0PE
Tel: 0642 780481

Styles Garden Centre
Moles Lane
Marldon
Paignton
Devon TQ3 1SY
Tel: 0803 873056

Syon Park Garden Centre
Syon Park
Brentford
Middlesex TW8 8JG
Tel: 081 568 0134

Trebaron Garden Centre
350 Common Edge Road
South Shore
Blackpool
Lancashire FY4 5DY
Tel: 0253 691368

Van Hage's Garden Centre
Great Amwell
Ware
Hertfordshire
SG12 9RP
Tel: 0920 870811

Weaver Vale Garden Centre
Winnington Lane
Northwich
Cheshire CW8 4EE
Tel: 0606 79965
Clarence Webb & Co. Ltd

Webbs Garden Centre
Burneside Road
Kendal
Cumbria LA9 4RT

Webbs of Wychbold
Wychbold
Droitwich
Hereford & Worcester WR9 0DG
Tel: 0527 861777

Wheatcroft Garden Centre
Landmere Lane
Edwalton
Nottingham NG12 4DE
Tel: 0602 216060

Whitehall Garden Centre
Corsham Road
Lacock
Chippenham
Wiltshire SN15 2LZ
Tel: 0249 730204

Whiteleys Garden Centre
Whitegate
Leeds Road
Mirfield
West Yorkshire WF14 0DQ
Tel: 0924 495944

Willington Garden Centre
Willington
Nr Bedford
Bedfordshire MK44 3QP
Tel: 0234 838777

Wilmslow Garden Centre
Manchester Road
Wilmslow
Cheshire SK9 2JN
Tel: 0626 525700

Wilton House Garden Centre
Salisbury Road
Wilton
Salisbury
Wiltshire SP2 0BJ
Tel: 0722 742280

Wolden Nurseries & Garden Centre
Cattlegate Road
Crew's Hill
Enfield
Middlesex EN2 9DW
Tel: 081 363 7003

Worsley Hall Garden Centre
Leigh Road
Boothstown
Worsley
Manchester M28 4LJ

CANADA

Agassiz Agricultural & Horticultural
Association
Box 78
Agassiz
British Columbia
V0M 1A0

Alberta Horticultural Association
Box 1712
Camrose
Alberta T4V 1X6
Tel: 403 672 4818

Saskatchewan Horticultiural Association
Extension Division
University of Saskatchewan
Saskatoon
Saskatchewan S7N0N0

Société d'Horticulture et d'Ecologie
   du Nord de Montreal
Mr J Blais
10125 Ave Curotte
Montreal
Quebec H2C 2YS

Newfoundland Horticultural Society
Mrs S Gale
PO Box 10099
St Johns
Newfoundland

Manitoba Horticultural Society
908 Norquay Building
Winnipeg
Manitoba R3C 0P8

Ontario Horticultural Association
Agricultural & Horticultural Societies Branch
Ontario Ministry of Agriculture
Parliament Buildings
Toronto
Ontario N7A 1A9

Ornamental Horticultural Society
Jardin van den Hende
Universite Laval
Ste. Foy
PQ Province of Quebec T5J 1HE

Canadian Horticultual Council
Suite 210
1101 Prince of Wales Drive
Ottawa
Ontario K2C 3W7
Tel: 613 226 4187

AUSTRALIA

Royal Horticultural Society of New South Wales
Mrs J W Slattery
12 Eddystone Road
Mexley
Sydney NSW 2207

Royal Agricultural & Horticultural Society of
   South Australia
Mr G T Campbell
Shouground
Wayville South Australia 5034

Royal Horticultural Society of Queensland
Mrs D L Young
Box 1921 Brisbane

Australian Flora Foundation
Dr M Reed
GPO Box 205 Sydney 2001

Index

Abutilon, 18
Acalypha hispida, 32
  A. wilksiana, 32
Achimenes, 142
  A. erecta, 142
  A. grandiflora, 142
  A. longiflora, 142
Adiantum, 14, 33
Aechmea fasciata, 120
Aeschynanthus speciosus, 22
African daisy, 175
African hemp, 113
African violets, 12, 14, 26, 212
Agapanthus, 18
Aglaonema, 14, 16, 20, 34
  A. commutatum, 34
  A. crispum, 34
  A. roebelenii, 34
Airplane plant, 47
Aloe, 24
Aloe vera, 35
Alpine violet, 164
Aluminium plant, 99
Amaryllis, 179
Amethyst flower, 151
Ampelopsis, 36
Ananas bracteatus striatus, 37
Angel wings, 45
Anthurium, 26
  A. scherzerianum, 38
Aphelandra squarrosa, 143
Arabian coffee plant, 52
Arabian violet, 14, 171
Araucaria heterophylla, 39
Arachis hypogaea, 29
Ardisia crenata, 144
Areca palm, 18, 48
Argyranthemum frutescens chrysaster, 158
Artillery plant, 99
Arum lily, 223
Asian bell tree, 100
Asparagus, 14
  A. densiflora meyerii, 128
  A. falcatus, 128
  A. plumosus, 129
  A. sprengeri, 22, 128
Asparagus fern, 129
Aspidistra, 16, 20, 40
  A. elatior, 40
  A. lurida, 40
Asplenium nidus, 130
Avocados, 28
Azalea, 16, 26
  A. indica, 145

Baby primrose, 205
Baby rubber plant, 96
Baby tears, 195
Baby's tears, 112
Bamboo, 41
Bambusa vulgaris, 41
Banjo fiddle, 78
Barbados aloe, 35
Barbados lily, 179

Barbeton daisy, 175
Basket selaginella, 108
Bathroom, plants in, 14
Bead plant, 195
Beaucarnea, 20, 24
  B. recurvata, 42
Begonia, 6, 14
  B. elatior, 26, 146, 147
  B. rex, 19, 43
  B. tuber-hybrida 'Harlequin', 147
  B. tuberosa, 146
Begonia rex vine, 49
Beloperone guttata, 148
Billbergia rhodocynea, 120
Bird's nest, 123
Bird's nest fern, 130
Bizzie lizzie, 183
Black-eyed Susan, 221
Black-gold philodendron, 97
Blechnum braziliense, 131
  B. gibbum, 131
Bleeding heart vine, 160
Blue dracaena, 54
Blue passion flower, 201
Blue-flowered torch, 124
Blushing bromeliad, 122
Boston fern, 136
Bottle brush plant, 120
Bougainvillea, 18, 20, 24
  B. glabra, 149
Bouvardia, 150
  B. grandiflora, 150
  B. longiflora, 150
Brachychiton, 24
  B. rupestris, 44
Breeding plants, 8
Bride's flower, 219
Bromeliads, 119
Browallia, 151
  B. speciosa, 151
  B. viscosa, 151
Brunfelsia, 152
  B. pauciflora calycina, 152
Burgundy mound, 199
Bush violet, 151
Butterfly flower, 211
Butterfly palm, 48
Button fern, 137

Cabbage tree, 54
Cacti, 12, 24
Caladium, 19
  C. bicolor, 45
Calamondin orange, 159
Calceolaria herbeohybrida, 153
  C. integrifolia, 153
Calla lily, 223
Campanula, 26
  C. carpatica, 154
  C. isophylla, 154
  C. poscharskyana, 154
Campanulatus, 18
Canary Islands date palm, 98
Canary Islands ivy, 12, 86

Canna hybrida, 155
  C. indica, 155
Canna lily, 155
Cape ivy, 23
Cape jasmine, 174
Cape leadwort, 204
Cape primrose, 14, 220
Capsicum annuum, 156
Care cards, 8
Cartwheel plant, 122
Cast-iron plant, 40
Cattleya bowringiana, 18
Celosia cristata, 157
  C. plumosa, 157
Chamaedorea elegans, 46
Chenille plant, 32
Cherry pie, 177
Chilean pouch or slipper flower, 153
China rose, 209
Chinese evergreen, 14, 16, 34
Chinese grape, 36
Chinese hibiscus, 178
Chinese primrose, 205
Chlorophytum, 14, 20, 22
  C. comosum 'Variegatum', 47
Christ plant, 168
Christmas cactus, 214
Christmas pepper, 156
Christmas pride, 210
Christmas star, 169
Chrysalidocarpus lutescens, 14, 18, 48
Chysanthemum, 16, 158
  C. frutescens, 158
  C. indicum, 26, 158
  C. morifolium, 158
Cissus antarctica, 23, 49
  C. discolor, 49
  C. striata, 49
Citrus, 18
  C. mitis, 159
Claw cactus, 214
Clerodendrum thomsonae, 160
Cliff brake, 137
Climbing lily, 176
Climbing plants, 22, 24, 25
Clivia miniata, 161
Cloak fern, 134
Clog plant, 182
Cockscomb, 157
Coconut palm, 50
Cocos nucifera, 50
Codiaeum variegatum pictum, 51
Coffea arabica, 52
Coffee beans, 29
Coffee tree of commerce, 52
Coleus, 20
  C. blumei, 53
Columnea, 22, 162
  C. banksii, 162
  C. gloriosa, 162
  C. stavangar, 162
Common gardenia, 174
Common ivy, 84
Compost, 243

Conservatories, 18, 19
Coral bead plant, 195
Coral berry, 144
Cordyline australis, 54
  C. congesta, 55
  C. indivisa, 54
  C. stricta, 55
  C. terminalis, 19, 54
Corridors, plants in, 16
Crassula argentea, 56
Creeping fig, 79
Creeping moss, 108
Crossandra infundibuliformis, 163
Croton, 19
Crown of thorns, 168
Cryptanthus, 57
  C. bivattatus, 57
  C. bromeliades, 57
  C. forsterianus, 57
  C. tricolor, 57
Ctenanthe oppenheimeriana, 58
Cupressus, 59
  C. macrocarpa, 59
Cycas revoluta, 60
Cyclamen, 16, 26
  C. persicum, 164
Cymbidium orchids, 196
Cyperus papyrus, 61
Cyrtomium falcatum, 132

Davallia, 14
  D. canariensis, 133
Deadheading, 237
Desert cacti, 24, 28
Devil's ivy, 16, 24, 69
Didymochlaena truncatula, 134
Dieffenbachia, 62
  D. compacta, 62
  D. exotica, 19
  D. picta, 62
Dionaea muscipula, 29, 63
Dipladenia boliviensis, 166
  D. sanderi, 166
Diseases, 245
Displaying plants, 8
Dizygotheca elegantissima, 64
  D. laciniata, 64
Dougal plant, 107
Dracaena, 20
  D. deremensis, 65
  D. fragrans 'Massangeana', 66
  D. marginata tricolor, 67
  D. marginata, 19, 24, 67
  D. reflexa, 68
Dragon tree, 66
Dry atmosphere plants, 22, 23
Dumb cane, 62
Dust, 237
Dwarf banana plant, 193
Dwarf ladyfinger banana, 193
Dwarf lemon, 184

Earth star, 57
Easter cactus, 208
Echeveria, 20, 167
  E. agavoides, 167
  E. pumila, 167
Egyptian paper plant, 61
Elkhorn fern, 138
Emerald fern, 128
Emerald tree, 100

English ivy, 84
Epipremnum, 12, 14, 24
  Epipremnum aureum, 69
Euonymus japonica, 70
Euphorbia lophogona, 168
  E. milii, 168
  E. pulcherrima, 169
  E. trigona, 71
Eustoma, 24
  E. grandiflorum, 170
Exacum, 14
  E. affinae, 171

Fairy primrose, 16, 205
False aralia, 64
False caster oil plant, 73
False Jerusalem cherry, 217
Fatshedera lizei, 16, 72
Fatsia japonica, 72, 73
Feeding plants, 236
Ferns, 127
Ficus, 18
  F. 'Curly', 74
  F. benjamina, 19
  F. benjamina 'Starlight', 74
  F. benjamina 'Variegata', 74
  F. decora, 77
  F. diversifolia, 76
  F. elastica robusta, 77
  F. longifolium, 74
  F. lyrata, 19, 78
  F. nitida, 74
  F. pumila, 79
  F. radicans 'Variegata', 80
Fiddleleaf, 97
Fiddle-leaf fig, 78
Finger aralia, 64
Firecracker flower, 163
Firecracker plant, 167
Fishbone fern, 136
Fittonia, 81
  F. argyroneura, 81
  F. verschaffeltii, 81
Flame nettle, 53
Flame of the woods, 184
Flame sword, 126
Flaming Katie, 186
Flamingo flower, 38
Florist's cineraria, 215
Florist's cyclamen, 164
Florist's gloxinia, 216
Flowering plants, 141
Foliage plants, 31
Foradora jasmine, 219
Forest cacti, 24
Freckle face, 88
Fuchsia, 22, 172, 173
Fun plants, 28, 29

Garden centres, 6
Garden rooms, 18, 19
Gardenia, 14
  G. jasminoides, 174
Geranium, 202
Geraniums, cascade, 22
Gerbera jamesonii, 175
German violet, 171
Gloriosa, 18
  G. rothschildiana, 176

Glory bower, 160
Glory lily, 176
Goldfish plant, 22, 162, 182
Good luck palm, 46
Good luck plant, 54
Goosefoot plant, 114
Grape ivy, 16, 23, 103
Greek vase plant, 120
Grevillea robusta, 82
Grooming, 237
Ground nut, 29
Guzmania lingulata major, 121
Gynura x. sarmentosa, 83

Hallways, plants in, 16
Hanging baskets, 22, 24
Happy wandering Jew, 116
Hare's foot fern, 133
Heart-leafed philodendron, 97
Hedera, 24
  H. canariensis, 12, 84
  H. helix, 6, 72, 84
Heliotrope, 177
Heliotropium arborescens, 177
  H. peruvianum, 177
Hen and chickens, 167
Herbs, 12
Hibiscus, 19, 24
  H. rosa-sinensis, 178
Hippeastrum hybrids, 179
Hippeastrum leopoldii, 179
Holly fern, 132
Hot water plant, 142
House lime, 113
Howea, 18, 87
  H. belmoreana, 87
  H. forsteriana, 87
Hoya bella, 14, 180
Hoya carnosa, 22, 180
Humbleplant, 192
Humidity, 25, 235
Hydrangea, 181
  H. macrophylla, 181
Hypocryta glabra, 182
  H. nummularia, 182
Hypoestes, 12
  H. sanguinolenta, 88

Impatiens hawkeri hybrida, 183
  I. walleriana, 183
Inch plant, 116
Indian azalea, 145
Indian laurel, 74
Indian rubber plant, 77
Indian shot, 155
Italian bellflower, 154
Ivy, 6
Ivy tree, 72
Ixora chinensis, 184
  I. coccinea, 184
  I. javanica, 184
  I. stricta, 184

Jade tree, 56
Japanese aralia, 73
Japanese spindle tree, 70
Jasminum officinal, 185
  J. polyanthum, 185
Joseph's coat, 51
Jungle geranium, 184

Kafir lily, 161
Kalanchoe, 24, 26
  K. blossfeldiana, 186
  K. manginii, 22, 186
Kangaroo ivy, 49
Kangaroo vine, 49
Kentia palm, 18, 87
Kitchen, plants in, 12

Lacy tree philodendron, 97
Lady palm, 18, 101
Laelia purpurata, 18
Lantana, 188
Leaf begonia, 43
Leaf shine, 237
Leea coccinea, 89
Lemon geranium, 203
Leopard lily, 62
Leptospermum scoparium, 189
Licuala grandis, 90
Light, 228
Lilium, 190
  L. auratum, 190
  L. citronella, 190
  L. fiesta, 190
  L. longiflorum eximium, 190
  L. regale, 190
  L. speciosum, 190
Lily, 190
Lipstick vine, 22
Lisianthus russelianus, 170
Lollipop plant, 200
Lotus berthelotii, 22

Madagascar dragon tree, 67
Madagascar jasmine, 14, 219
Maidenhair fern, 14, 33
Mandevilla sanderi, 166
Manuka, 189
Maranta, 19
  M. leuconeura, 14, 91
  M. tricolor, 14, 91
Medicine plant, 35
Medinilla magnifica, 191
Mexican breadfruit plant, 92
Mexican leaf star, 169
Mexican violet, 171
Microlepia strigosa, 135
Mimosa pudica, 192
Miniature wax plant, 180
Mind your own business, 25, 112
Mini bulrush, 107
Miniature grape vine, 49
Mint geranium, 203
Mistletoe fig, 76
Money plant, 56
Monkey plant, 210
Monsteria deliciosa, 16, 92
Monterey cypress, 59
Morning, noon and night, 152
Mosaic plant, 81
Moses in the basket, 102
Moth orchid, 16, 198
Mother of thousands, 22
Mother-in-law plant, 45
Mother-in-law's tongue, 104
Moulded wax, 167
Mozambique lily, 176
Musa cavendishii, 193

Natal vine, 103
Neoregelia carolinae, 122
Nephrolepis, 16, 136
  N. cordata, 136
  N. exaltata bostoniensis, 136
Nephrolepis ferns, 14
Nephthytis, 114
Nerium oleander, 194
Nertera depressa, 195
  N. granadensis, 195
Never-never plant, 58
Nidularium, 123
  N. fulgens, 123
  N. innocentii, 123
  N. innocentii striatum, 123
Norfolk Island pine, 39
Nut orchid, 142

Oleander, 18, 194
Orchid phalaenopsis, 198
Orchids, cymbidium hybrids, 196
Ornamental chilli pepper, 156
Osteospermum, 199
  O. fruticosum, 199

Pachystachys lutea, 200
Painted lady, 167
Painted net leaf, 81
Palm Beach belle, 186
Palm lily, 54
Paper flower, 149
Paphiopedilum, 16
Paradise palm, 87
Parasol plant, 106
Parlour ivy, 97
Parlour palm, 46
Passiflora, 23
  P. caerulea, 201
  P. violacea, 201
Passion flower, 23
Patient lucy, 183
Peace lily, 218
Peanut, 29
Pebble trays, 24
Pelargonium, 24, 202
  P. crispum, 203
  P. domesticum hybridus, 202
  P. peltatum, 202
  P. tomentosum, 203
  P. x. fragrans variegatum, 203
  P. x. hortorum, 202
  P. zonale, 202
Pellaea rotundifolia, 137
Pellionia, 14
  P. pulchra, 93
Peperomia, 14
  P. caperata, 94, 95
  P. clusifolia, 95
  P. glabella 'Variegata' 95
  P. obtusifolia, 96
  P. variegata, 96
Pepper face, 96
Persian violet, 171
Pests, 244
Phalaenopsis, 16
Philodendron, 19, 20, 97
  P. 'Emerald Queen', 97
  P. melanochrysum, 97
  P. panduriforme, 97

P. panduriforme 'Burgundy', 23
P. pertusum, 16
P. scandens, 12, 14, 16, 22, 97
P. selloum, 16, 97
Phoenix canariensis, 24, 98
Piggyback plant, 14, 115
Pilea cadieri, 99
Pine lily, 118
Pineapple, 28
  variegated red, 37
Pink allemande, 166
Pink jasmine, 185
Pink quill, 124
Plants, natural colours, 8
Platycerium, 16, 138
  P. alcicorne, 138
Plumbago auriculata, 204
  P. capensis, 204
  P. indica, 204
Plume asparagus, 128
Plume flower, 157
Poinsettia, 169
Poison primrose, 205
Pocketbook plant, 153
Polka dot plant, 88
Ponytail plant, 42
Poor man's orchid, 211
Porcelain flower, 180
Portulaca grandiflora, 204
Pots, 8
Potting mix, 243
Potting on, 242
Prairie gentian, 170
Prayer plant, 91
Primrose, 26, 205
Primula, 205
  Primula acaulis, 26, 205, 206
  P. malacoides, 16, 26, 205, 206
  P. obconica, 26, 205, 206
  P. sinensis, 205
  P. vulgaris, 205
Propagation, 238, 239
Pruning, 240
Pteris, 139
  P. cretica, 139
  P. ensiformis evergemiensis, 139
Purple passion vine, 83
Pygmy rose 209

Queensland bottle tree, 44

Rabbit's foot fern, 14, 133
Rabbit's tracks, 91
Radermachera, 100
Rainbow star, 57
Raphis, 101
  R. excelsa, 18, 101
  R. humilis, 101
Red herringbone plant, 91
Red hot cattail, 32
Repotting, 242
Resurrection plant, 110
Rhipsalidopsis, 208
  R. gaertneri, 208
  R. rosea, 208
Rhoeo bermudensis, 102
  R. discolor, 102
Rhoicissus capensis, 23, 103
  R. rhomboidea, 16, 103

Ribbon fern, 139
Rio tradescantia, 116
Rooting fig, 80
Rosa chinensis, 209
Rose bay, 194
Rose dipladenia, 166
Rose grape, 191
Rose moss, 204
Rose of Jericho, 110
Ruellia, 210
  R. macrantha, 210
  R. makoyana, 210

Saffron spike, 143
Sago palm, 60
Sail plant, 218
St Bernard's lily, 47
Saintpaulia, 12, 14, 26, 212, 213
Sansevieria, 20
  S. trifasciata, 104
Sapphire flower, 151
Satin pellionia, 93
Saxifraga stolonifera, 22, 105
Scarlet star, 121
Scarlet trompetilla, 150
Schefflera, 16, 20, 106
  S. arboricola 'Trinette', 106
  S. 'Nora', 106
Schizanthus retusus, 211
Schlumbergera, 214
  S. bridgesii, 214
  S. truncata, 214
Scindapsus, 16
  S. aureus, 23, 24, 69
  S. 'Marble Queen', 24
Scirpus cernuus, 107
Selaginella apoda, 108
  S. kraussiana, 109
  S. martensii, 110
  S. rubra, 108
Senecio cruentis hybridus, 215
  S. rowleyanus, 111
Sensitive plant, 192
Sentry palm, 87
Shrimp plant, 148
Shrub verbena, 188
Sicklethorn, 128
Silky oak, 82
Silver leaf net, 81

Silvery wandering Jew, 116
Sinningia hybridus, 216
Slipper orchid, 16
Snake plant, 104
Snakeskin plant, 81
Solanum, 217
  S. capsicastrum, 217
  S. pseudocapsicum, 156, 217
Soleirolia soleirolii, 25, 112
Song of India, 68
Sparmannia africana, 113
Spathiphyllum, 16, 218
  S. floribunda, 218
  S. wallisii, 218
Spice berry, 144
Spider plant, 14, 20, 22, 47
Spineless yucca, 118
Spreading clubmoss, 109
Spurge, 71
Staghorn fern, 16, 138
Star of Bethlehem, 154
Starfish plant, 57
Stephanotis, 14, 23
  S. floribunda, 219
Stiff pheasant leaf, 57
Strawberry geranium, 105
Streptocarpus, 14, 220
  S. saxorum, 220
  S. wenlandii, 220
String of pearls, 111
Striped dracaena, 65
Sweet bouvardia, 150
Sweetheart plant, 12, 14, 97
Swiss cheese plant, 16, 23, 92
Sword fern, 16, 136
Syngonium, 114
  S. podophyllum, 23
  S. 'White Butterfly', 14, 22, 114

Tea tree, 189
Temperature, 230
Thanksgiving cactus, 214
Thunbergia alata, 221
Ti plant, 54
Tillandsia cyanea, 124
  Tillandsia lindenii, 124
Tolmiea menziesii, 14, 115
Torenia fournieri, 222
  T. f. alba, 222

  T. f. grandiflora, 222
Tradescantia, 12, 22, 116
  T. albiflora 'Albo-vittata', 116
  T. albiflora tricolor, 116
  T. flumensis, 116
Trailing African daisy, 199
Trailing plants, 24, 25
Trailing selaginella, 109
Trailing velvet plant, 210
Training, 241
Transvaal daisy, 175
Tree ivy, 16
Tree of kings, 54
True aloe, 35
Trumpet lily, 223

Umbrella tree, 106
Urn plant, 120

Variegated red pineapple, 37
Velvet plant, 83
Venus fly trap, 29, 63
Vriesea splendens, 126

Wandering Jew, 116
Water melon pilea, 99
Watering, 232-4
Wax flower, 219
Wax plant, 22
Weeping fig, 74
White sails, 16
Windowsills, plants on, 20
Winter cherry, 217
Winter colour, 26, 27
Wishbone plant, 222

Yellow palm, 48
Yellow sage, 188
Yesterday, today and tomorrow, 152
Yucca, 16, 20, 24
  Y. elephantipes, 118

Zantedeshia, 223
  Z. aethiopica, 223
  Z. elliottiana, 223
  Z. rehmannii, 223
Zebra plant, 143
Zebrina pendula, 116
Zygocactus truncatus, 214

Acknowledgements

There are a number of people I would like to thank for their work and help on this book.

First, thanks go to Jacqui Hurst for her lovely photographs and Sally Maltby for her beautiful watercolours and line drawings which illustrate the book.

A big thank you also to: Susan Haynes and Suellen Dainty for their research; Geoff Hayes for the design of the book; Mrs Peter Bowen, Alison Cathie and Paul Whitfield for opening up their homes to our photographer for the location sections at the front; Marks & Spencer PLC; Floreac, Belgium; Jan Kochem at Lemflora, Denmark; the Royal Horticultural Society, the Garden Centre Association and Chivers Flowers of London.

Finally, thanks to Kyle Cathie, Caroline Taggart and Beverley Cousins at Kyle Cathie Limited for their hard work, and to all those in my company whom I have pestered from time to time.

Photographs

Grateful acknowledgement is made for permission to reproduce the following photographs: Andrew Lawson, page 24; Boys Syndication, 12; Eisenbeiss, page 36; Flower Council of Holland, pages 35, 41, 61, 108, 132, 134, 150, 167, 179, 195; Hugh Palmer, pages 18, 19, 25; Mercurius UK Ltd, pages 57, 63, 82, 101, 102, 113, 119, 124, 135, 144, 155, 156, 157, 161, 167, 176, 177, 188, 211, 217, 221, 222; Photo Horticultural, pages 93, 210.